JN260567

ALEJANDRO ARAVENA
THE FORCES IN ARCHITECTURE

アレハンドロ・アラヴェナ　フォース・イン・アーキテクチャー

TOTO出版

ALEJANDRO ARAVENA　THE FORCES IN ARCHITECTURE

First published in Japan on July 28, 2011
Fifth published on March 25, 2020

TOTO Publishing (TOTO LTD.)
TOTO Nogizaka Bldg. 2F, 1-24-3 Minami-Aoyama, Minato-ku, Tokyo 107-0062, Japan
[Sales] Telephone: +81-3-3402-7138　Facsimile: +81-3-3402-7187
[Editorial] Telephone: +81-3-3497-1010
URL: https://jp.toto.com/publishing

Author: Alejandro Aravena
Content Editor: Víctor Oddó
Publisher: Takeshi Ito
Book Designer: Masahiro Eigen
Printer: Tokyo Inshokan Printing Co., Ltd.

Except as permitted under copyright law, this book may not be reproduced, in whole or in part, in any form or by any means, including photocopying, scanning, digitizing, or otherwise, without prior permission. Scanning or digitizing this book through a third party, even for personal or home use, is also strictly prohibited.
The list price is indicated on the cover.

ISBN978-4-88706-320-4

ALEJANDRO ARAVENA
THE FORCES IN ARCHITECTURE
アレハンドロ・アラヴェナ　フォース・イン・アーキテクチャー

Contents

The Forces in Architecture

Alejandro Aravena Architects
HOUSE FOR A SCULPTOR
MATHEMATICS SCHOOL
EASTER ISLAND HIGH SCHOOL
MONTESSORI SCHOOL
GARIB HOUSE
MEDICAL SCHOOL
BICENTENNAL TOWER OF COMMUNICATIONS
SIAMESE TOWERS
PIREHUEICO HOUSE
SCHOOL OF ARCHITECTURE
VERBO DIVINO SCHOOL
ST. EDWARD'S UNIVERSITY DORMS
SAO PAULO HOUSE
VITRA CHILDREN'S WORKSHOP
ORDOS 100 HOUSE
PILGRIM LOOK OUT POINT
CHAIRLESS FOR VITRA
BANSI BANK
PLAYA ONDA RESORT
KUNSTMUSEUM BASEL EXTENSION
OCEAN WINERY
MEDELLIN MUSEUM OF MODERN ART
ETLIN HOUSE
CAREY HOUSE
ANACLETO ANGELINI INNOVATION CENTER

ELEMENTAL
QUINTA MONROY HOUSING
RENCA HOUSING
HOUSING COMPLEX SOCIAL CENTERS
BARNECHEA HOUSING
MONTERREY LAS ANACUAS HOUSING
MAKE IT RIGHT FOUNDATION
METROPOLITAN PROMENADE
EARTHQUAKE AND TSUNAMI RESPONSE
    WATER DISTRIBUTION
    ELEMENTAL SHELTER
    CONSTITUCION PLAN FOR SUSTAINABLE RECONSTRUCTION

Interview with Alejandro Aravena

Biography
Bibliography
Credits

フォース・イン・アーキテクチャー	6
アレハンドロ・アラヴェナ・アーキテクツ	13
彫刻家の家	18
数学部研究棟	20
イースター島の高校	24
モンテッソーリ・スクール	26
ガリブ邸	28
医学部棟	30
建国200年記念電波塔	36
シャム・タワー	38
ピリウェイコの住宅	46
建築学部棟	48
ヴェルボ・ディヴィーノ大学	52
セント・エドワード大学 学生寮	54
サンパウロの住宅	62
ヴィトラ・チルドレンズ・ワークショップ	64
オルドス100	68
巡礼路の展望台	72
チェアレス	80
バンシ銀行	82
プラヤ・オンダ・リゾート	84
バーゼル美術館増築	86
オーシャン・ワイナリー	94
メデジン近代美術館	100
エトリン邸	104
ケアリー邸	106
アナクレート・アンジェリーニ・イノヴェーション・センター	108
エレメンタル	119
キンタ・モンロイの集合住宅	122
レンカの集合住宅	132
集合住宅の集会所	136
バルネチアの集合住宅	138
モンテレイの集合住宅 ラス・アナクァス	140
メイク・イット・ライト財団	144
メトロポリタン・プロムナード	146
地震・津波対策	152
水の配給	154
エレメンタル・シェルター	156
コンスティトゥシオン市のサステイナブルな復興計画	158
アレハンドロ・アラヴェナ　インタヴュー	164
略歴	195
書誌	196
クレジット	199

THE FORCES IN ARCHITECTURE
フォース・イン・アーキテクチャー

What informs the form of a project?

We spend a lot of time identifying and designing the right question (not just the answer) that a project is expected to solve (there is nothing worse than responding well to the wrong question).

In a project's equation, there are some terms that are unavoidable. Like gravity or nature. Gravity it's a fact and as a consequence our projects' weight. Nature works with different magnitudes and as a consequence we try not to loose the big picture in our projects. Both of them introduce atavistic, primitive forces that impose a certain discipline to forms. They work as filters against arbitrariness. We like that.

But even if counterintuitive, there are other forces in architecture that are much stronger and it is better to agree with them. One of those forces is the strength of daily customs and everyday life – the search for the shortest distance across a field that a shortcut offers, the search for a nice morning light for a bedroom or the possibility to darken it at night, the proliferation of curtains that try to reduce undesired glare in curtain-wall office spaces that may be too modern for eyes that haven't changed in millenniums – are traces of the force of customs.

All these forces should inform the form of architecture (and if not taken into consideration, they transform it anyhow). This book documents these forces in play.

なにがプロジェクトのフォルムを決めるのか。

私たちは、単に答えを出すためにではなく、然るべき問いを設定するためにも、十分に時間をかける。その問いを解決することが、プロジェクトの役目なのだから（見当違いな問いに律儀に応えてしまうことほど不毛なことはない）。

プロジェクトの方程式には不可避の項もある。たとえば重力や自然がそうである。重力は事実であり、プロジェクトに重さがあることの帰結でもある。かたや自然はさまざまな度合いで作用するので、私たちはプロジェクトの全体像を見失ってはいけない。重力にせよ自然にせよ原始的な力をフォルムに隔世遺伝させ、そうしてフォルムをいくぶん規定していく。これが恣意性を取り除くフィルターの働きをしてくれる。

普通は気づかないかもしれないが、ほかにも建築に作用する力はいろいろある。むしろ先のふたつよりずっと強力なので、これには素直に従いたい。一例が、生活習慣と日常生活の影響力である。野原を最短距離で横断するための近道を探ること、寝室にさわやかな朝日を採り入れ、逆に夜は暗くすること、あるいは何千年も前から進化していない人間の眼にはまぶしすぎる、オフィスのカーテンウォール越しに射す現代的な光を和らげようとカーテンを吊るすこと、すべては生活習慣の力の痕跡なのである。

いずれの力も、建築のフォルムを決める（仮にこれらを無視したとしても、どのみちフォルムは変わる）はずである。本書は、これらの力の作用の記録である。

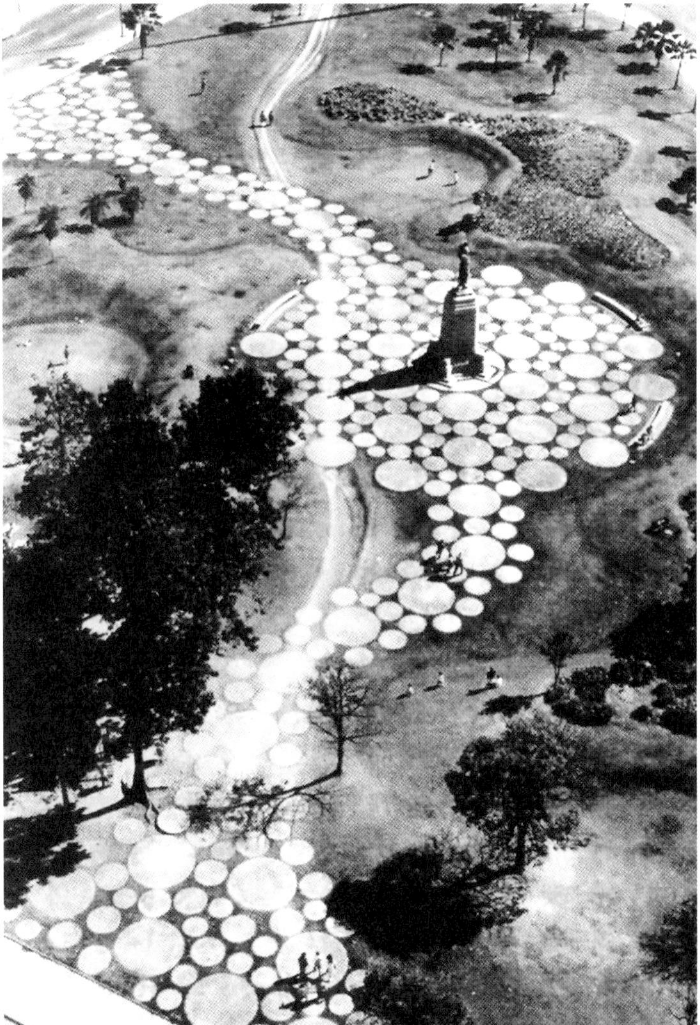

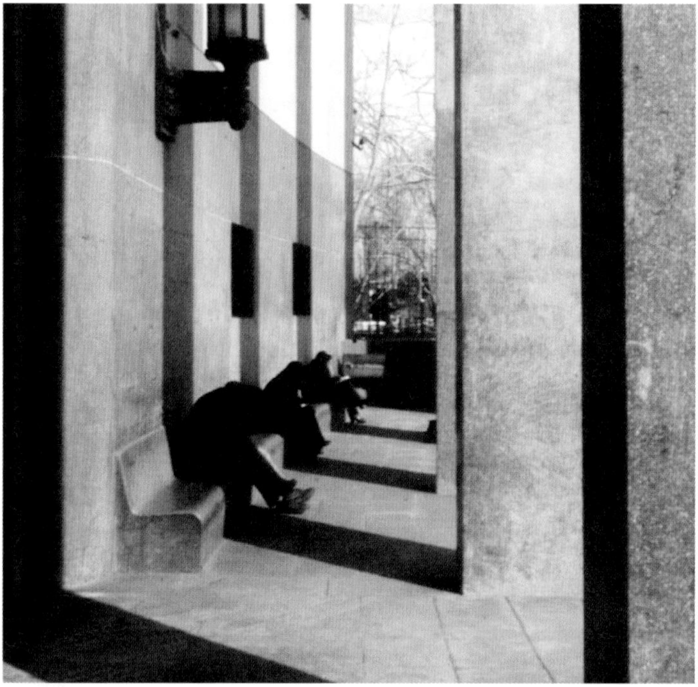

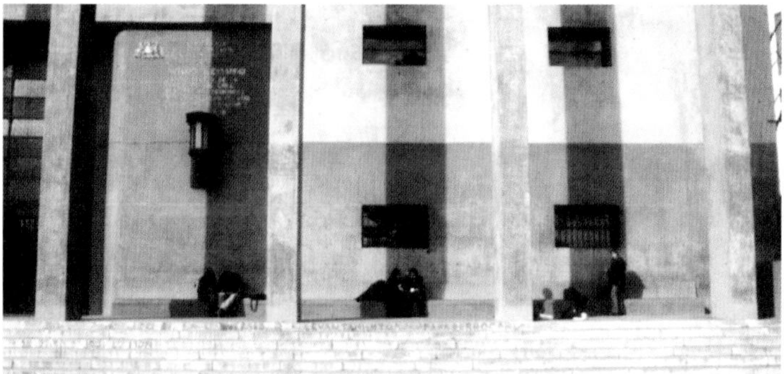

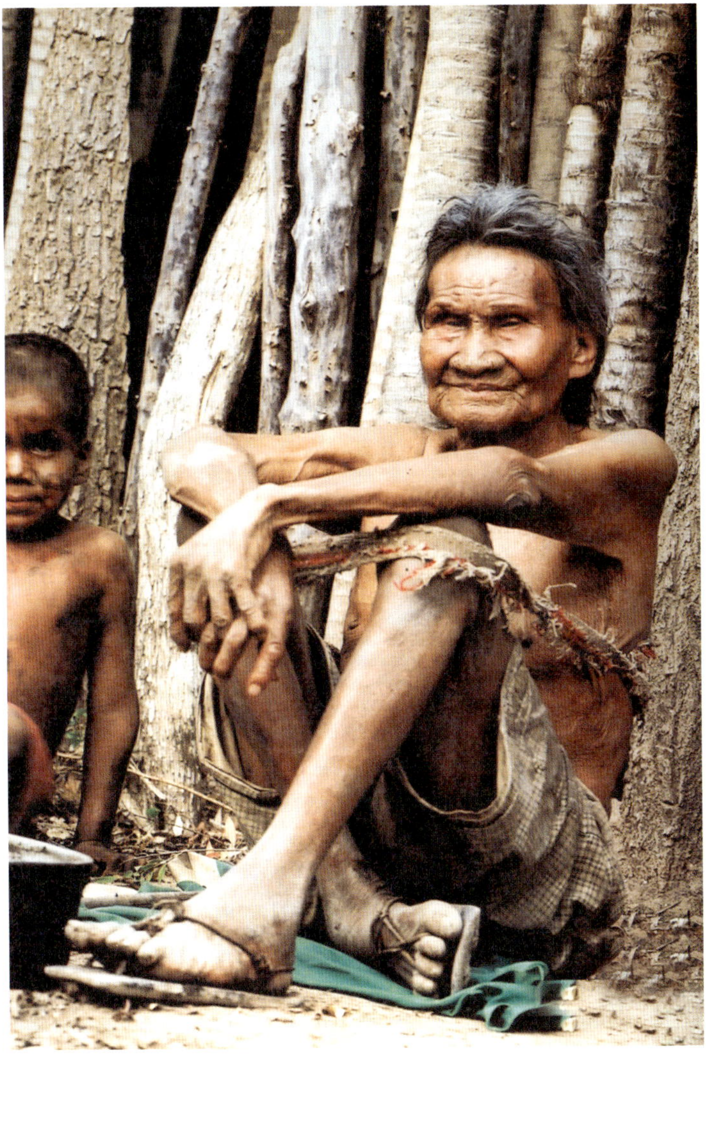

TIME LINE

1994	1995	1996	1997	1998	1999	2000	2001	2002	200

- Alejandro Aravena Architects (1994)
- Finalist in the Mies van der Rohe Award (1999)
- XII Architecture Biennale of Santiago (2001)
- Elemental (2001)
- Harvard visiting professor (2000)

Alejandro Aravena Architects
- House for a Sculptor
- Mathematics School
- Easter Island High School
- Montessori School
- Garib House
- Medical School
- Bicentennal Tower of Communications
- Siamese Towers
- Pirehueico House
- School of Architecture
- Verbo Divino School
- St. Edward's University Dorms
- Sao Paulo House
- Vitra Children's Workshop
- Ordos 100 House
- Pilgrim Look Out Point
- Chairless for Vitra
- Bansi Bank
- Playa Onda Resort
- Kunstmuseum Basel Extension
- Ocean Winery
- Medellin Museum of Modern Art
- Etlin House
- Carey House
- Anacleto Angelini Innovation Center

ELEMENTAL
- Quinta Monroy Housing
- Renca Housing
- Housing Complex Social Centers
- Barnechea Housing
- Monterrey Las Anacuas Housing
- Make It Right Foundation
- Metropolitan Promenade

Feb. 27 Richter 8.8
- Earthquake and Tsunami Response
- Water Distribution
- Elemental Shelter
- Constitución Plan for Sustainable Reconstruction

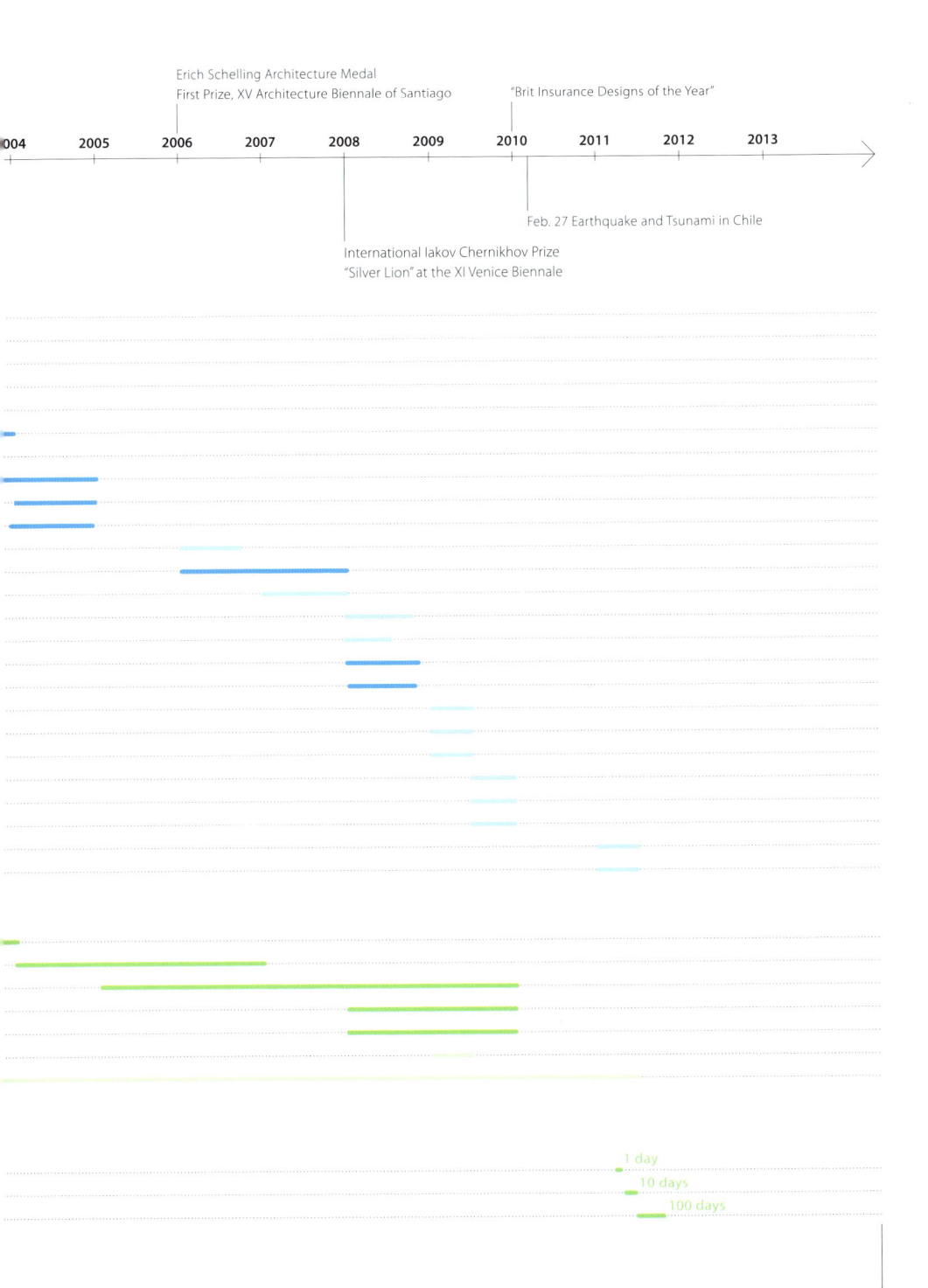

Erich Schelling Architecture Medal
First Prize, XV Architecture Biennale of Santiago

"Brit Insurance Designs of the Year"

2004   2005   2006   2007   2008   2009   2010   2011   2012   2013

Feb. 27 Earthquake and Tsunami in Chile

International Iakov Chernikhov Prize
"Silver Lion" at the XI Venice Biennale

1 day
10 days
100 days

11

ALEJANDRO ARAVENA ARCHITECTS

House for a Sculptor

Mathematics School

Easter Island High School

Montessori School

Garib House

Pirehueico House

Medical School

Siamese Towers

Sao Paulo House

Ordos 100 House

Alejandro Aravena Architects

Bansi Bank

St. Edward's University Dorms

Vitra Children's Workshop

Kunstmuseum Basel Extension

Anacleto Angelini Innovation Center

Pilgrim Look Out Point

Ocean Winery

Medellin Museum of Modern Art

Etlin House

Alejandro Aravena Architects: Projects in the World

- Austin, Texas, USA
- Guadalajara, MX
- Jalisco, MX
- Isla Saboga, PA
- Medellin, CO
- Easter Island, CL
- Sao Paulo, BR
- Santiago, CL
- Pirehueico Lake, CL

Nierstein, DE
Weil am Rhen, DE
Basel, CH

Ordos, Inner-Mongolia, CN
Shanghai, CN

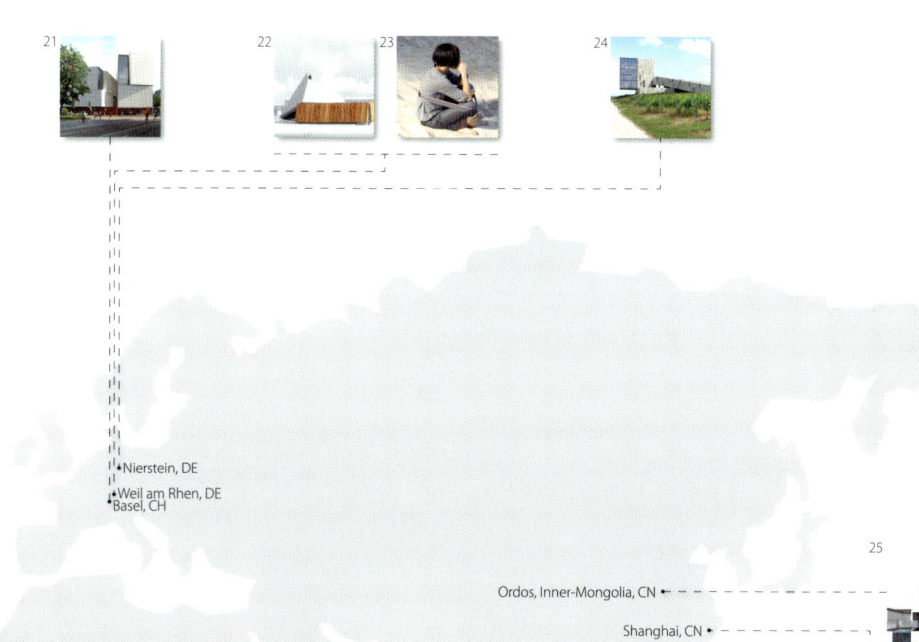

Work in Progress

1: Siamese Towers — p. 38
2: Medical School — p. 30
3: Bicentennal Tower of Communications — p. 36
4: Garib House — p. 28
5: Montessori School — p. 26
6: House for a Sculptor — p. 18
7: Mathematics School — p. 20
8: Anacleto Angelini Innovation Center — p. 108
9: Carey House — p. 106
10: School of Architecture — p. 48
11: Verbo Divino School — p. 52
12: Easter Island High Sschool — p. 24
13: Pirehueico House — p. 46
14: Bansi Bank — p. 82
15: Pilgrim Look Out Point — p. 72
16: Medellin Museum of Modern Art — p. 100
17: St. Edward's University Dorms — p. 54
18: Playa Onda Resort — p. 84
19: Sao Paulo House — p. 62
20: Etlin House — p. 104
21: Kunstmuseum Basel Extension — p. 86
22: Vitra Children's Workshop — p. 64
23: Chairless for Vitra — p. 80
24: Ocean Winery — p. 94
25: Ordos 100 House — p. 68
26: Novartis Shanghai Campus Office Building

HOUSE FOR A SCULPTOR
彫刻家の家

Like the client's nearby handmade brick studio, this house was very tight for budgetary reasons, but responded to her request that it be able to receive people for more social occasions. We thus designed a house experienced through its "triagonals," balancing the longest possible view of a given volume with the shortest distance to cross it.

施主が自ら建てたという隣の煉瓦造のアトリエと同様に、この住宅も非常に厳しい予算ではあったが、それでもここを社交の場としたいとする彼女の要望には応えることにした。室内の空間は「立体対角線(トライアゴナル)」を軸に構成されている。これは与えられたヴォリュームの範囲内で、奥行きを極力長く見せると同時に、移動距離を最短にするためである。

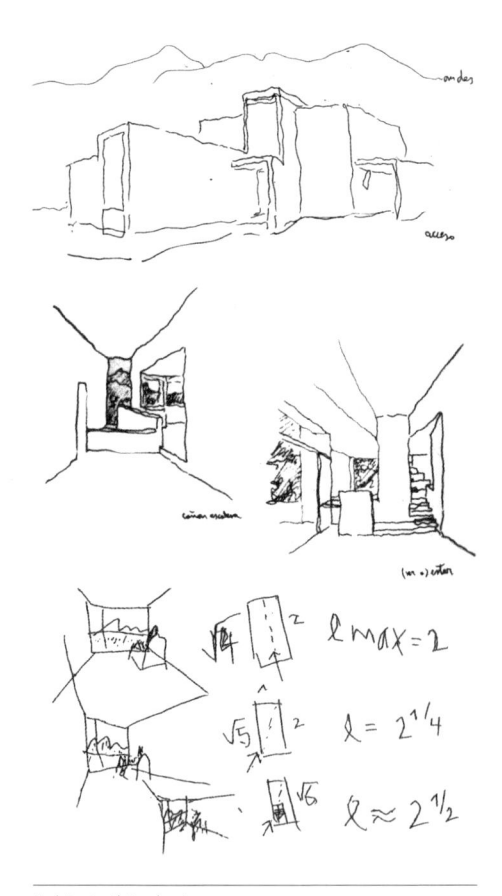

Second floor

Ground floor

Cross section

0　3　10m

Architect: Alejandro Aravena
Design/Construction Period: 1997
Building Area: 120m²
Location: Santiago, CHILE

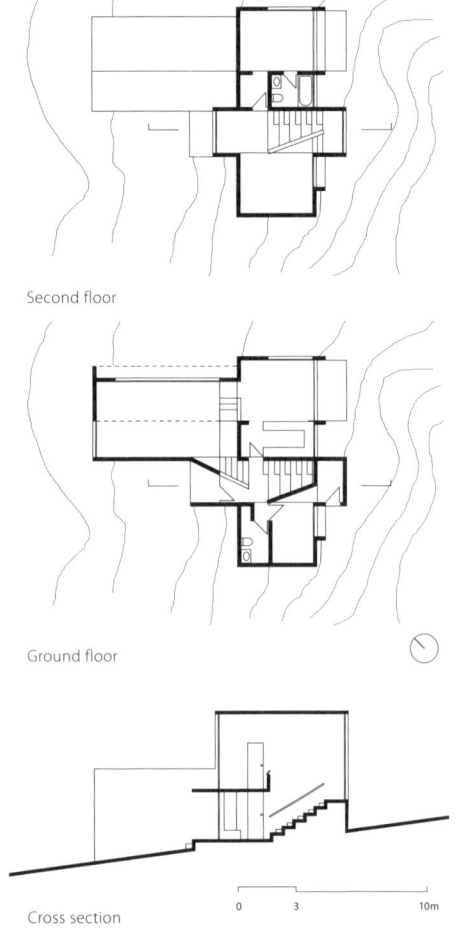

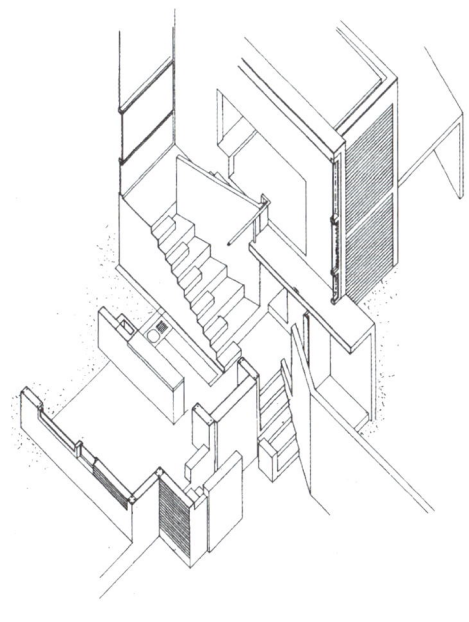

Axonometric view

MATHEMATICS SCHOOL
数学部研究棟

$2 + 1 = 1$

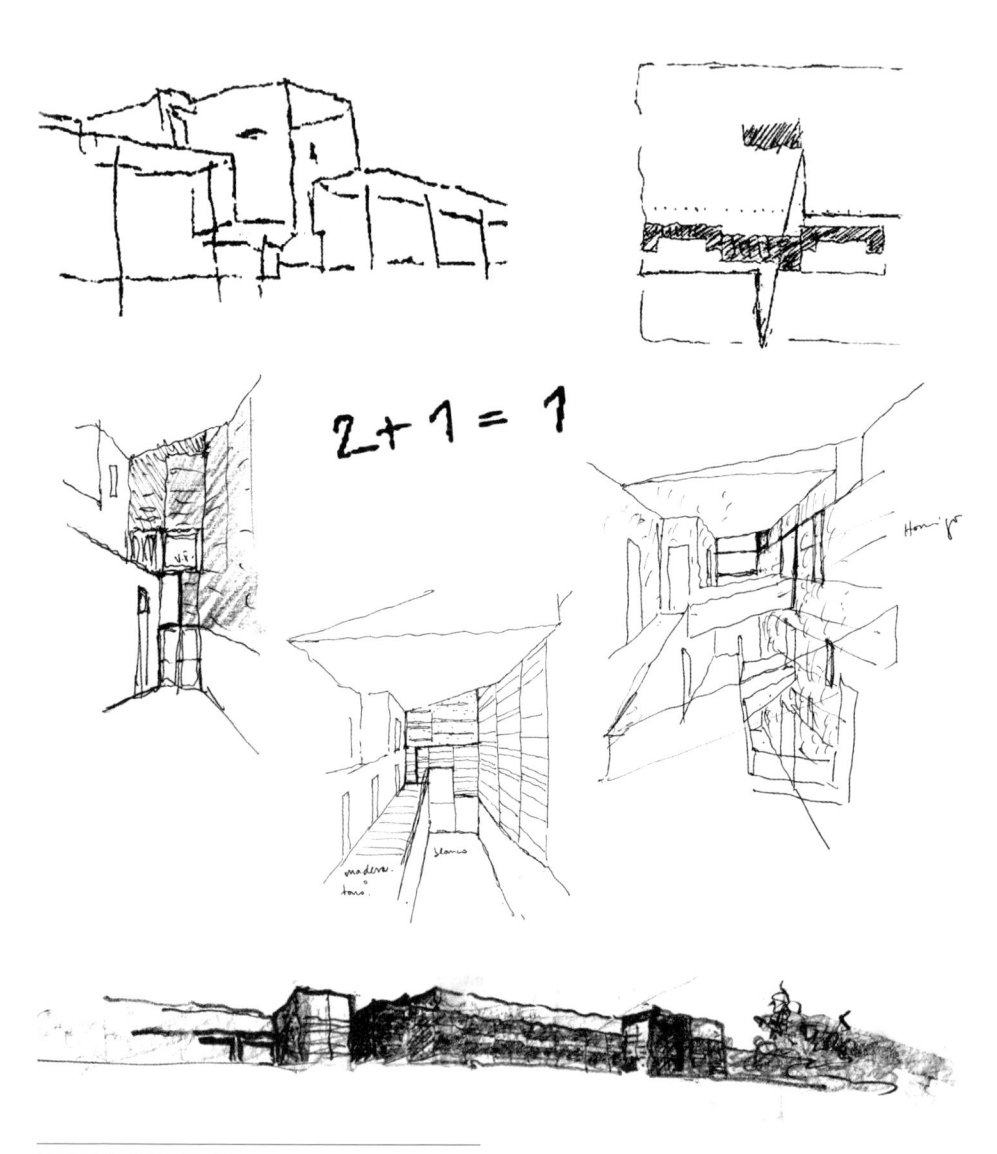

Architect: Alejandro Aravena
Collaborator: Luis Lucero
Design/Construction Period: 1998-1999
Building Area: 2,000m²
Location: The Catholic University of Chile, Santiago, CHILE

2+1=1

"A mathematician is a machine who transforms coffee into equations." We thought that joke expressed one of the dimensions by which knowledge is produced: the casual encounter of people. Besides the coffee room, we identified the corridor as a design opportunity, as the moment where you see other people before they disappear into the isolated retreat of the individual working unit. We decided to add the new building to two existing ones, so that after the operation we had fewer elements than at the beginning.

2+1=1

「数学者の手にかかるとコーヒーさえも方程式に変換されてしまう」。この冗談は、知が生み出されるひとつの相を言い当てているように思われた：知は人と人との遭遇によって生み出されると。だから私たちは、コーヒー・ルームに限らず廊下も格好のデザインの対象になると考えた。研究者たちがめいめいの個室に引きこもる前の、廊下を通る瞬間くらいしか、彼らの姿が人目に触れることはないからだ。ここでは既存の2棟の間に新たに1棟を増築することで全体が1つになり、当初よりも要素を減らした。

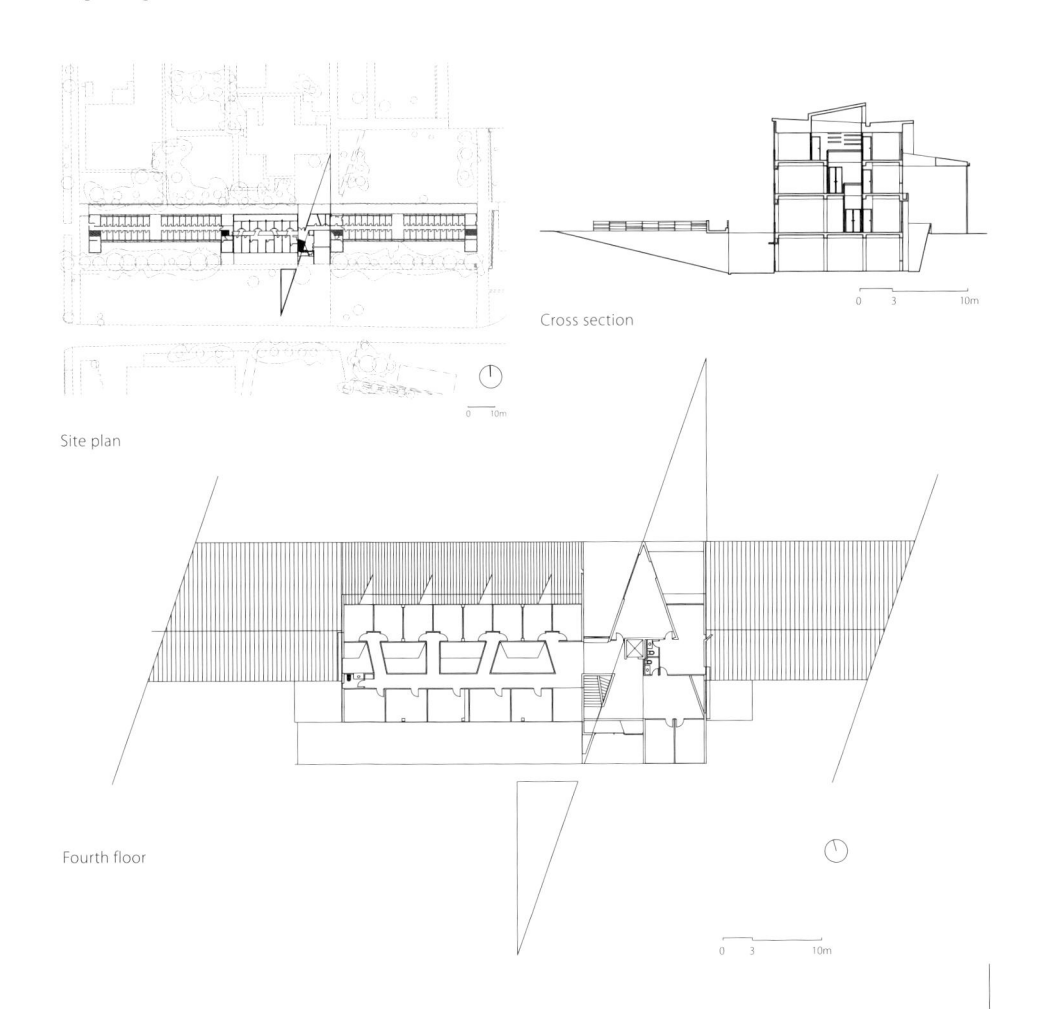

Site plan

Cross section

Fourth floor

North facade

South facade

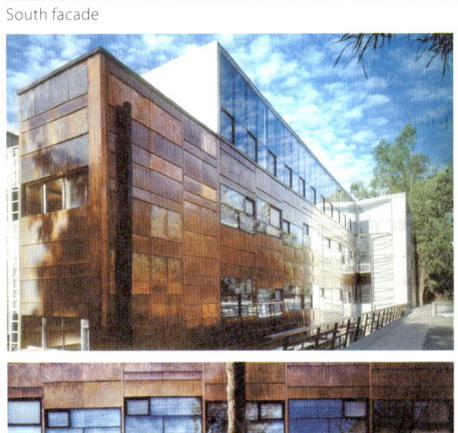

EASTER ISLAND HIGH SCHOOL
イースター島の高校

How can one work in a place where culture tends to be a cliché? How can one choose an architectural language that rejects folklore without getting alienated from the place? How can one work in place where the most abundant material is the horizon?

We thought of excavating a mass that domesticated the openness for the use of the school, but still allowed for the horizon to be experienced from every point of the project.

文化がクリシェと化してしまうような土地では、いったいなにができるというのか。はたしてどの建築言語を用いれば、民俗学を否定しつつもその土地から疎外されずにすむか。その土地に最も潤沢にある素材が地平線だとしたら、ほかになにを与えればいいのか。
私たちは、マッスを割り抜くことにした。割り抜いた内側には校舎としての広がりを取り込みつつ、なおかつ校内のどの地点からも地平線が望めるようにした。

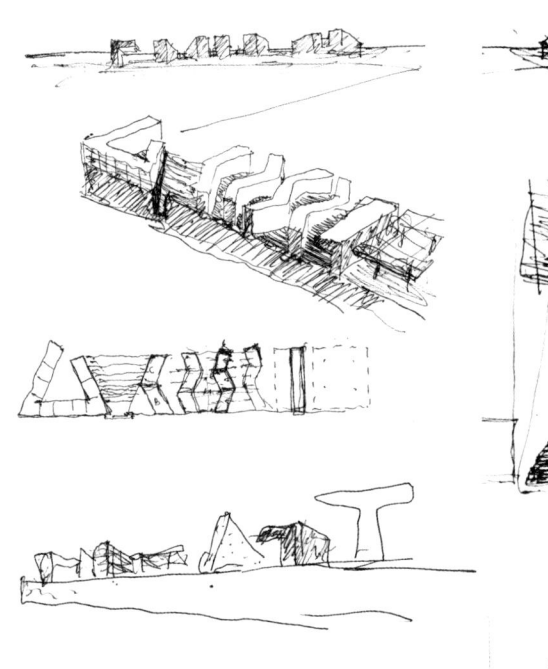

Architect: Alejandro Aravena
Partner Architect: Charles Murray
Collaborators: Jorge Christie, Francisco Chateau, Carolina Portugueis
Design Period: 1999
Building Area: 2,000m^2
Location: Easter Island, CHILE

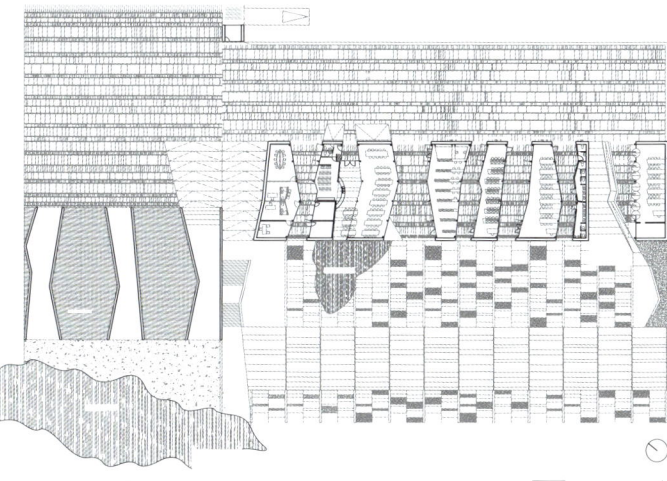

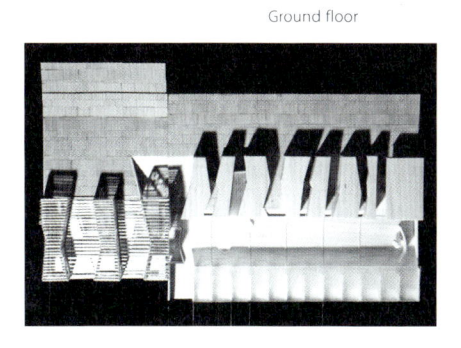

Ground floor

MONTESSORI SCHOOL
モンテッソーリ・スクール

The Montessori educational system is based on children's capacity of choosing their own schedule during the day. So classrooms need many corners to accommodate the different knowledge areas. We opted for volumes that have an articulated perimeter with many corners, still simple enough to allow for a calm architecture.

モンテッソーリ教育では、子供に日中の過ごし方を自主的に決めさせる。したがってどの教室にも複数のコーナーを設け、そこに各学習領域［生活・感覚・言語・数・文化］を割り振ることになる。建物のヴォリュームの角部を凹ませて角部を増やした。ただしあまり複雑にはせず、建築としての落ち着きを保つようにした。

Site plan

Ground floor / Changing room

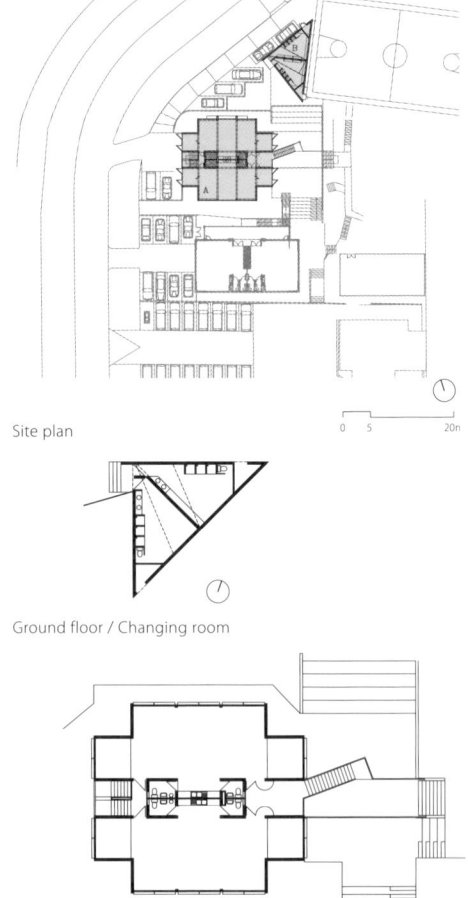

Ground floor / Classrooms

Architect: Alejandro Aravena
Partner Architects: Claudio-Blanco Architects
Collaborator: Marcela Guevara
Design/Construction Period: 2001
Building Area: 1,000m²
Location: Santiago, CHILE

27

GARIB HOUSE
ガリブ邸

Should we do a box (modern, abstract) in order to keep the pace of contemporary formal research that likely will be published, but also will very likely have a roof that leaks? Or do we do a more conventional sloped roof house that doesn't leak, but will never be published? The question was: to publish or to leak?

Since we were building on a sloped site, we chose not to choose: we did a box, but we made it follow the topography, had a slope and because of that, avoid leaks.

時代と足並みを揃えるつもりで箱（モダンで抽象的）の形態にこだわれば、雑誌には掲載されるだろうが、しかしそれでは雨漏りするのは目に見えている。あるいは昔ながらの勾配屋根にすれば、雨漏りはしないだろうが、雑誌にとり上げられる見込みはない。問題は、雑誌掲載をとるか、雨漏りをとるか。

幸い敷地は斜面にあったので、選択しないことを選択した。つまり箱は箱でも、地面の傾斜なりに建てれば雨漏りの心配もなくなる。

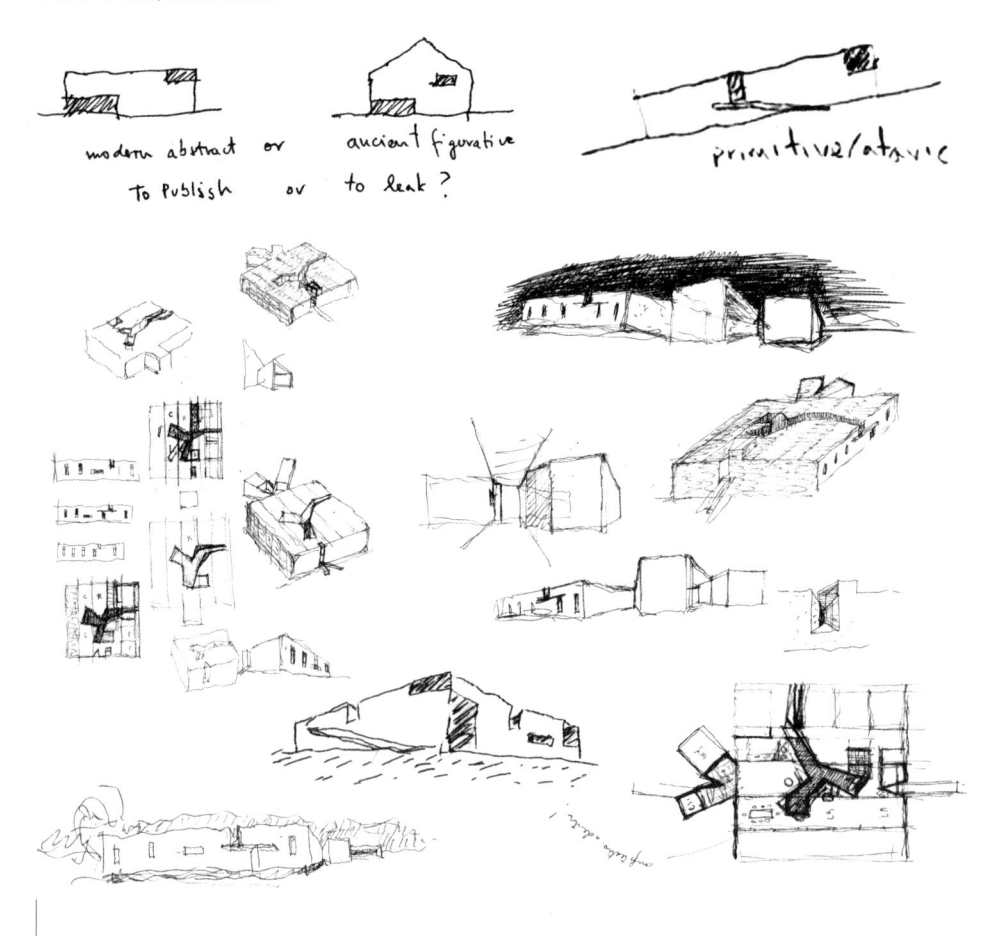

Ground floor

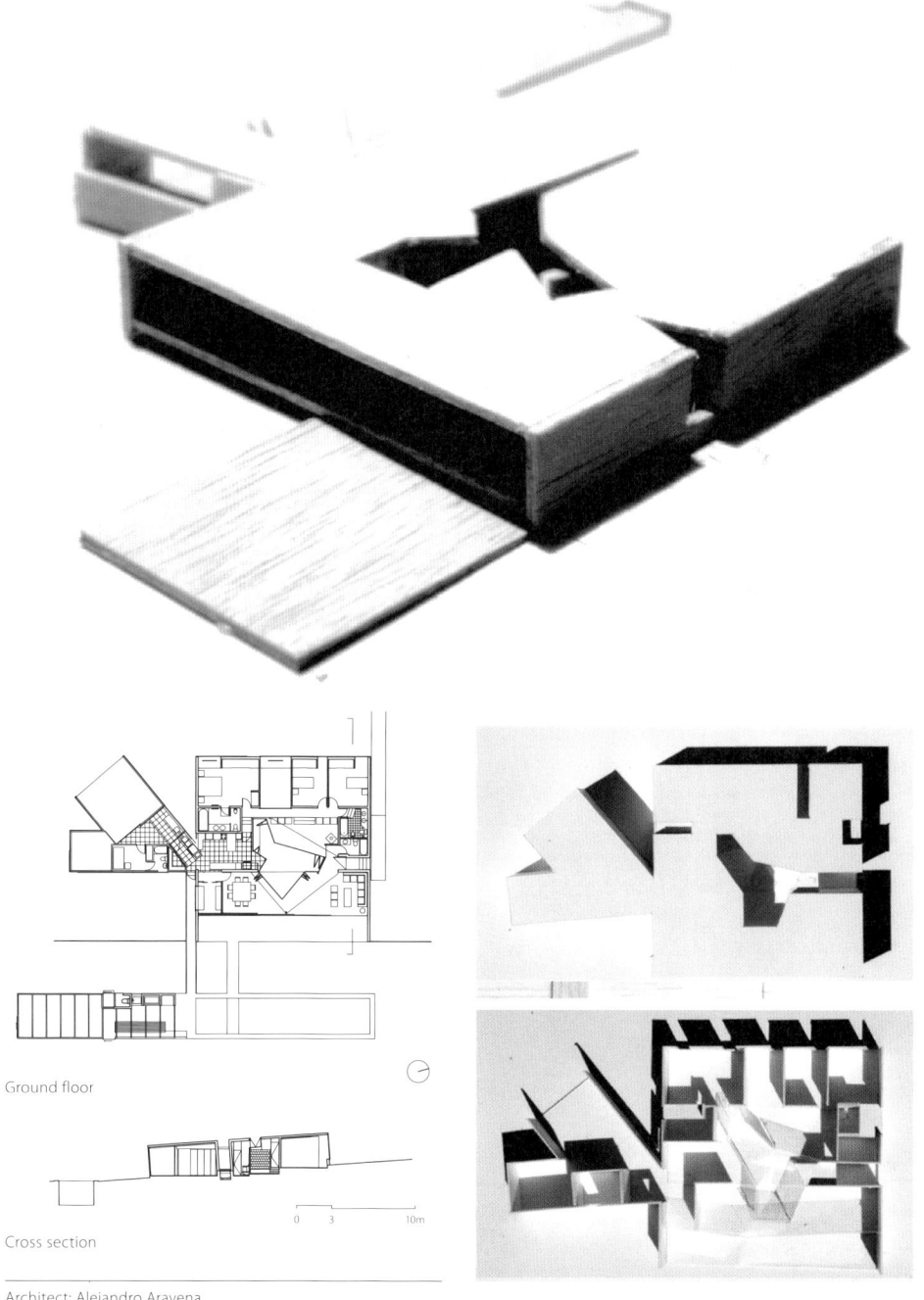

Cross section

0   3   10m

Architect: Alejandro Aravena
Partner Architect: Charles Murray
Design Period: 2001-2002
Building Area: 250m²
Location: Pirque, CHILE

MEDICAL SCHOOL
医学部棟

Hay 5 casos:
1. cono
2. embudo
3. paralelo
4. encuentro abierto
5. encuentro cerrado

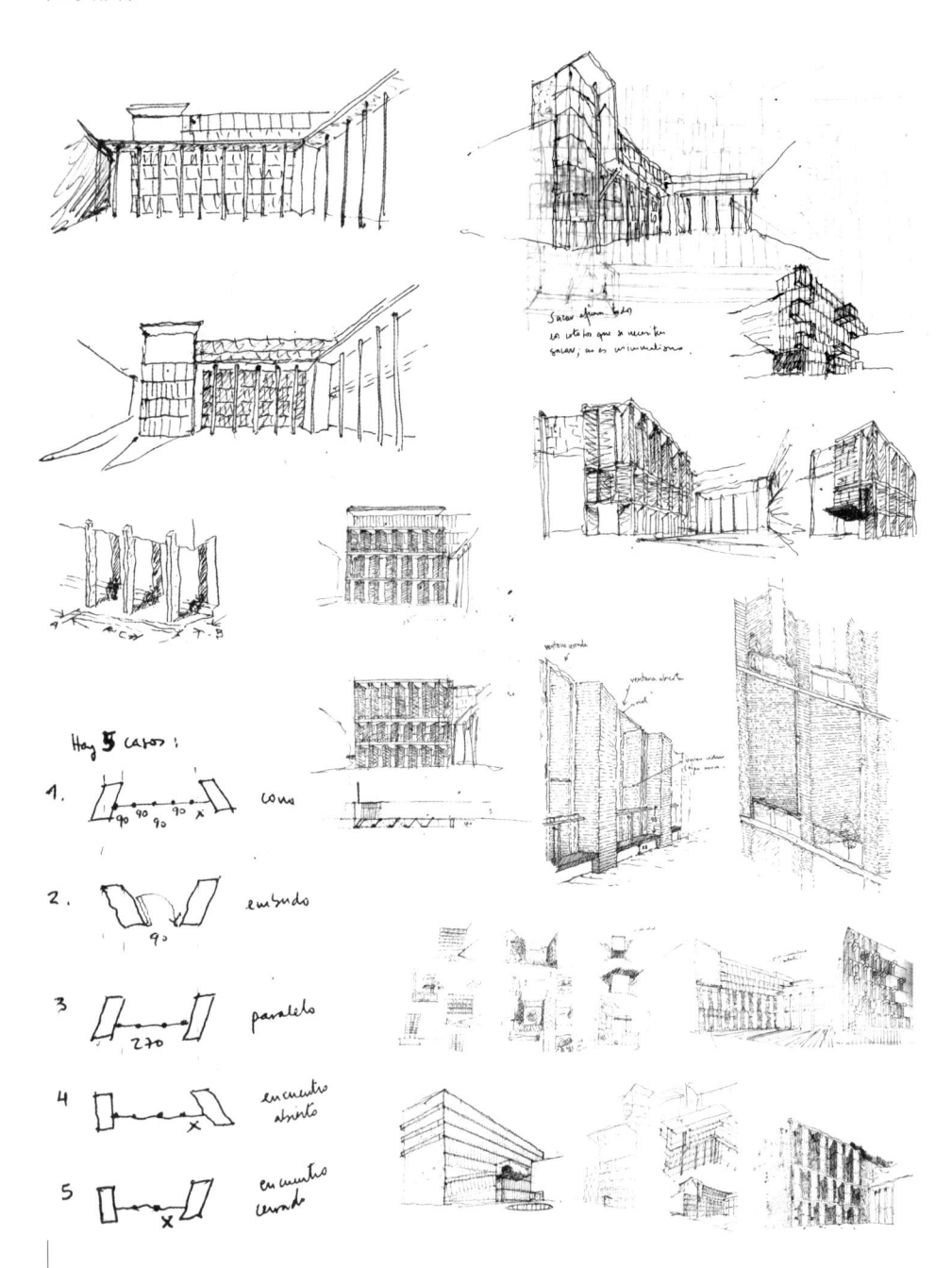

We were asked to design all kinds of classrooms – from seminars to auditoriums – in a very dense context. The only way out was to go high. Given that massive student occupancy in higher floors has always been hard to solve, we decided to bring the courtyard closer to each upper floor. This building is a vertical cloister.

非常に建て込んだ窮屈な土地に多種多様な教室——研究室から大講義室に至るまで——を設計することになった。これでは高層化するしかない。しかしながら利用頻度の高い施設を高層階に集中させるわけにもいかないので、各高層階に中庭を併設することにした。建物自体が高層の回廊となっている。

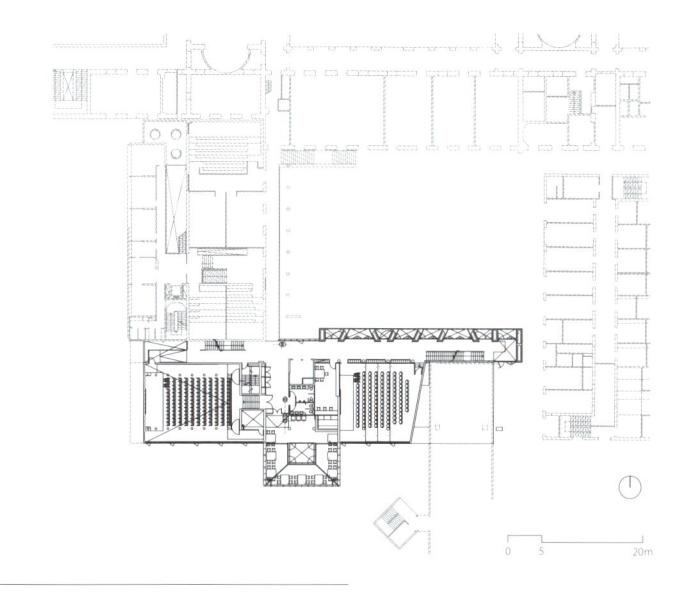

Third floor

Architect: Alejandro Aravena
Partner Architect : Fernando Perez
Collaborators: Luis Lucero, Lorena Andrade, Marcela Guevara, Ricardo Serpell, Philippe Blanc, Carolina Rodríguez, Claudio Valenzuela, Tomás Retamales
Design/Construction Period: 2001-2004
Building Area: 9,000m²
Location: The Catholic University of Chile, Santiago, CHILE

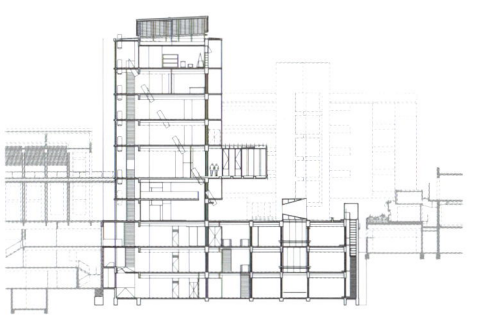

Cross section

Long section

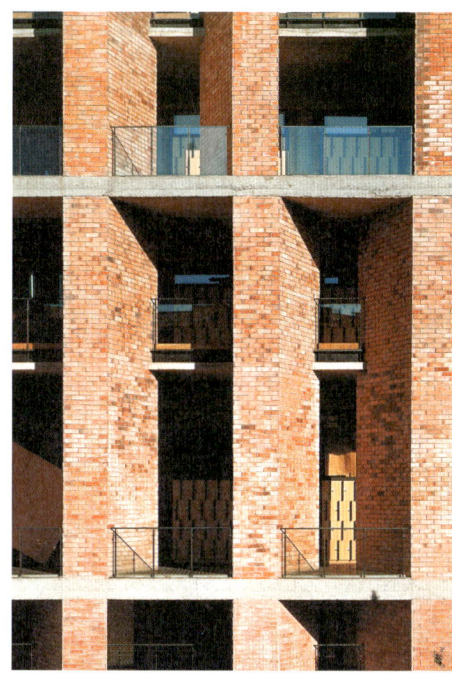

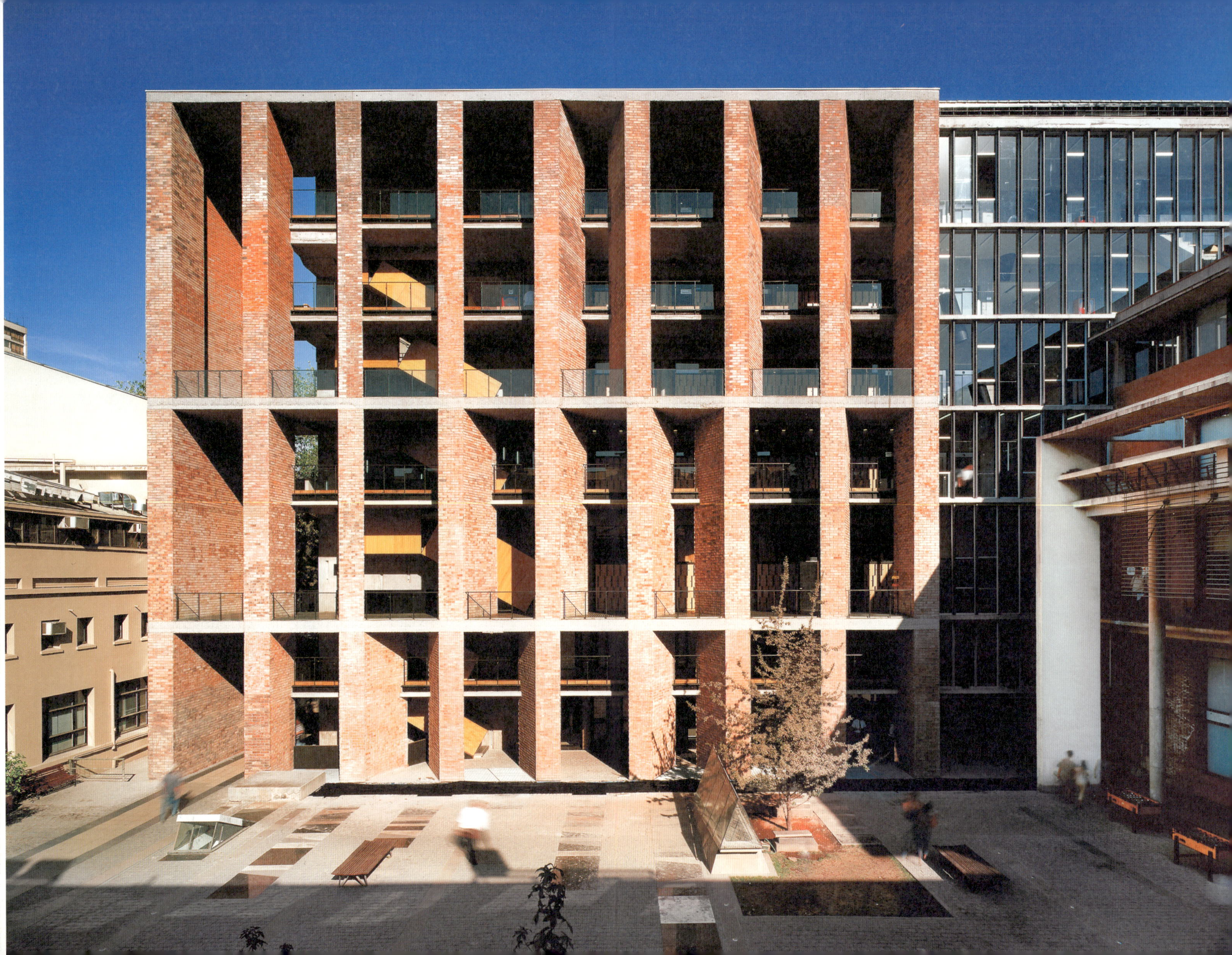

Library

Visual shots that go through the building vertically

35

BICENTENNIAL TOWER OF COMMUNICATIONS
建国200年記念電波塔

Chile is a seismic country. Santiago is surrounded by mountains. The competition guidelines asked for an "at least 300-meter-high tower." But the mountains in front of the lot were 270 meters high. In that case it was more efficient to do a thirty-meter high structure on top of the hill. So, unless we could achieve a one-kilometer high tower, there was no point in doing one. Instead of fighting gravity to achieve that height, we thought of having a gaseous tower as a kind of vertical zeppelin anchored to the ground and leveled using propellers. This was a problem of lateral forces instead of vertical ones.

チリは地震国である。その首都サンティアゴは山々に取り囲まれている。コンペ要綱には「高さ300m以上のタワー」とあった。ところが敷地正面の山の高さは270m。であれば山頂に高さ30mの構造物を建てたほうが合理的である。高さ1,000mのタワーを建てるのでもない限り、1棟に集約する意味はない。であれば重力と闘ってまで高さを稼ぐよりは、気球のタワーのようなものを大地に固定し、プロペラを使って平衡を保てばいいのではないか。ちょうど飛行船(ツェッペリン)を垂直に立てかけるような感じで。となると、鉛直力ではなく水平力の問題になる。

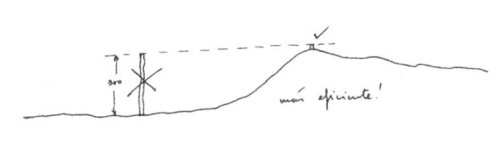

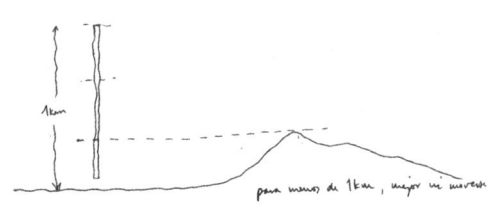

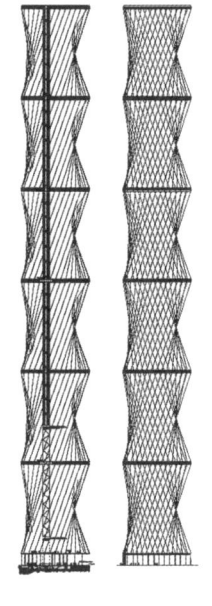

Conceptual reference

Architect: Alejandro Aravena
Partner Architect: Fernando Perez
Collaborators: Juan José Hurtado, Juan Ignacio Cerda
Design Period: 2002
Building Area: 10,000m²
Building Hight: 300m
Location: Santiago, CHILE

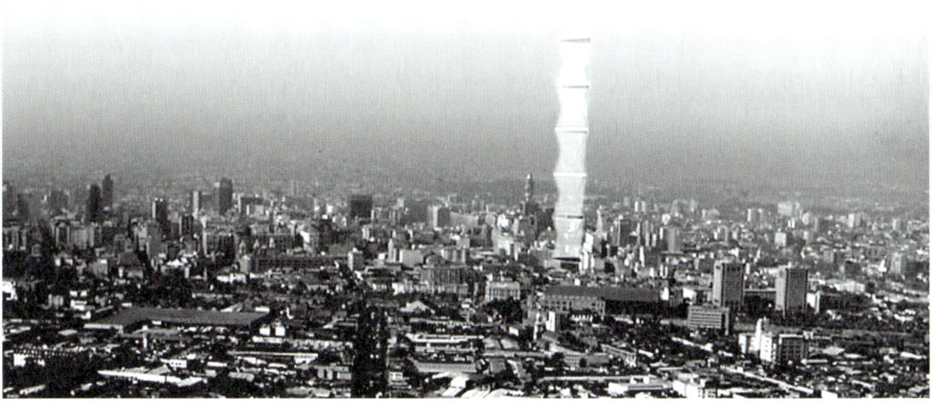

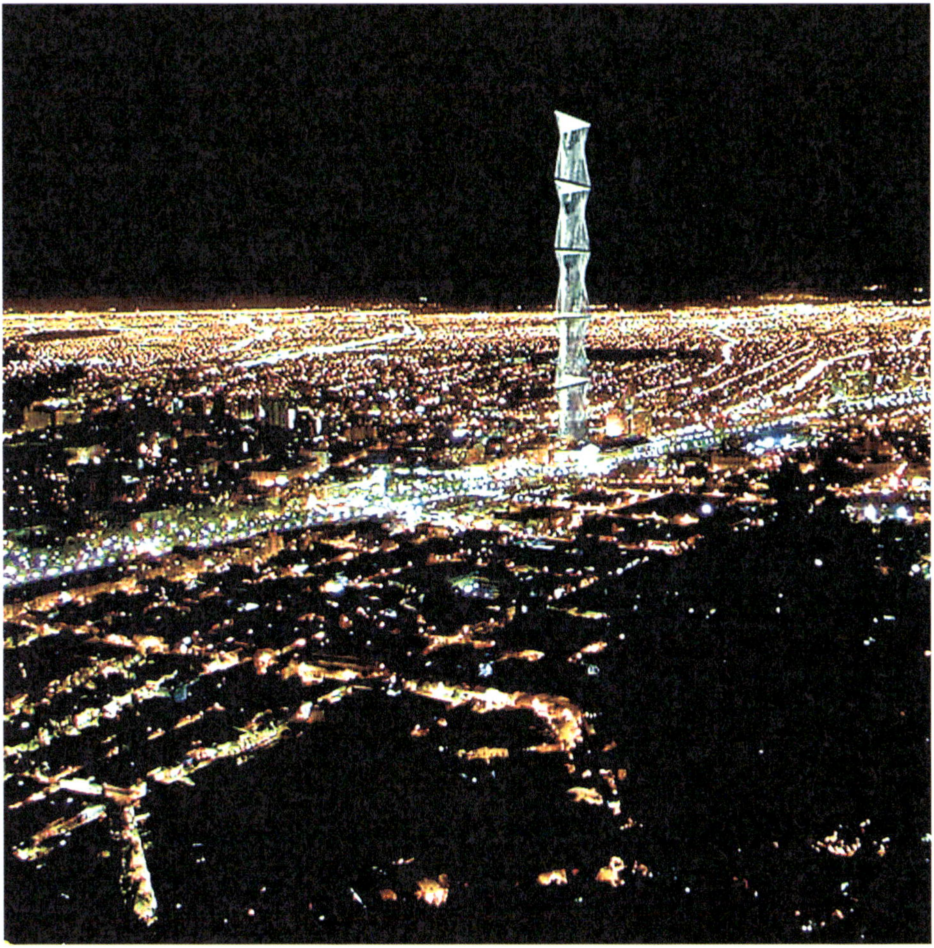

SIAMESE TOWERS
シャム・タワー

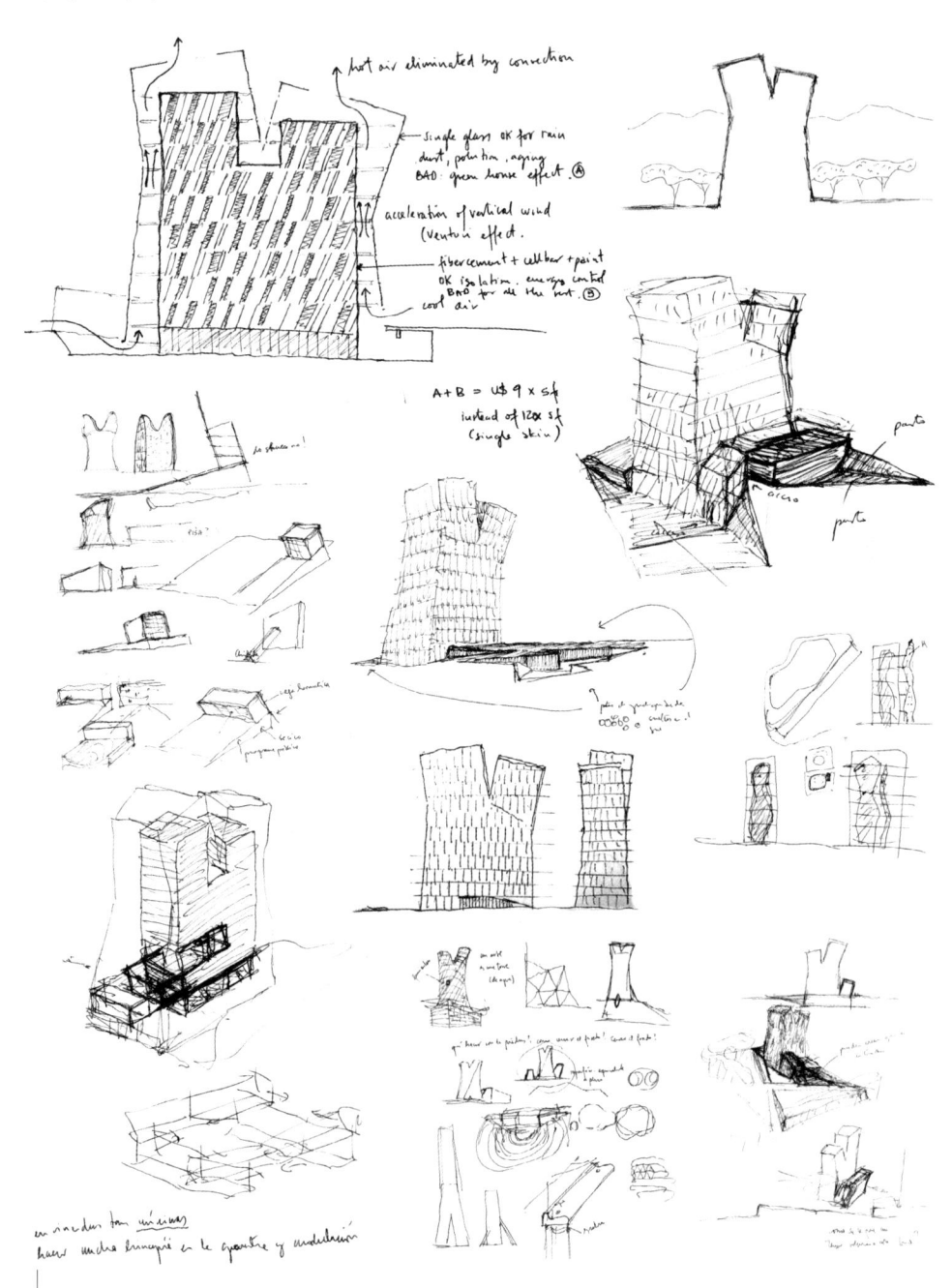

We were asked to design a glass tower. Glass is very inappropriate for Santiago's climate, because it generates the green house effect, even though it is a nice material to resist rain, pollution and aging. So we thought of using glass on the outside for what it's good and then do another building inside with efficient energy performance and allow air to flow in between the two. Convection of hot air creates a vertical wind, which is accelerated by the "waists" of the building by the Venturi effect, eliminating undesired heat gains before they reach the second building inside.

ガラス張りのタワーを設計することになった。あいにくだが、ガラスはサンティアゴの気候にはおよそ適さない。たしかにガラスは雨にも汚れにも強く耐久性もあるが、温室効果を引き起こす。そこでガラスを用いるのはさしあたり外観だけにして、その内側にエネルギー効率の良い建物をまた別につくり、両者の間にできた隙間を空気の通り道にする。暖気が対流することによって空気が上に流れ、さらに建物の「くびれ」ではヴェンチュリ効果によりこの流れが勢いを増して、内側の建物に対する熱負荷を軽減する。

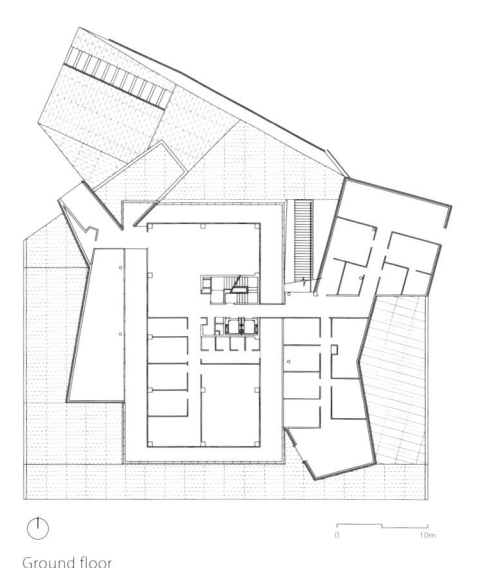

Site plan

Axonometric view

Long section

Ground floor

Architect: Alejandro Aravena
Partner Architects: Charles Murray, Alfonso Montero, Ricardo Torrejón
Collaborator: Emilio de la Cerda
Design/Construction Period: 2003-2005
Building Area: 5,000m^2
Location: The Catholic University of Chile, Santiago, CHILE

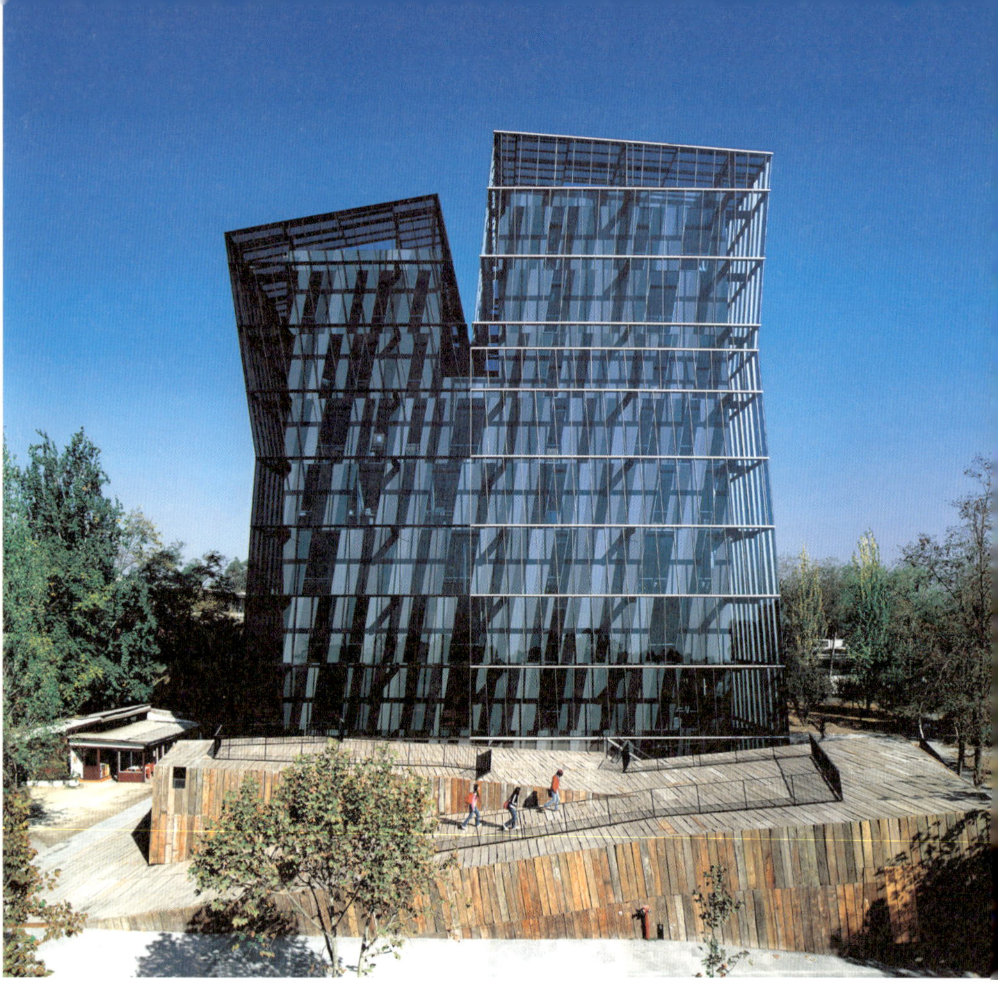

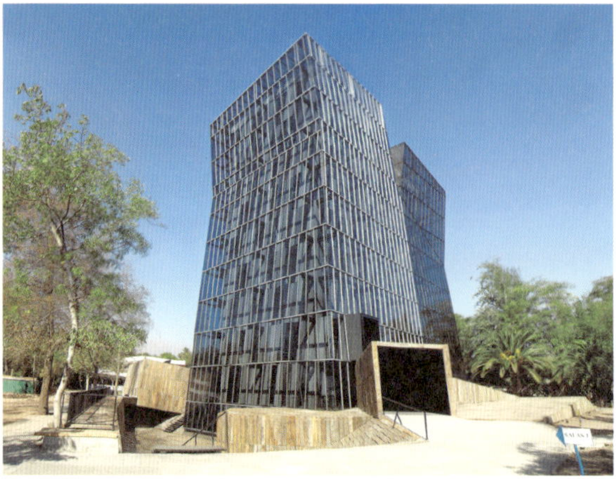

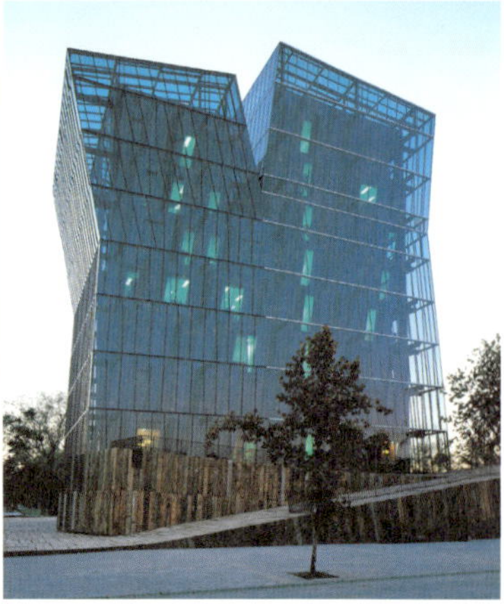

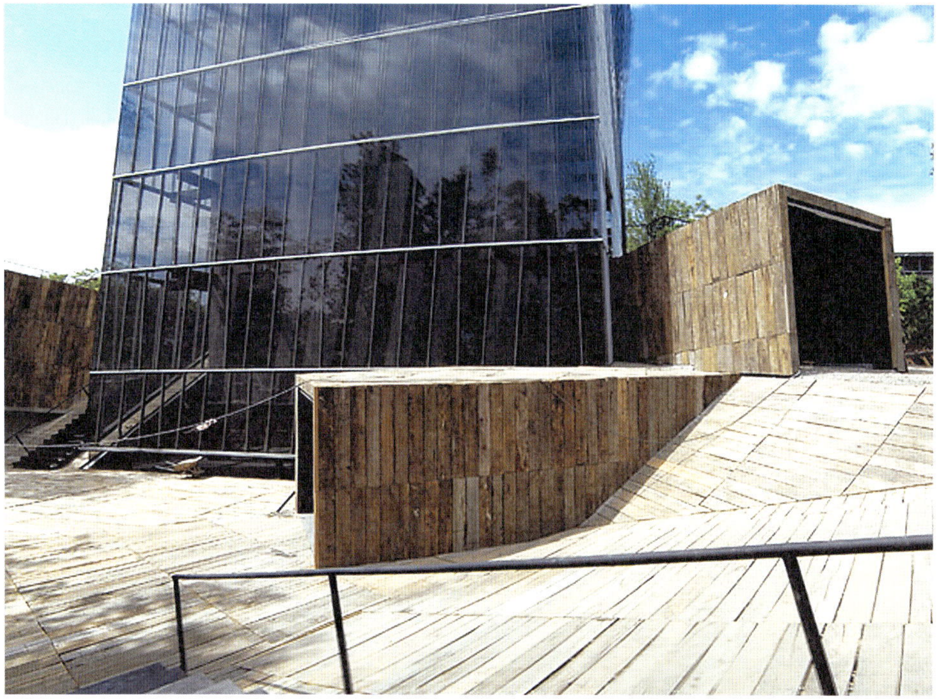
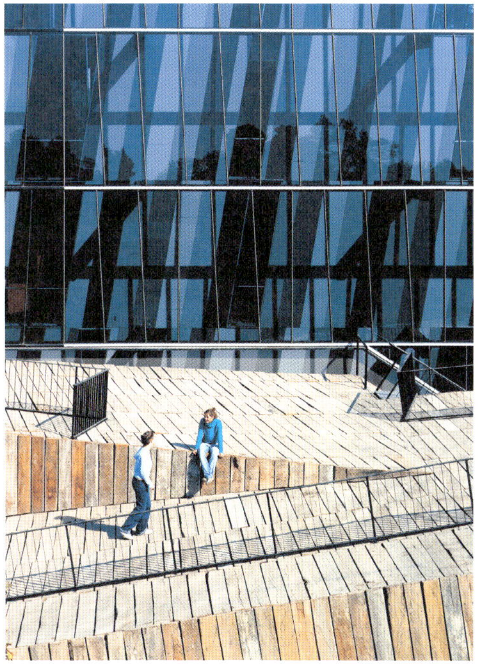
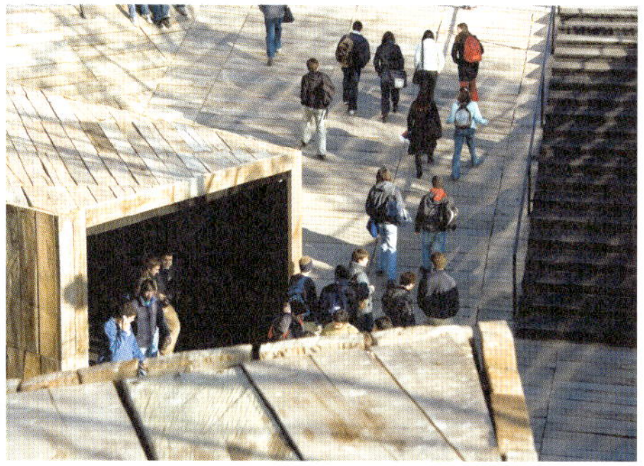
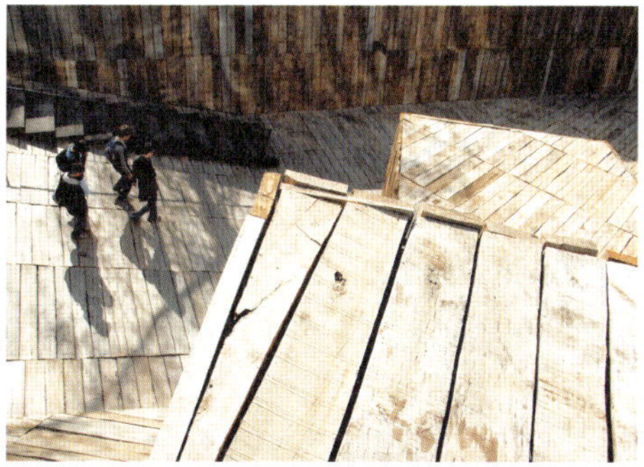
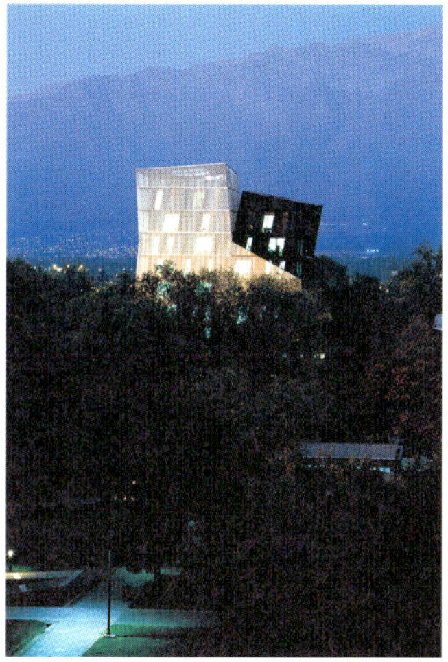
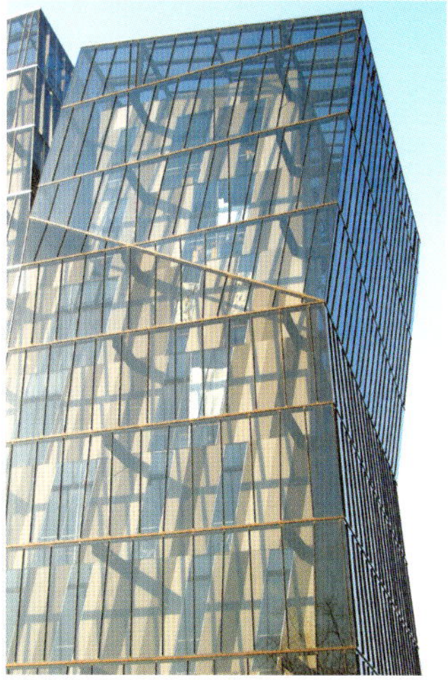
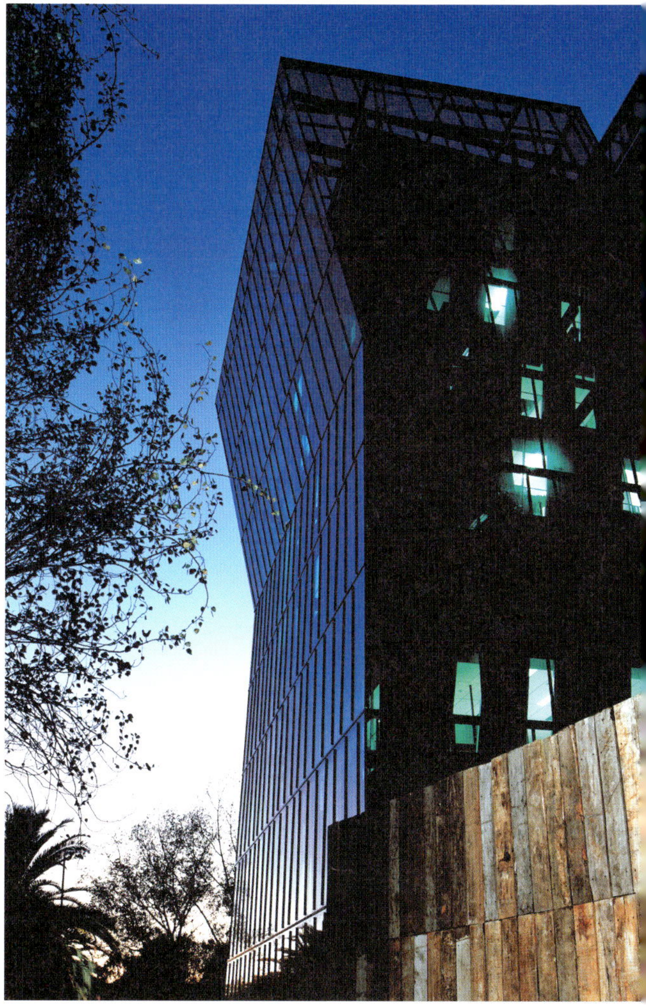
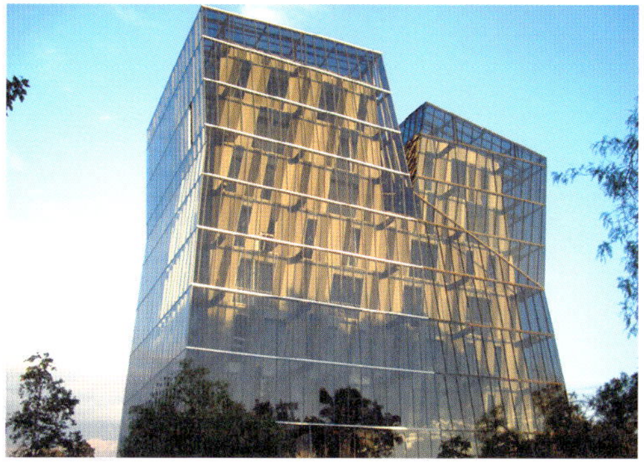
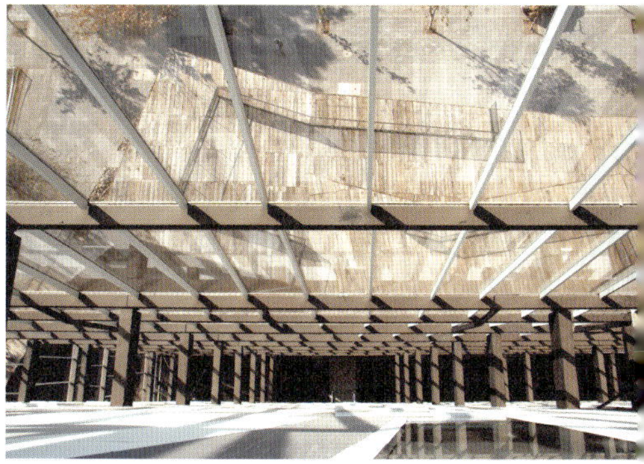

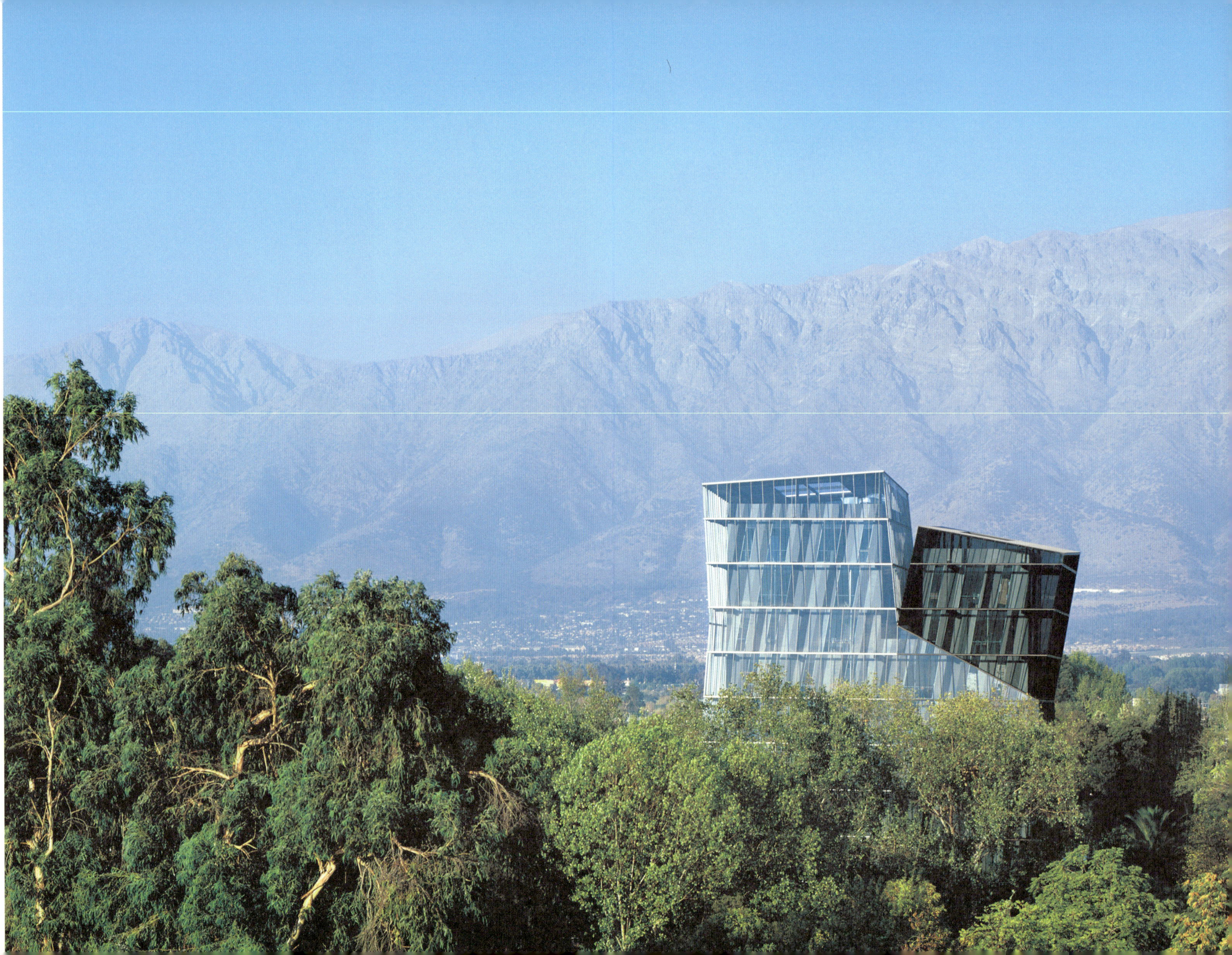

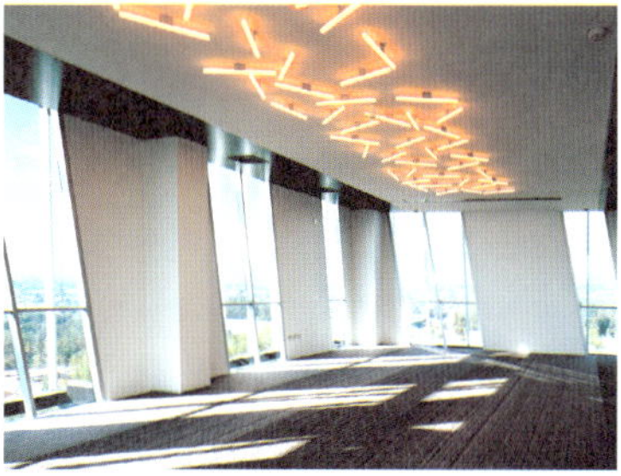

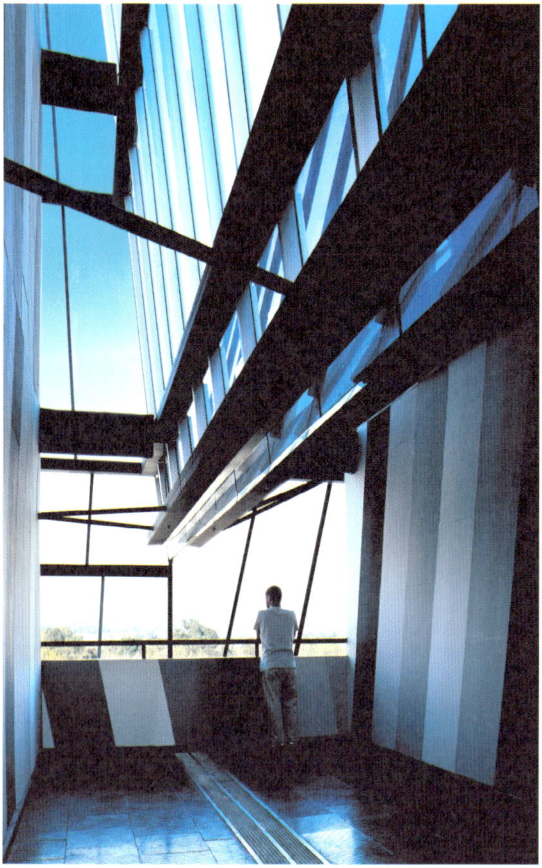

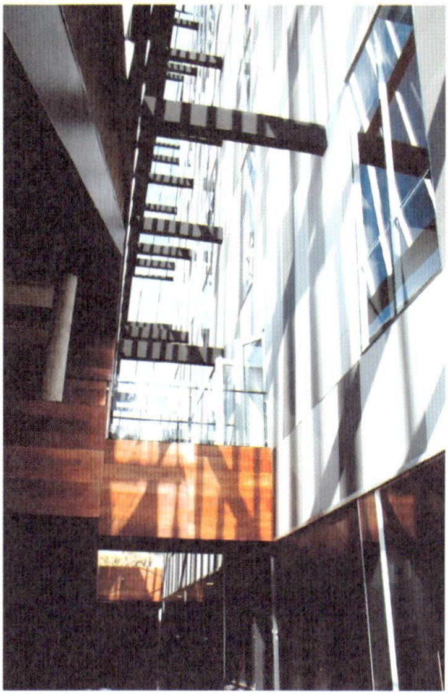

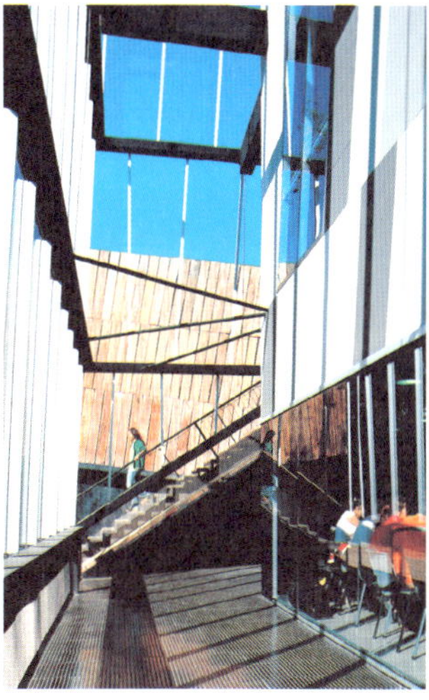

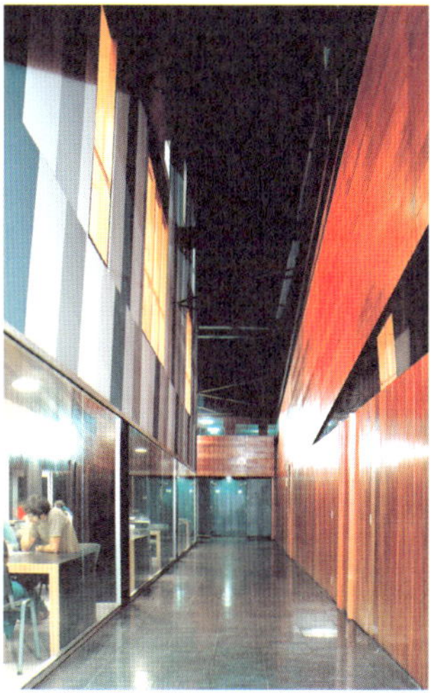

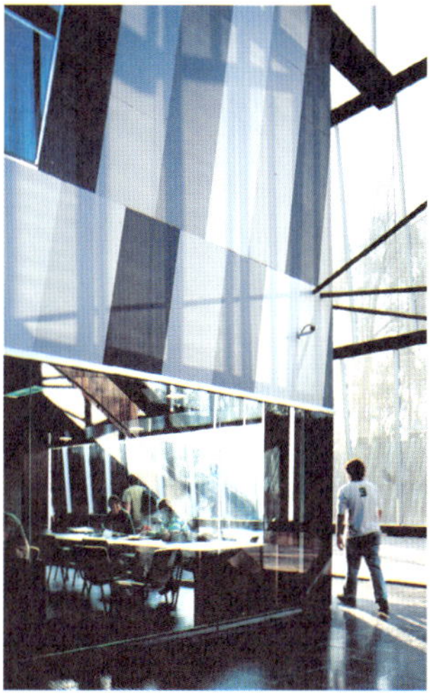

PIREHUEICO HOUSE
ピリウェイコの住宅

The client asked for a house with the color of the shadow. He wanted to restitute to the place the condition that was there before the intervention. We proposed a base able to resist the place and on top of it, a geometry that reacted to views and orientation, but also avoided strong winds and heavy rain.

影と同じ色の住宅が欲しい、と施主は言った。彼はその場所を手つかずの状態に戻したかったのだ。私たちは頑丈な基礎を据え、その上に眺望や方位を優先しながらも強風や豪雨にも耐えうる構造を載せた。

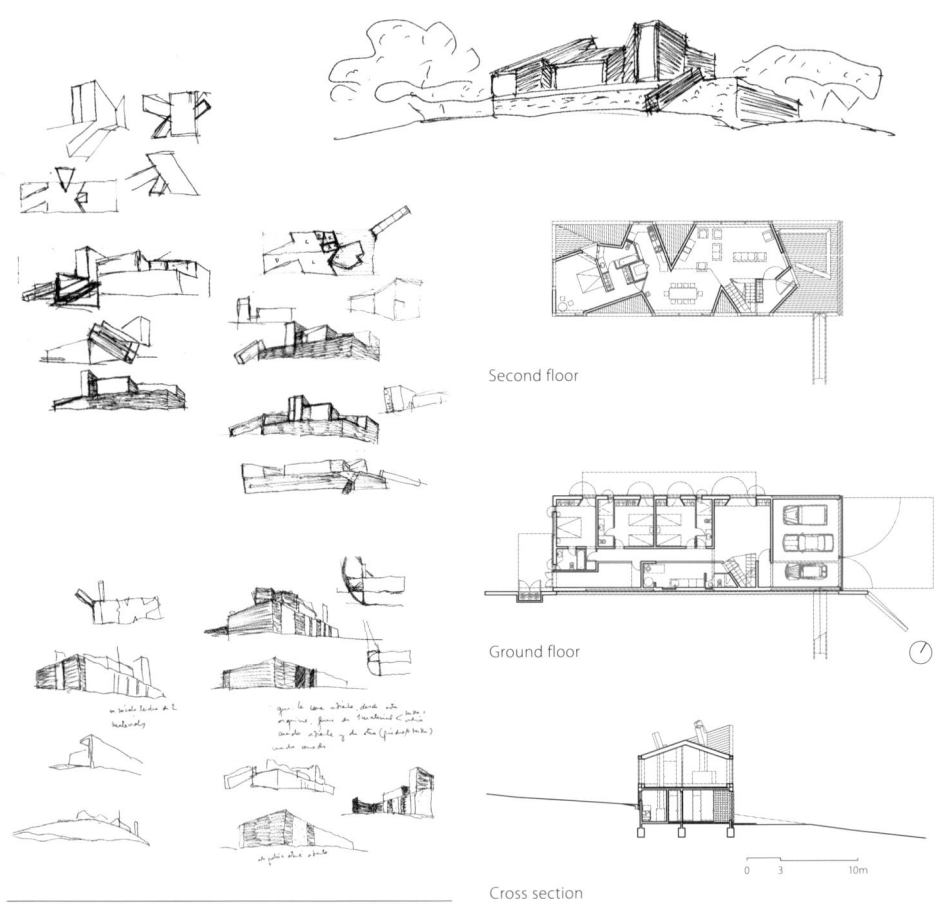

Second floor

Ground floor

Cross section

Architect: Alejandro Aravena
Partner Architects: Jorge Christie, Víctor Oddó
Design/Construction Period: 2003-2004
Building Area: 350m²
Location: Pirehueico Lake, CHILE

Alejandro Aravena Architects

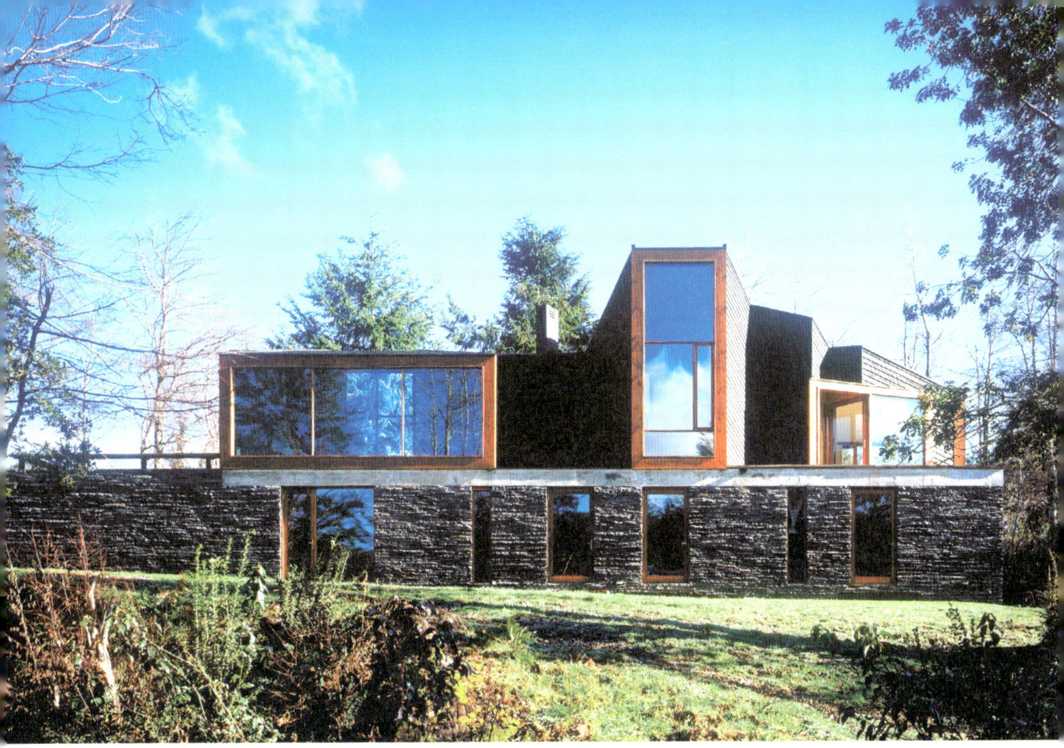
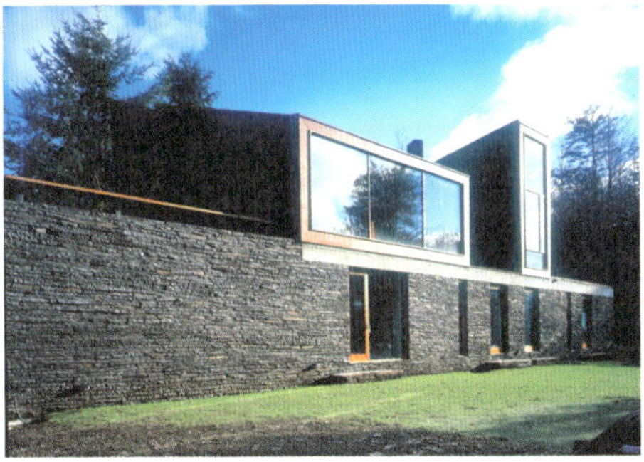
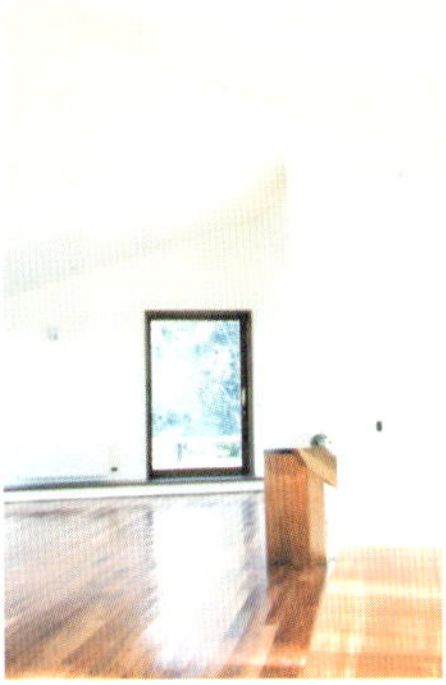
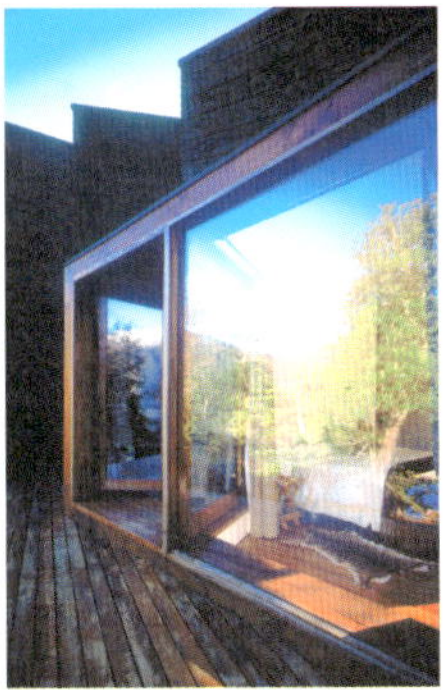
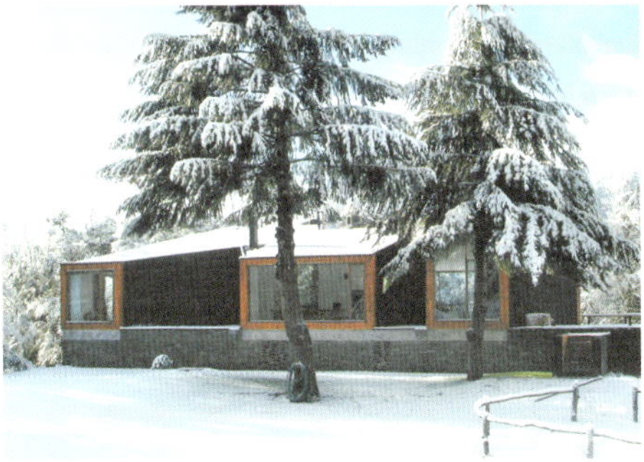
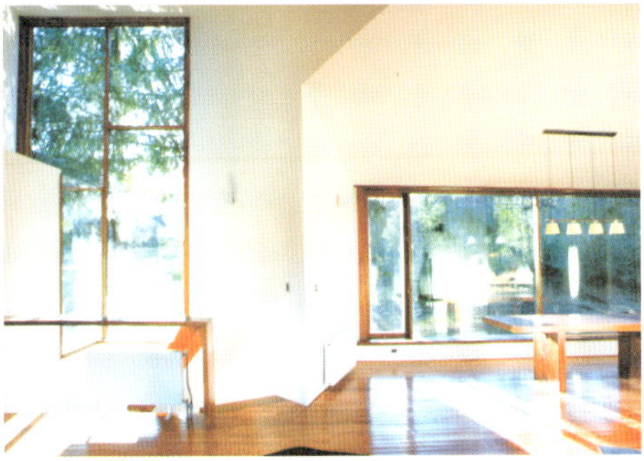

SCHOOL OF ARCHITECTURE
建築学部棟

We were asked to remodel a building from the Nineties. We wrapped a building that had too many lines with a rather tense and straight envelop that meliorated the energy performance, offered a more neutral volume towards the historical building in front and added a review spaces in between the two skins.

1990年代に建てられた校舎の改修を頼まれた。これがやたらと線の多い建物だったので、これにシャープですっきりとした覆いを被せた。おかげでエネルギー効率が上がり、また外観がニュートラルになったぶん正面の歴史的造物を引き立てることにもなった。新旧の外皮（スキン）の間には新たに講評スペースを設けた。

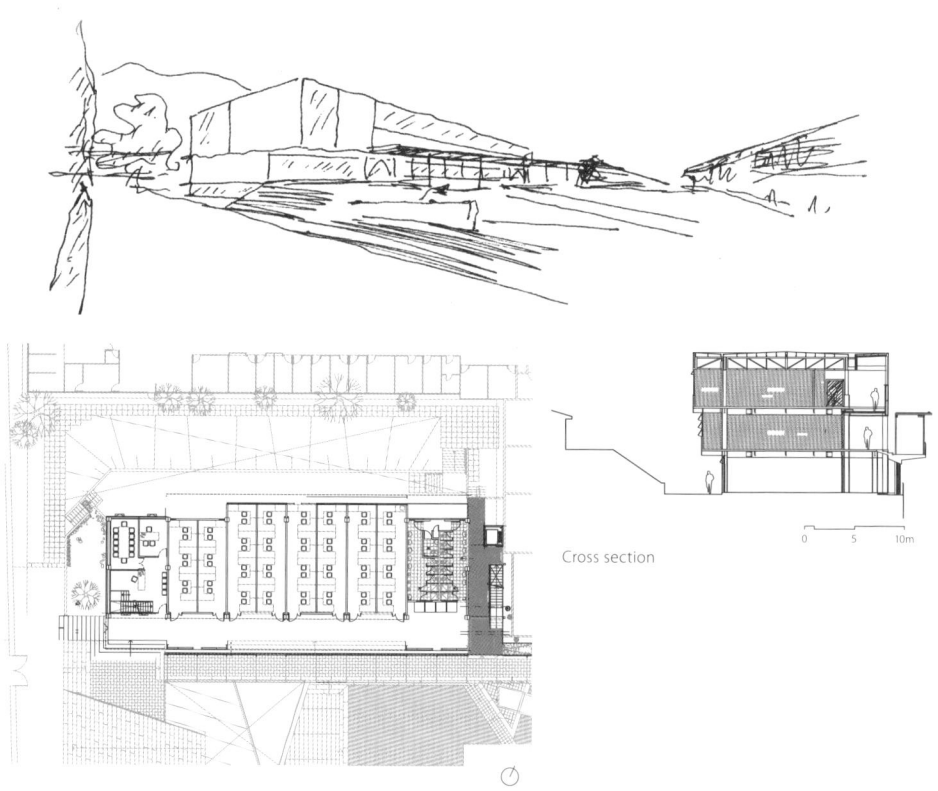

Cross section

Ground floor

Architect: Alejandro Aravena
Partner Architect: Lorena Andrade
Collaborators: Juan Hurtado, Carlos Bisbal, Armando Bahamondes, Luis Lucero
Design/Construction Period: 2004
Building Area: 1,500m²
Location: The Catholic University of Chile, Santiago, CHILE

Original state

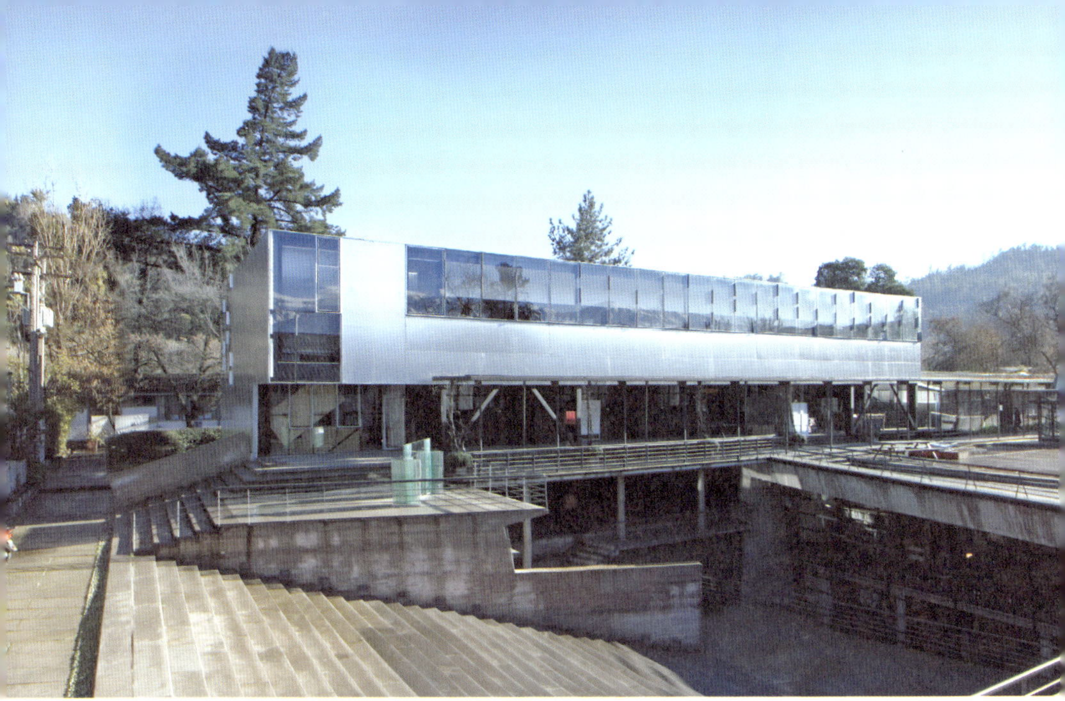

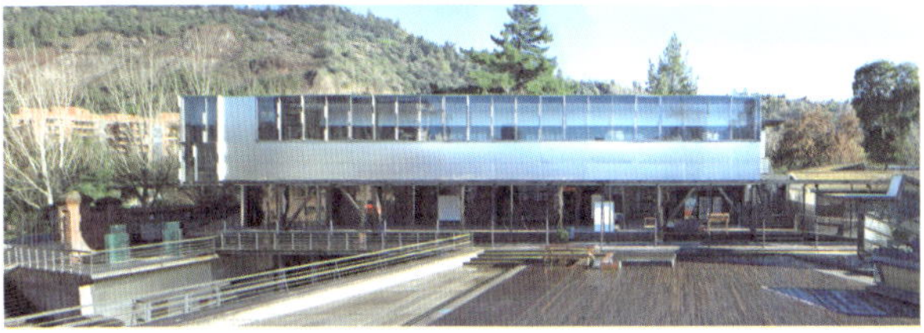

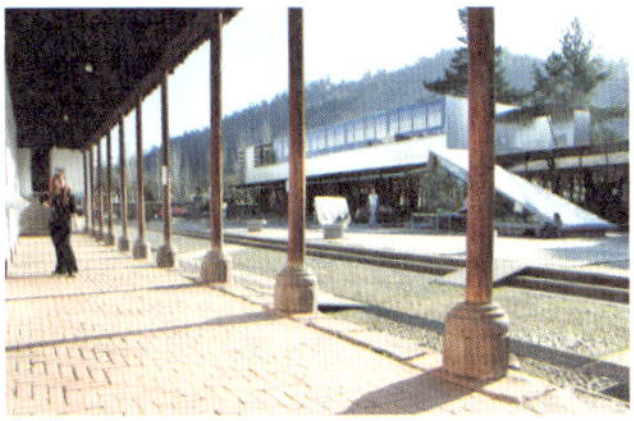

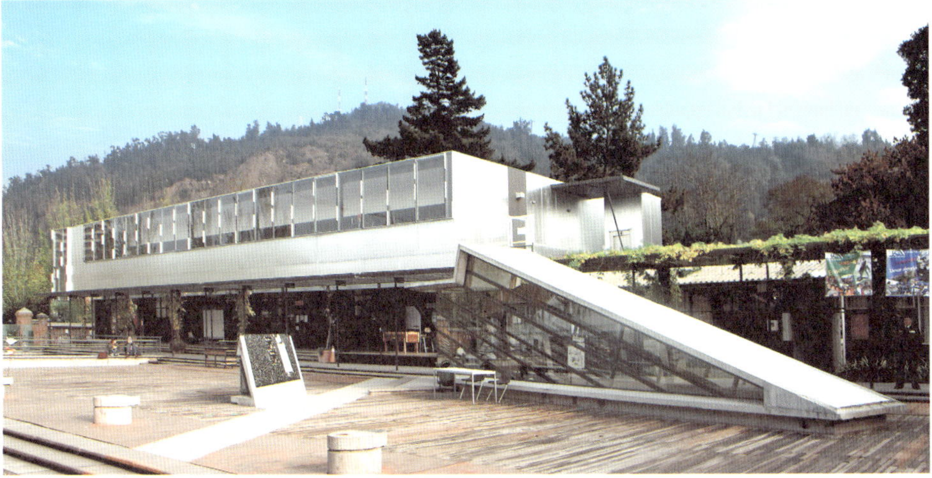

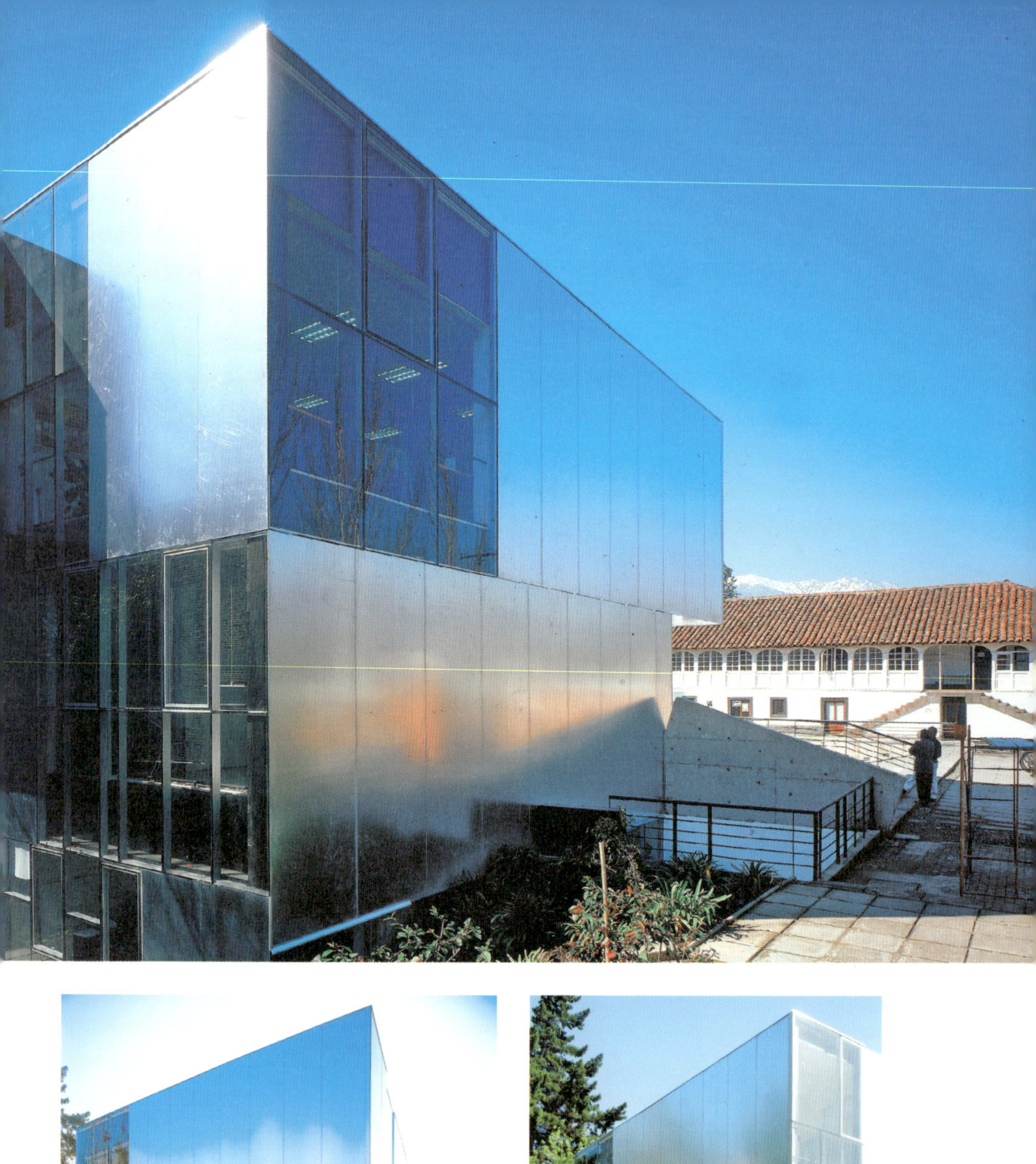

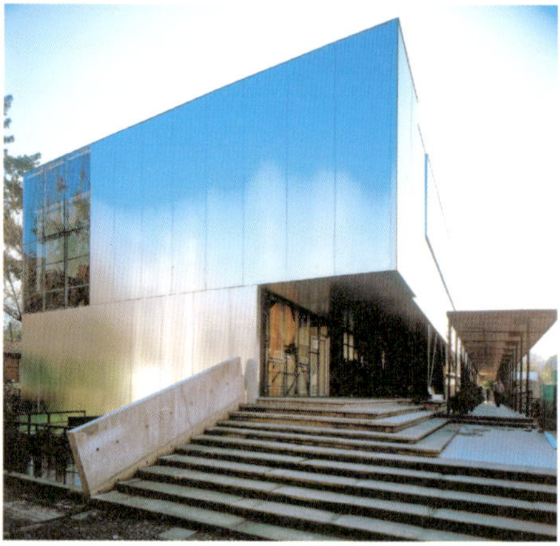

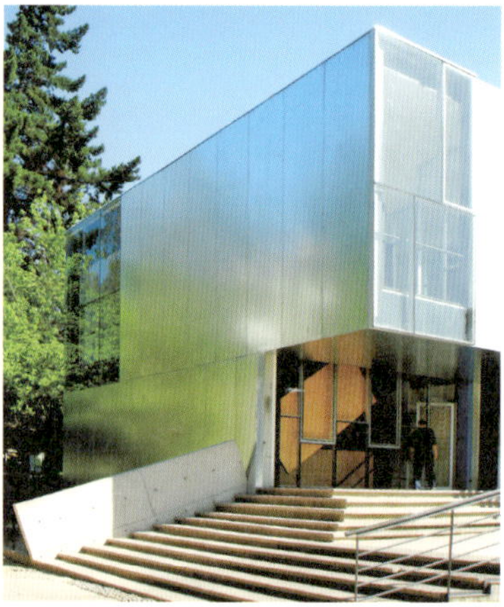

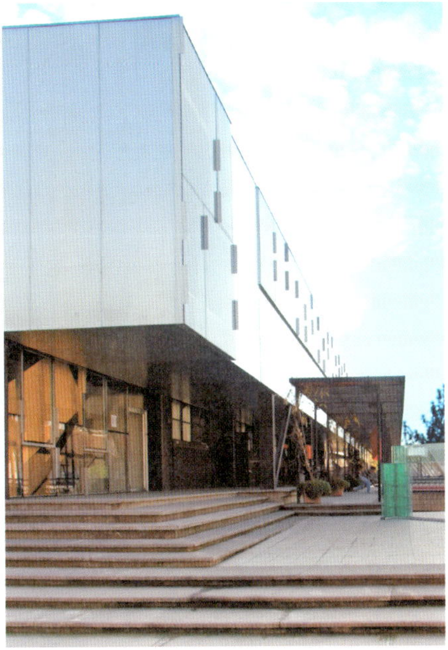

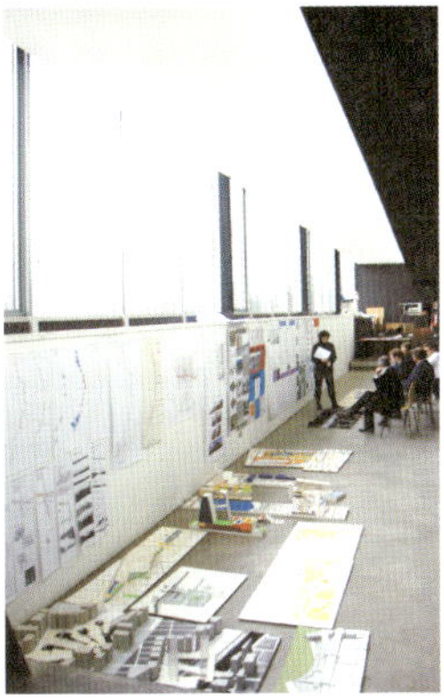

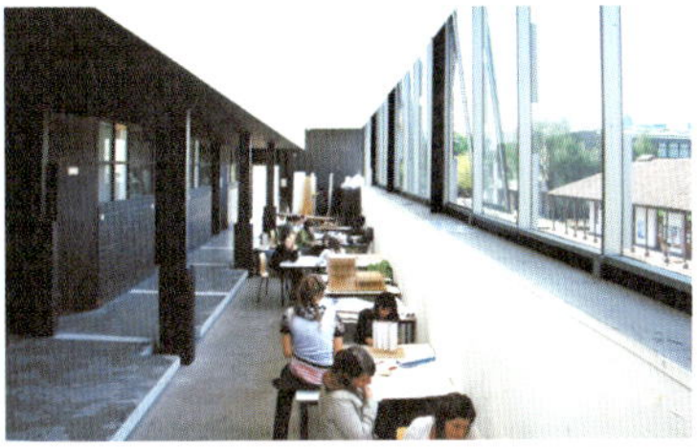

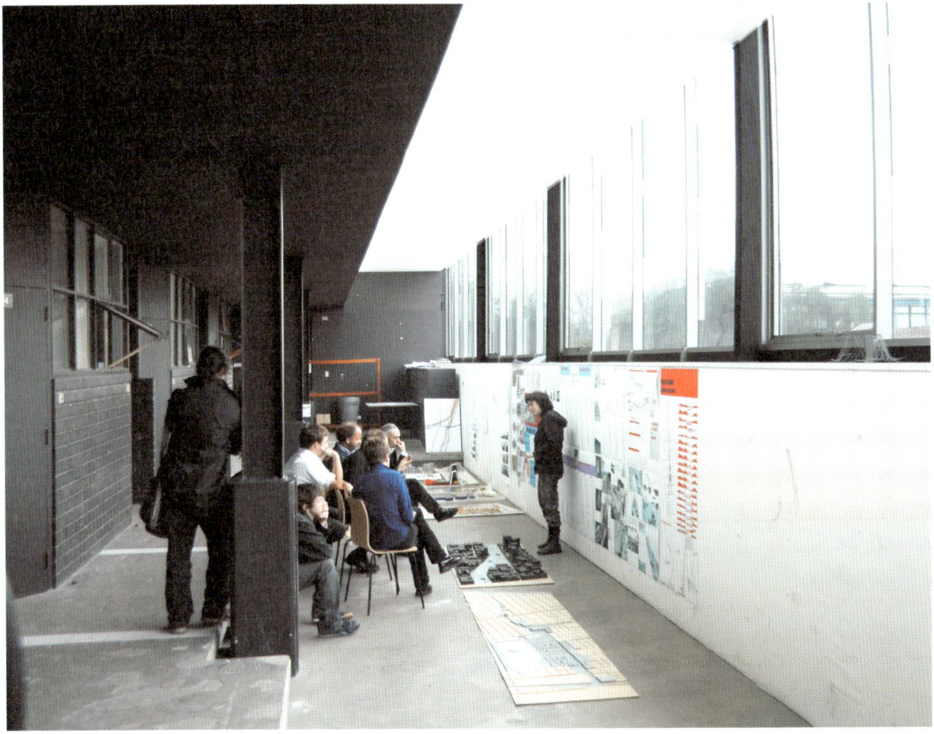

VERBO DIVINO SCHOOL
ヴェルボ・ディヴィーノ大学

After a quick analysis we arrived to the conclusion that there was not going to be enough space for the required built area and all the courtyards that the competition established after all the phase's implementation. So we thought of elevating the classrooms and use them as the roof for the covered courtyards. The circles wanted to occupy the territory from the very beginning though a primitive operation underscoring the origins of the school.

ざっと検討してみただけで結論は見えた。このコンペ所定の建築面積と中庭をすべて実現するほどの広さは、全工期を終えるころには残っていない、ということが。そこで教室群を頭上に持ち上げ、その階下に中庭を設ける。構内を円で埋め尽くしていくことは最初から決めていた。原始的なやり方ではあるが、これにより建学の精神をアピールする。

Conceptual references

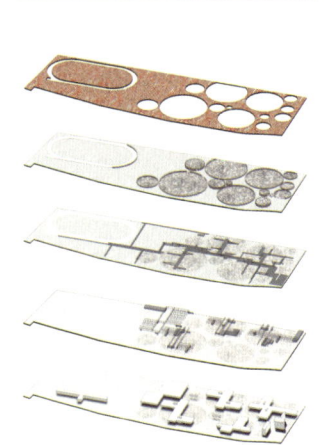

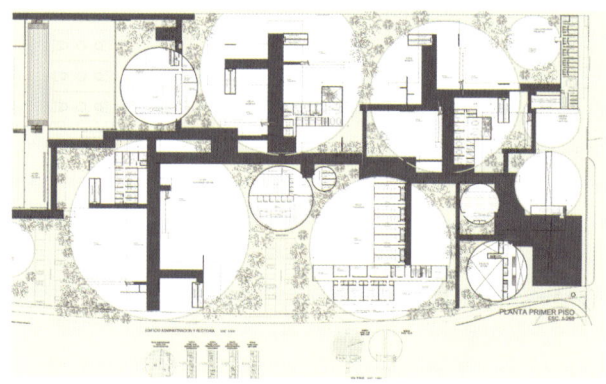

Ground floor

General view

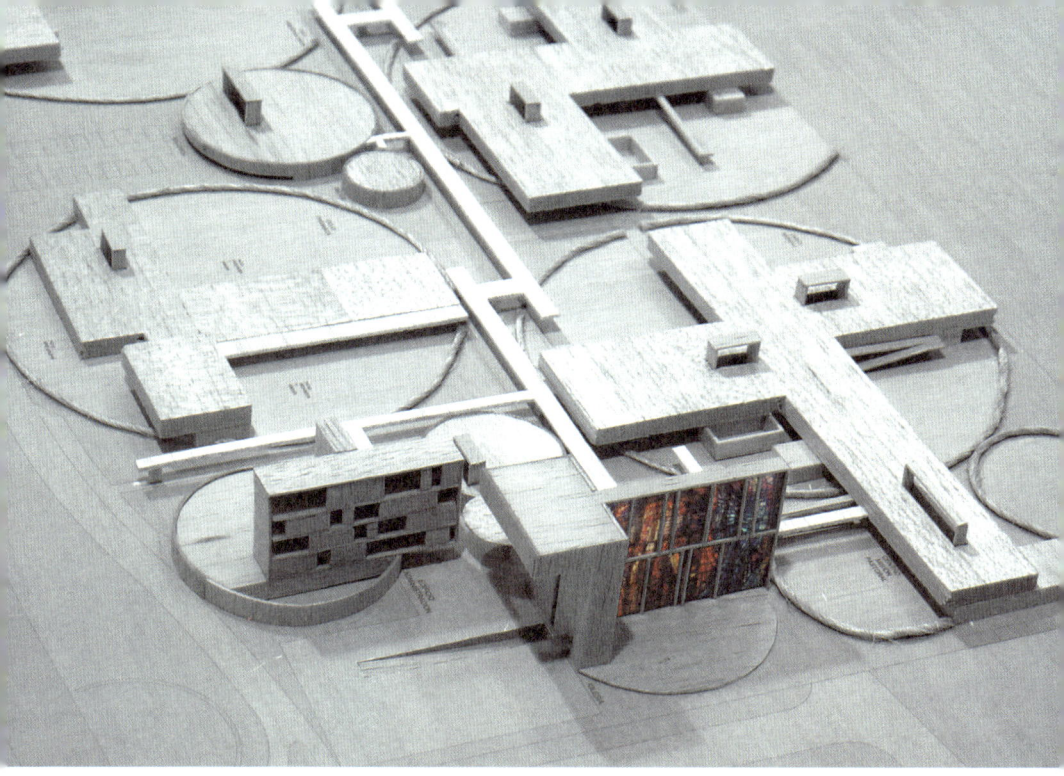

Architect: Alejandro Aravena
Partner Architects: Gica Fernandes, Blanco-Andrade Architects
Collaborators: Víctor Oddó
Design Period: 2006
Building Area: 10,000m²
Location: Santiago, CHILE

ST. EDWARD'S UNIVERSITY DORMS
セント・エドワード大学 学生寮

We needed to accommodate 300 beds, some social areas and some services for the whole campus in a narrow lot. We did three things: we created a plinth using the more public facilities to activate the ground floor, we carved the volume's core and placed there the social areas and we articulated the perimeter of the building as much as possible, increasing the linear meters of façade in order to guarantee views and natural light to each room. To be able to resist a tough environment, we opted for a sequence of skins that are hard and rough in the outer layer and become softer and more delicate towards the core.

全300床の寮ならびに社交場や食堂などの共用施設を、狭い敷地に詰め込まなければならなかった。私たちは3つの措置を講じた。まずは基壇を築き、そこに公共性の高い施設を集めて地上階を活性化する。次にこのヴォリュームのコアを割り抜き、そこを社交の場にあてる。最後は平面の輪郭を分節することで外壁の表面積を増やし、各室の眺望と採光を担保する。過酷な環境を耐え抜くために、外側のレイヤーには硬くて肌理の粗い材を用いたが、これを内側のコアに向けて柔らかで繊細な材に変えていった。

Image reference: Hamilton Pool Preserve, Austin, Texas, USA

Third floor

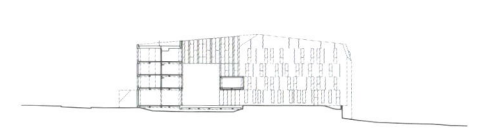

Cross section

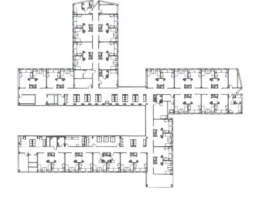

Second floor

Architect: Alejandro Aravena
Partner Architect: Ricardo Torrejón
Partner Architects Texas: Cotera + Reed
Collaborators CHILE: Victor Oddó, Rebecca Emmons
Collaborators Texas: Tiffani Erdmanczyk, Travis Hughbanks, Leyla Shams, Joyce Chen, Deb Ebersole
Design/Construction Period: 2006-2008
Building Area: 30,000m^2 (12,000m^2 dorms + 18,000m^2 parking)
Location: Austin, Texas, USA

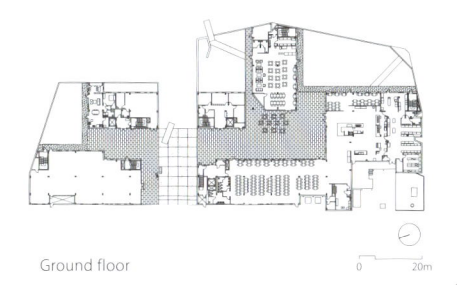

Ground floor

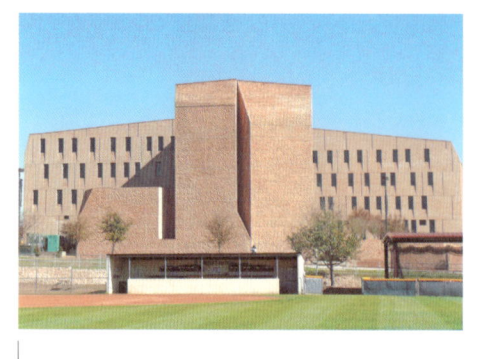

56 | Alejandro Aravena Architects

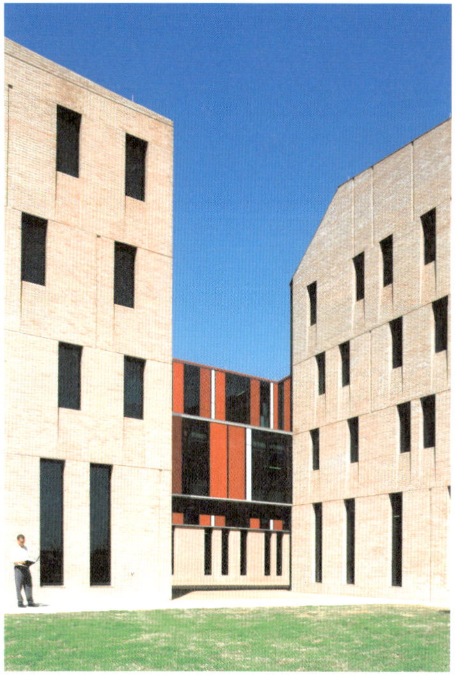
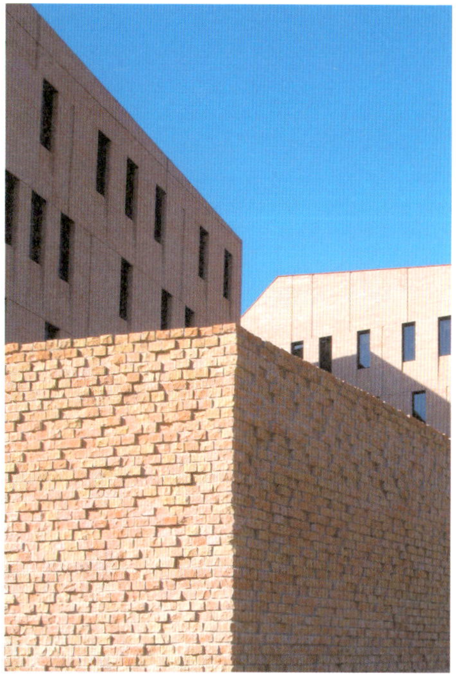
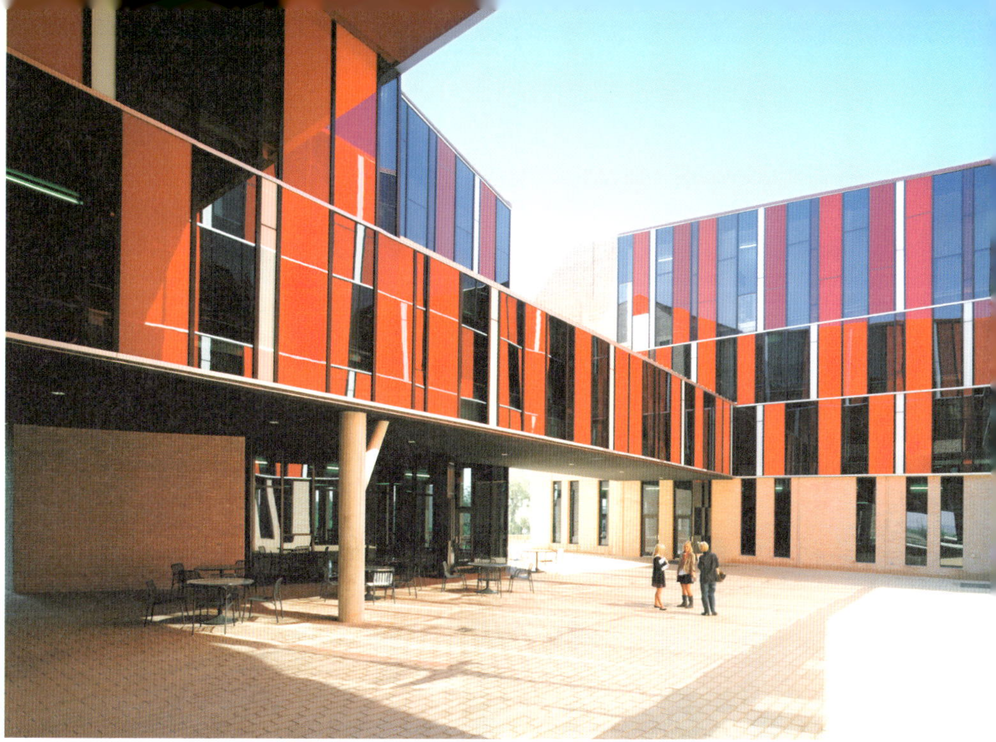
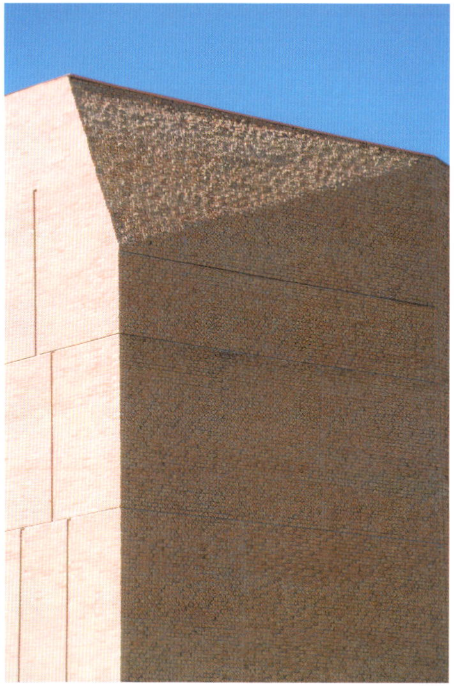
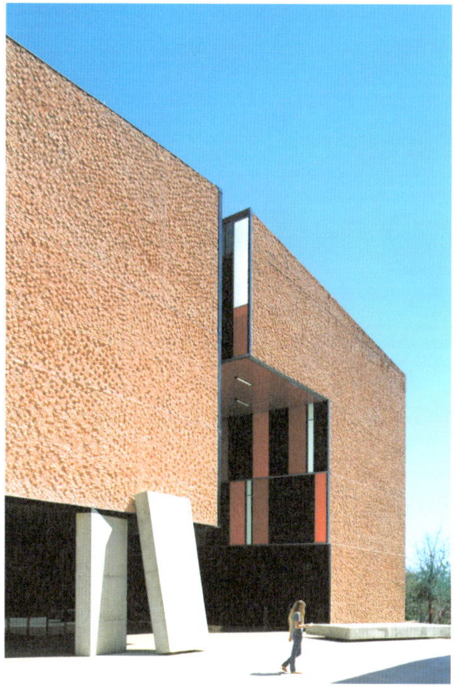
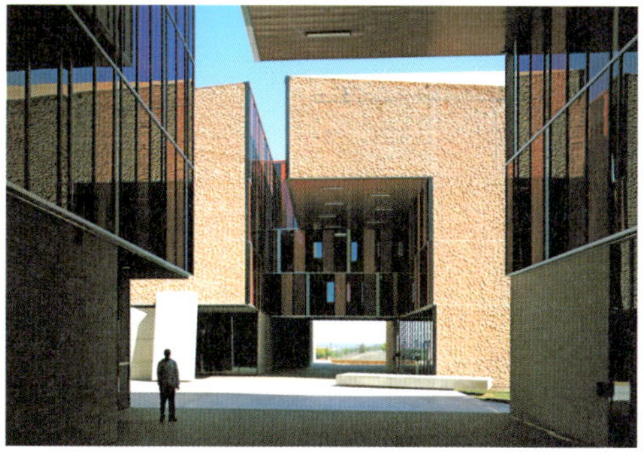
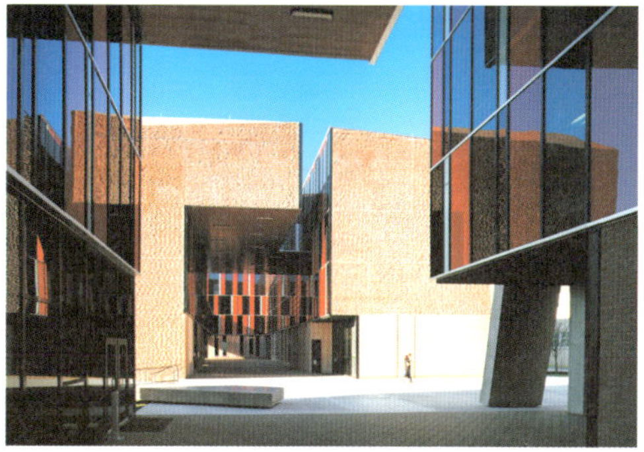
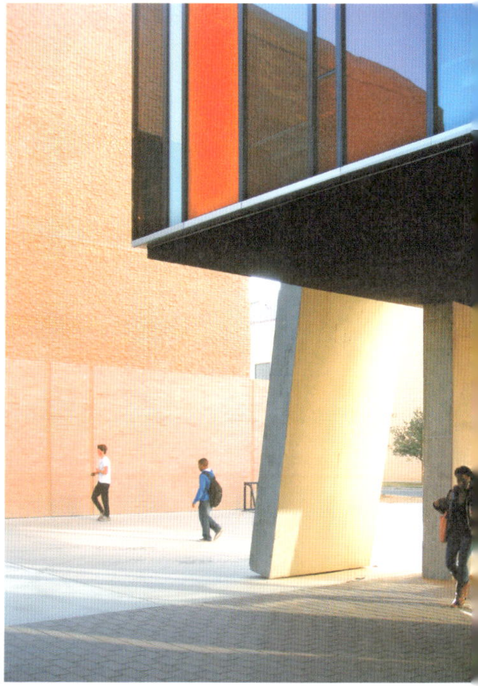

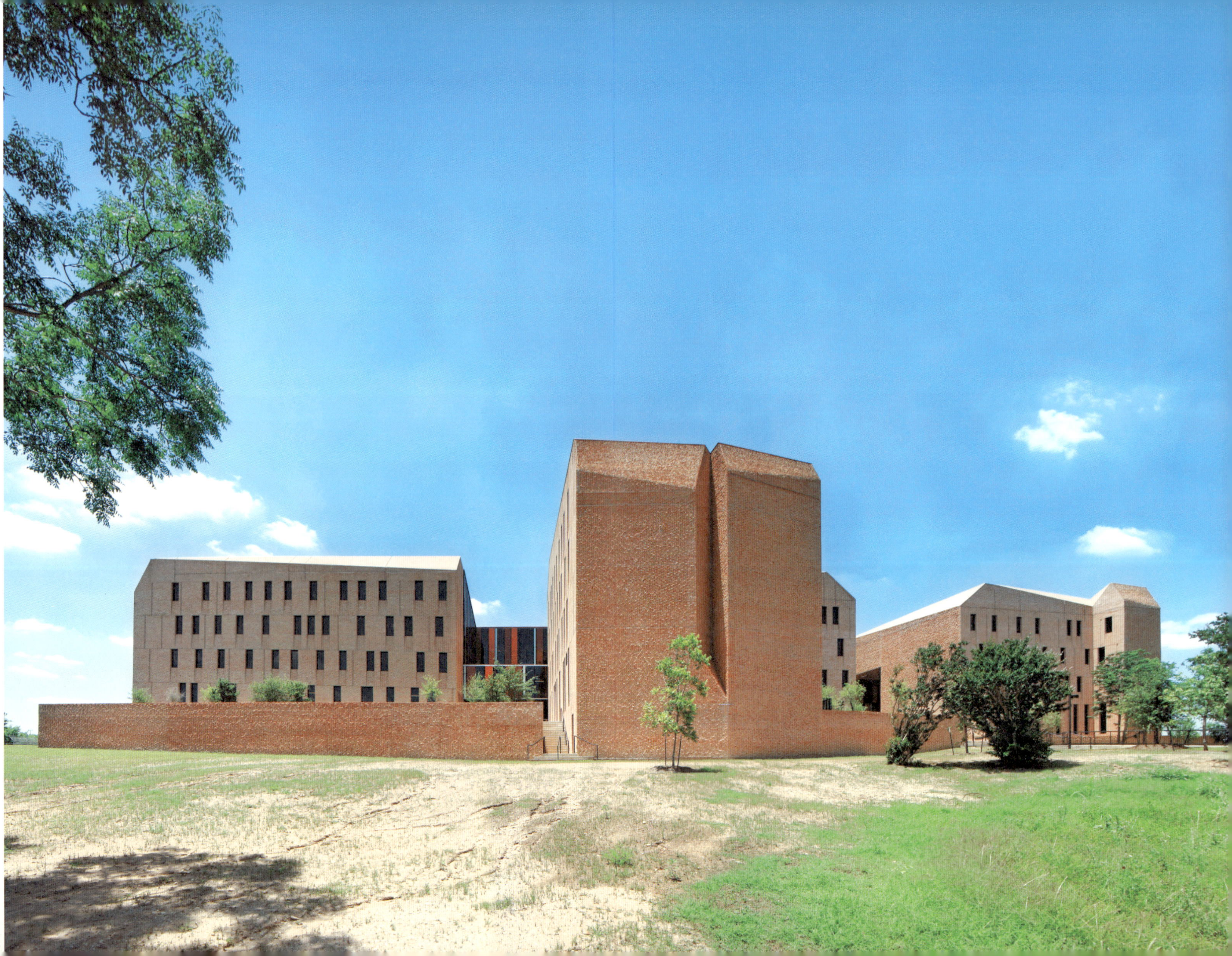

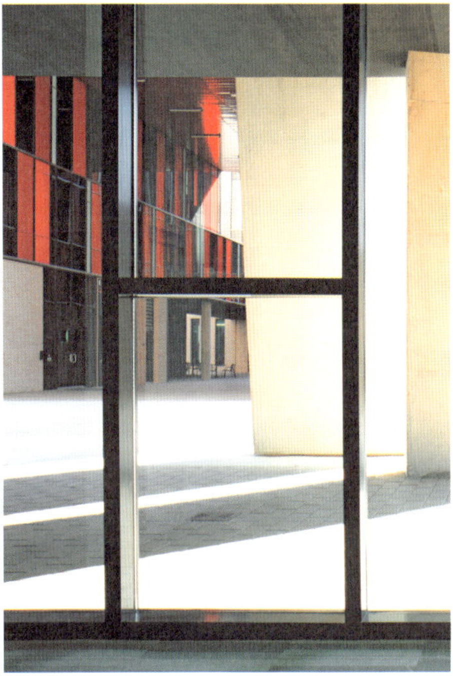

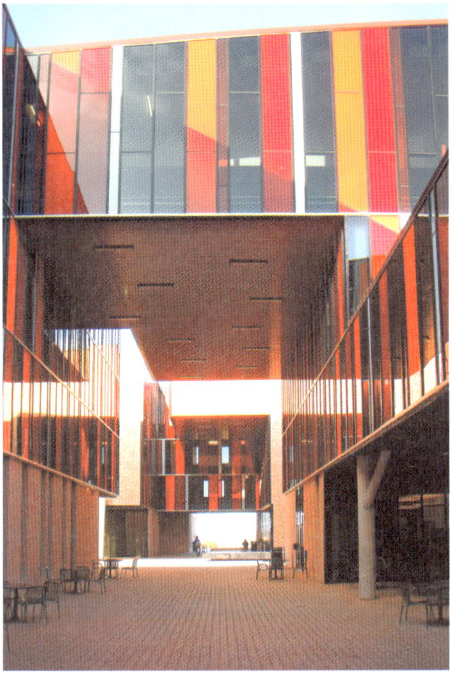

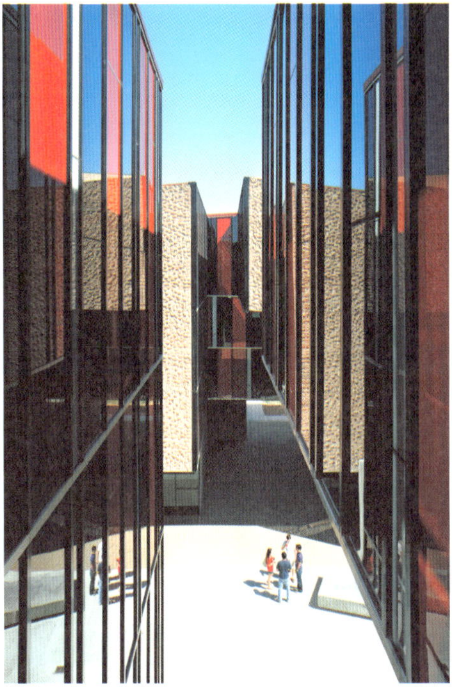

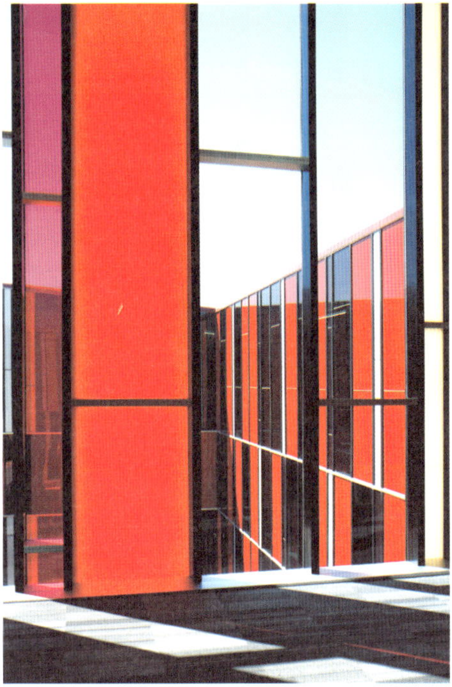

SAO PAULO HOUSE
サンパウロの住宅

Brazil has such a benevolent weather, that architecture should be nothing more than a mere intermediate space. This house, in a very tight and dense urban context, is raised in order to transform the entire lot into a living room: sometimes as an outdoor garden, sometimes as a terrace covered by the bedrooms volume whose geometry tries to amplify the perimeter exposed to natural light and cross ventilation.

ブラジルほどの温暖な気候ならば、建築は単なる媒介空間でいい。都会の密集地に建つこの住宅は、敷地一面を居間にあてるために頭上に持ち上げられた。この居間は、あるときは屋外庭園と化し、またあるときは屋根付きのテラスと化す。その屋根に相当する寝室を収めたヴォリュームは、日の射す側と風の抜ける側の表面積を増やしていく。

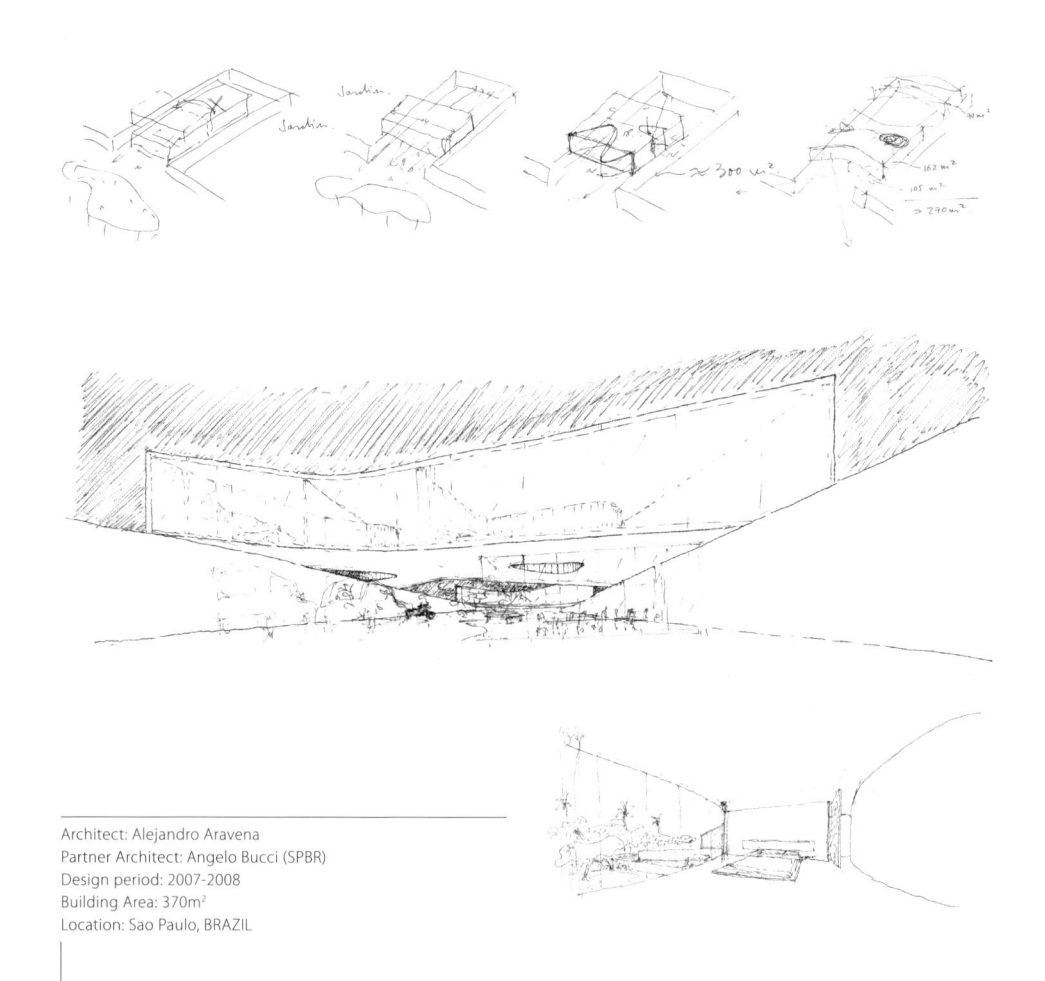

Architect: Alejandro Aravena
Partner Architect: Angelo Bucci (SPBR)
Design period: 2007-2008
Building Area: 370m^2
Location: Sao Paulo, BRAZIL

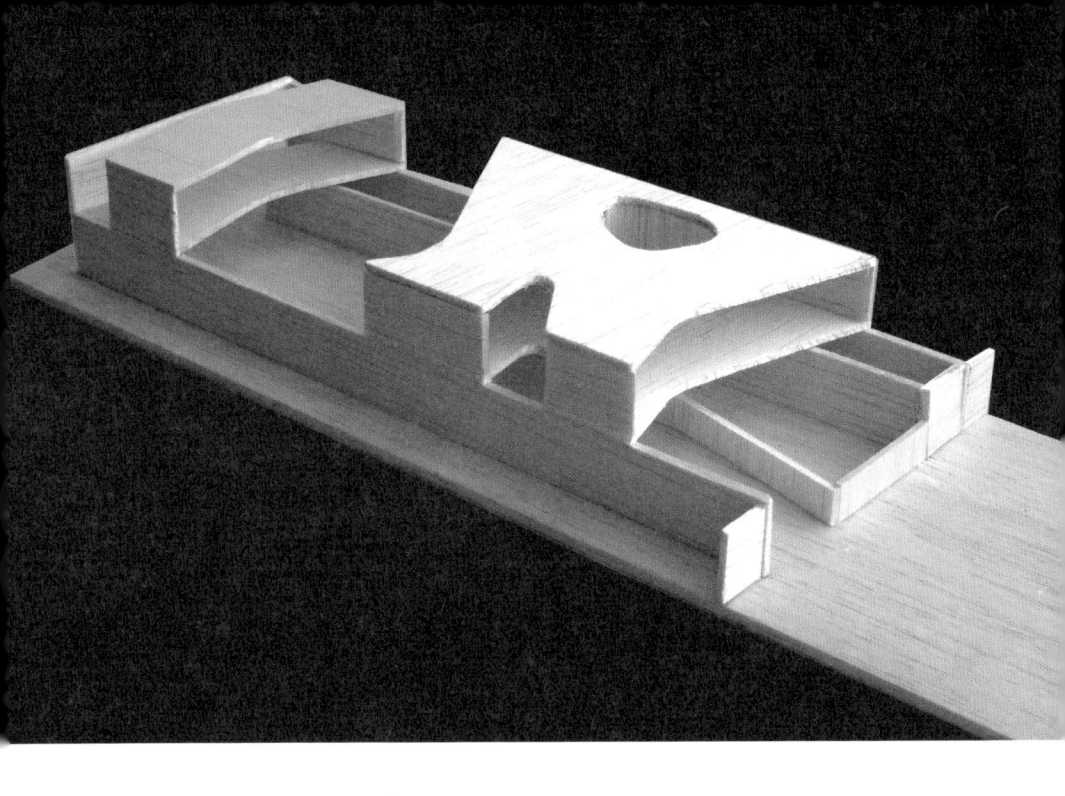

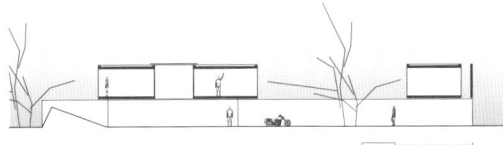

Long section

Second floor

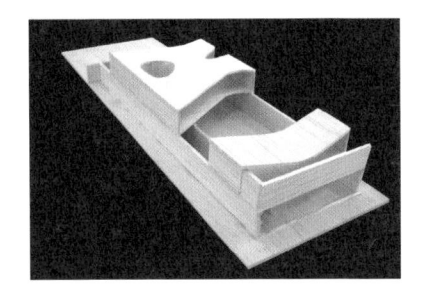

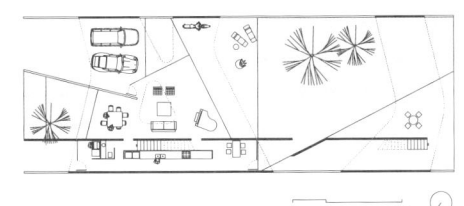

Ground floor

VITRA CHILDREN'S WORKSHOP
ヴィトラ・チルドレンズ・ワークショップ

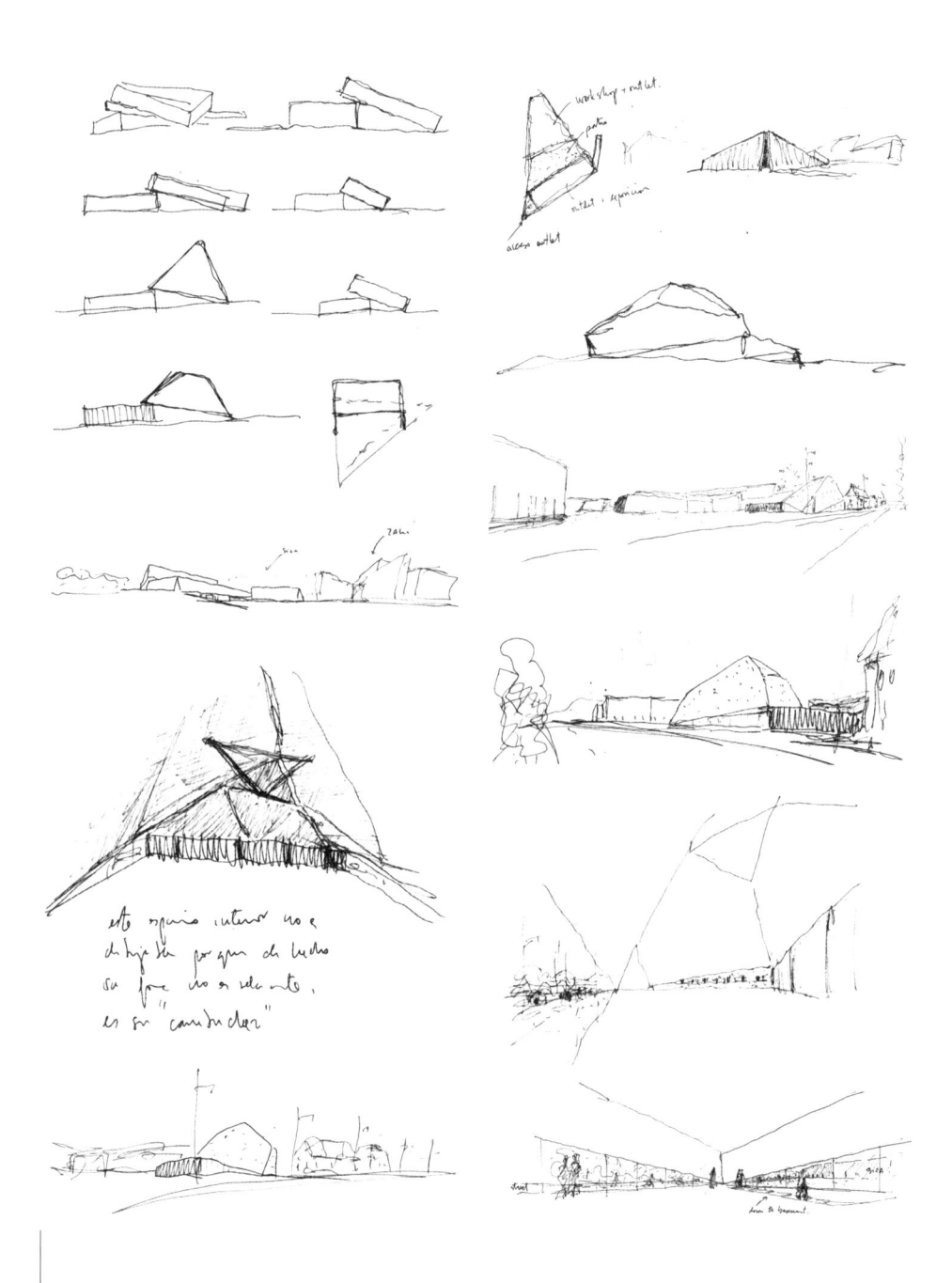

The client asked us for a direct, happy, low-carbon footprint, flexible building for hosting children workshops using encouraging materials. Once the problem is framed like that, not too many options are left: Wood and Reet. We followed archaic building systems traceable in the region, so that the form was disciplined before even starting design.

子供向けワークショップは、元気の出るような素材を使って、ストレートで楽しく低炭素型のフレキシブルな建物にしたい、とのことだった。課題が明快なだけに、選択肢も絞られてくる。材料は木と葦。この地域に古くから伝わる構法に則ったので、デザインをしなくても形態はおのずから限定された。

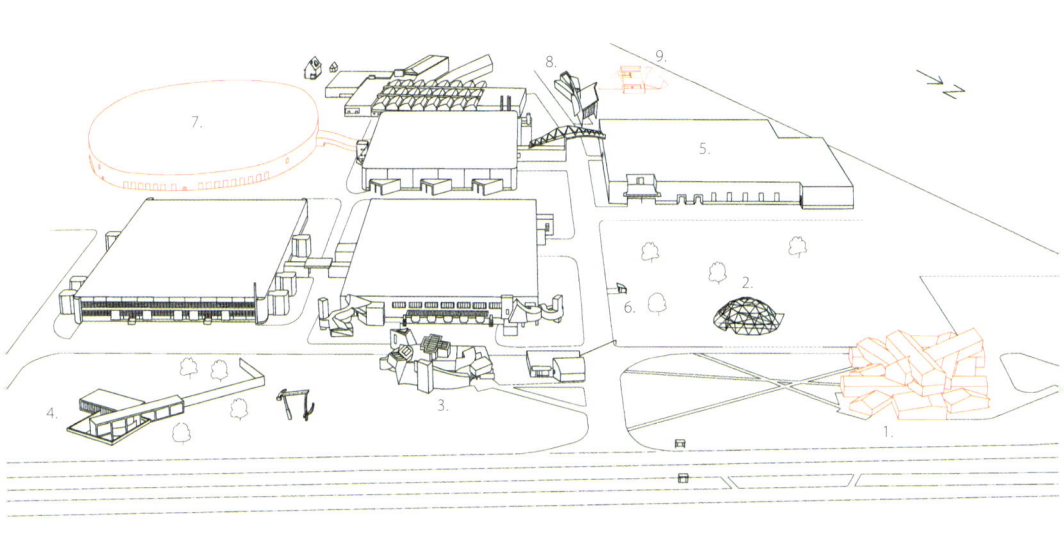

1. Herzog & de Meuron
2. Buckminster Fuller
3. Frank Gehry
4. Tadao Ando
5. Álvaro Siza
6. Jean Prouvé
7. SANAA
8. Zaha Hadid
9. Alejandro Aravena

Reet   Wood

Architect: Alejandro Aravena
Partner Architects CHILE: Ricardo Torrejón, Víctor Oddó
Partner Architect GERMANY: Osolin Plüss
Design Period: 2008
Building Area: 600m²
Location: Campus Vitra, Weil am Rhein, GERMANY

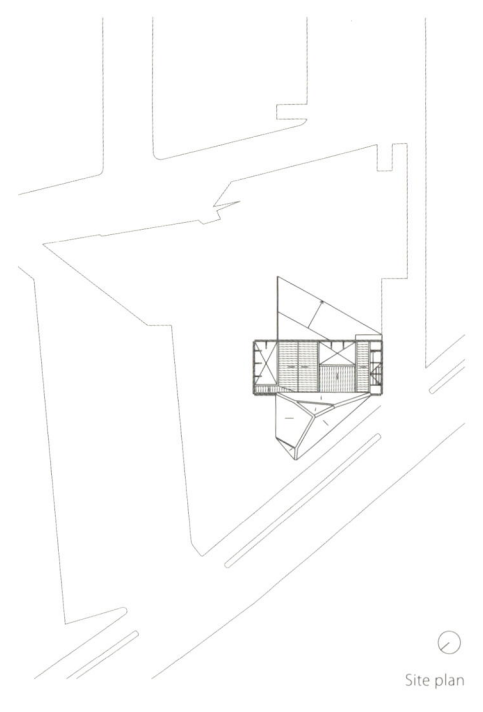

Site plan

66 | Alejandro Aravena Architects

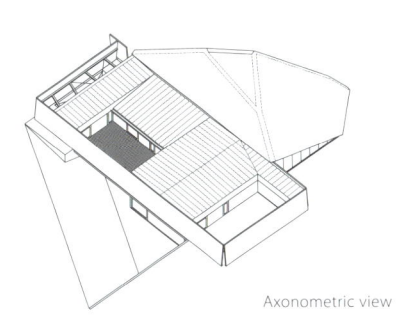

Axonometric view

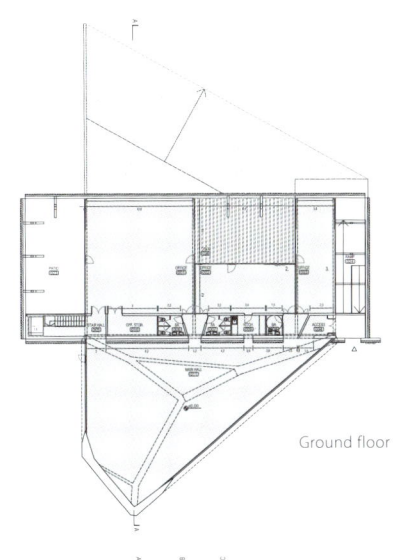

Ground floor

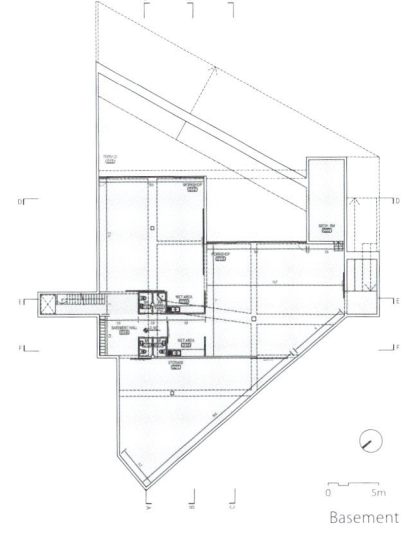

Basement

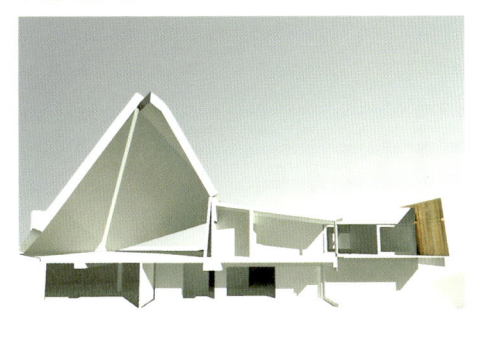

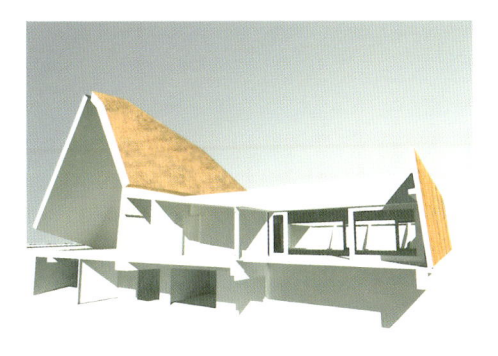

0 5m

ORDOS 100 HOUSE
オルドス 100

There are two strategies to follow when dealing with big-scale landscapes: to define a limit and domesticate the space within (introversion) or to gain height to dominate the vastness (extroversion). We decided to do both and have a smooth transition from one to another.

広大なランドスケープを扱うにはこつがふたつある。ひとつは範囲を限定してその内側の空間を飼い慣らす方法（内向型）。もうひとつは高さを出して周囲の広がりを支配する方法（外向型）。私たちはこの両方を採って、それらを滑らかに継ぎ合わせた。

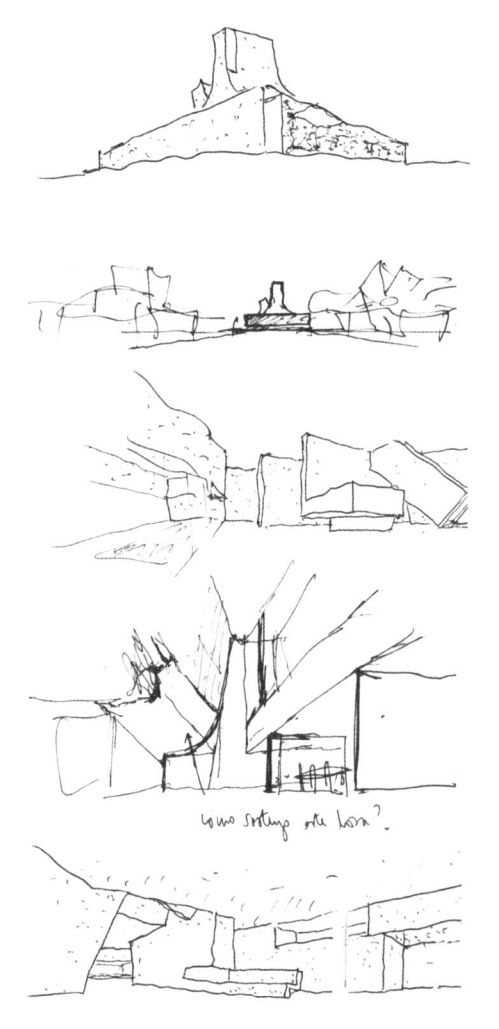

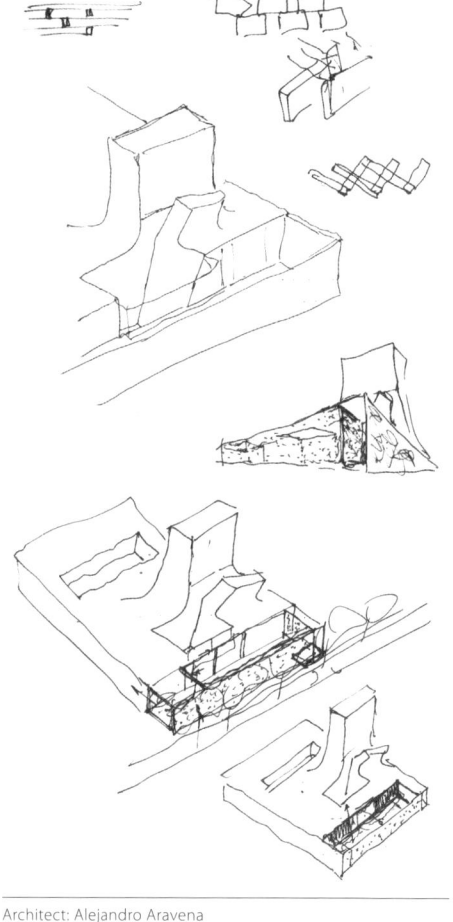

Architect: Alejandro Aravena
Partner Architects: Ricardo Torrejón, Víctor Oddó
Design period: 2008
Building area: 900m^2
Location: Ordos, Inner-Mongolia, P.R. CHINA

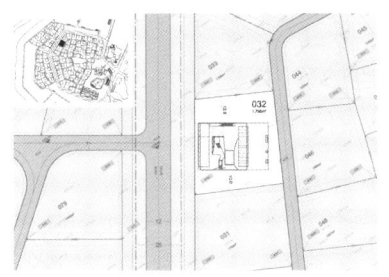

Site plan

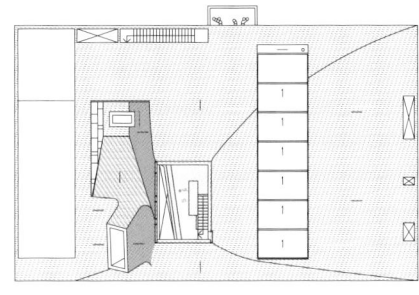

Studio floor

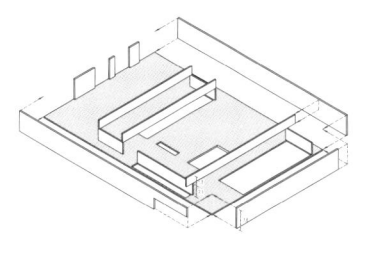

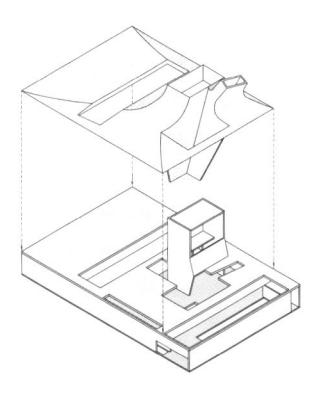

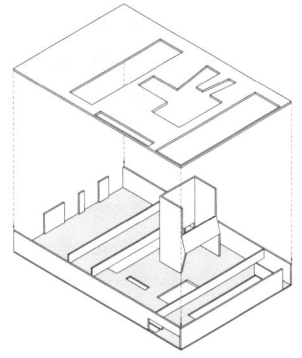

Ground floor

Axonometric view

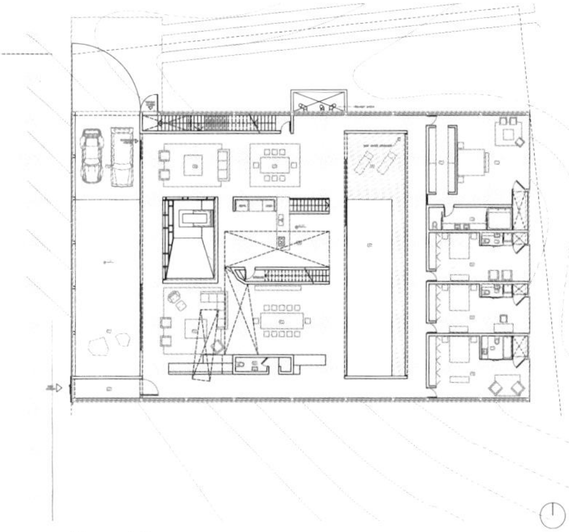

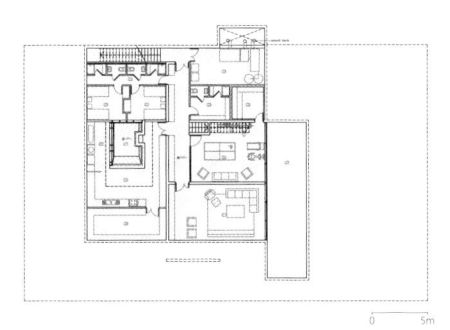

Basement

0 5m

69

It is made out of black core bricks, broken in half, with their rough surface facing out. This will be the outward texture of the whole volume, including roofs and exterior pavements.

Alejandro Aravena Architects

71

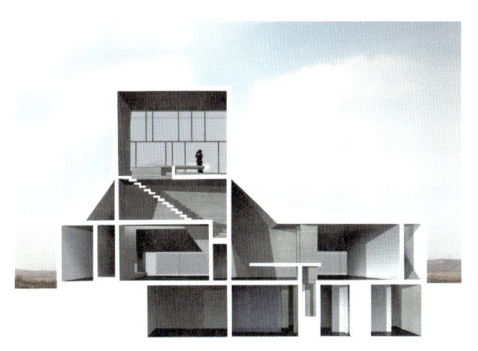

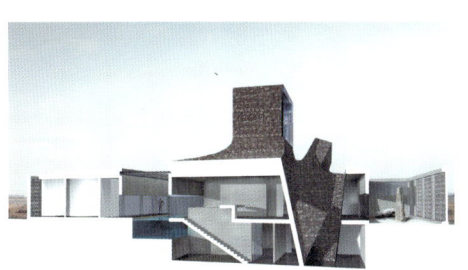

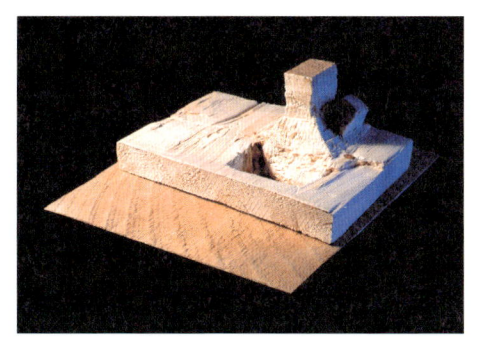

PILGRIM LOOK OUT POINT
巡礼路の展望台

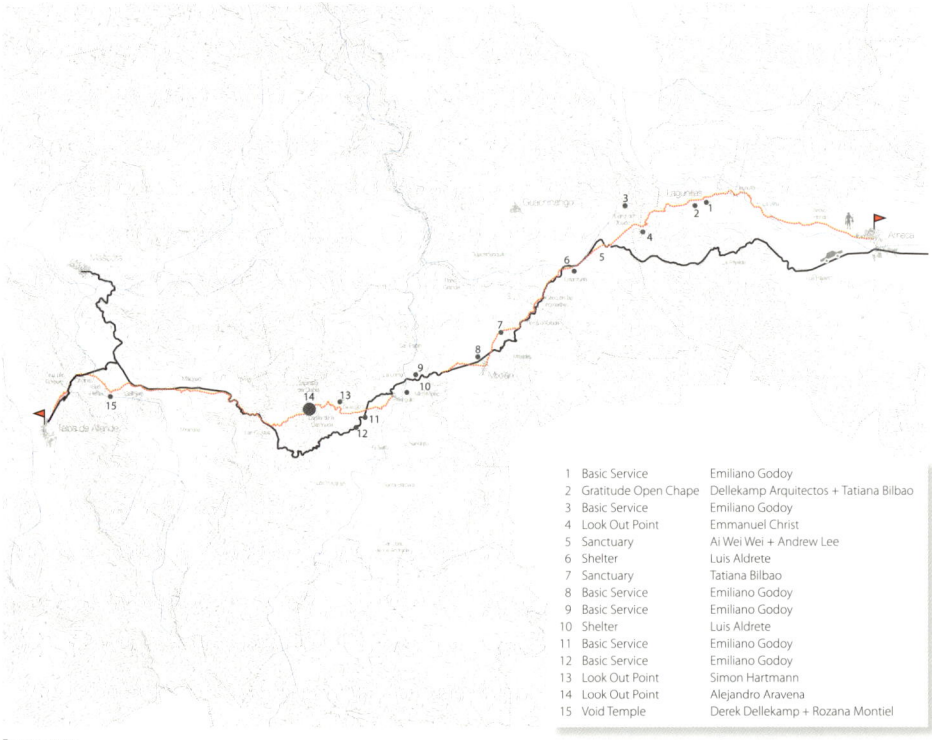

1	Basic Service	Emiliano Godoy
2	Gratitude Open Chape	Dellekamp Arquitectos + Tatiana Bilbao
3	Basic Service	Emiliano Godoy
4	Look Out Point	Emmanuel Christ
5	Sanctuary	Ai Wei Wei + Andrew Lee
6	Shelter	Luis Aldrete
7	Sanctuary	Tatiana Bilbao
8	Basic Service	Emiliano Godoy
9	Basic Service	Emiliano Godoy
10	Shelter	Luis Aldrete
11	Basic Service	Emiliano Godoy
12	Basic Service	Emiliano Godoy
13	Look Out Point	Simon Hartmann
14	Look Out Point	Alejandro Aravena
15	Void Temple	Derek Dellekamp + Rozana Montiel

Route map

Alejandro Aravena Architects

Building in a remote place should generate an architecture able to age as if it were a natural element. So, we thought of a kind of hollowed stone, bent to rest calmly on the hill side, and whose only purpose is to offer pilgrims a resting place with dark shadows, cross-ventilation and a view over the path they walked for a hundred kilometers to arrive there.

僻地に建てるなら、自然の一部であるように風化していく建築が望ましい。ということで、空洞の石のようなものを思いついた。これを折り曲げて山腹にそっと据える。唯一の用途は、巡礼者に休息の場を提供することである。内部には暗い影が落ち、風が抜ける。外に目をやれば、ここまで延々100kmと辿ってきた道が見晴らせる。

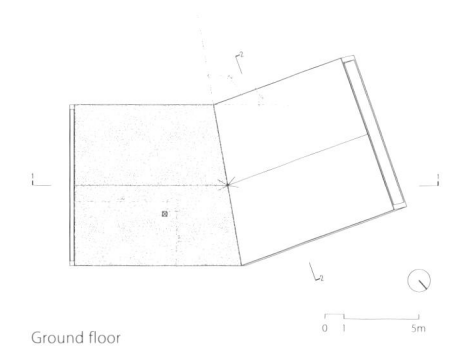

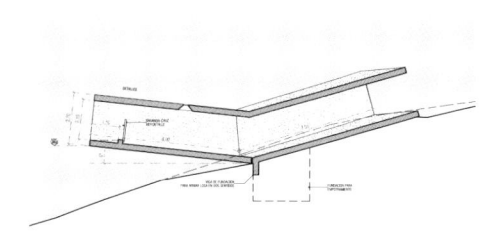

Ground floor

Long section

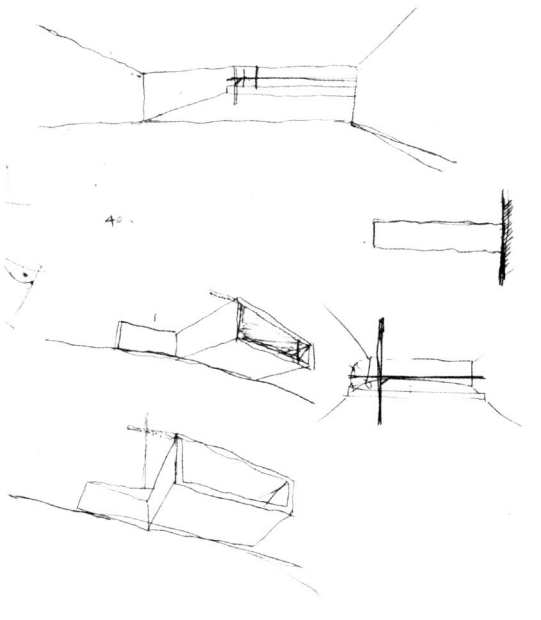

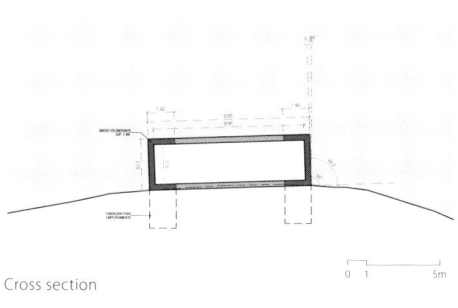

Cross section

Architect: Alejandro Aravena
Partner Architects: Diego Torres, Víctor Oddó
Design/Construction Period: 2008-2010
Building Area: 148m^2
Location: Pilgrim route Ameca-Talpa, Jalisco, MEXICO

74 | Alejandro Aravena Architects

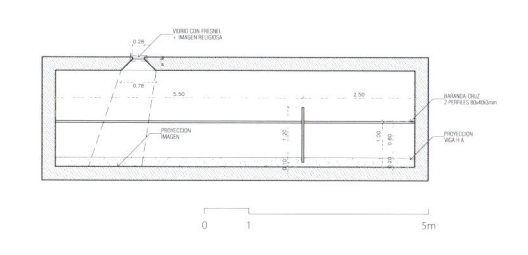

Projection image of the Virgin Mary on the floor and walls

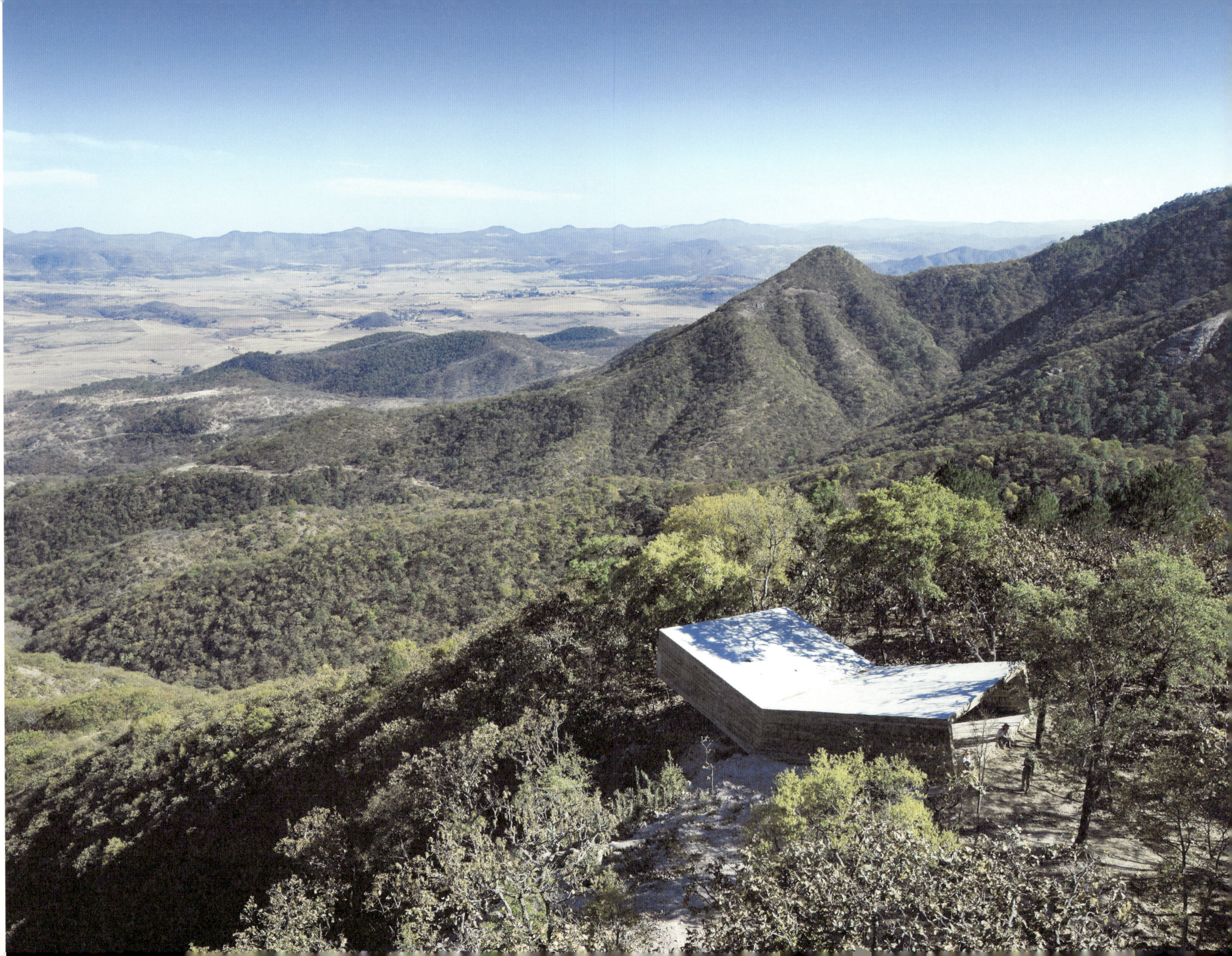

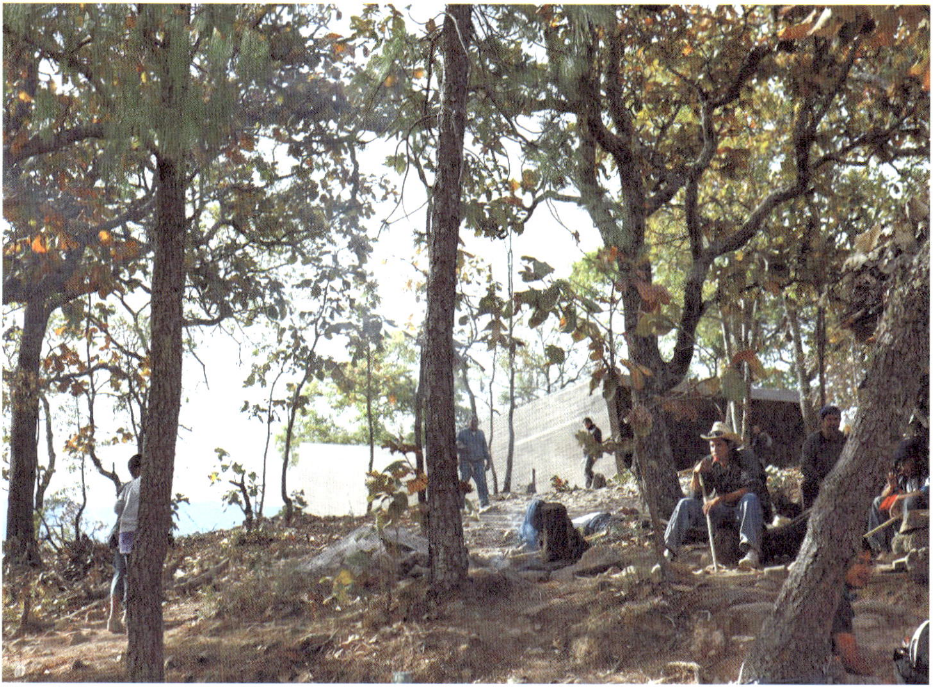
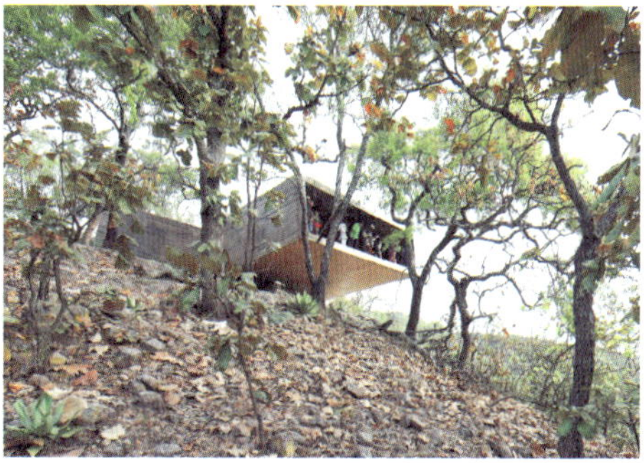
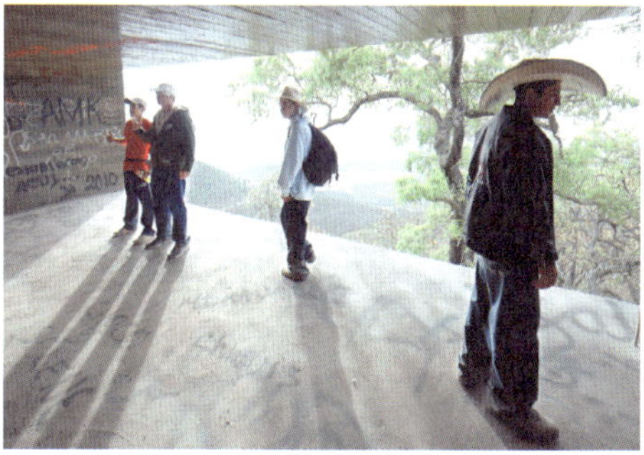
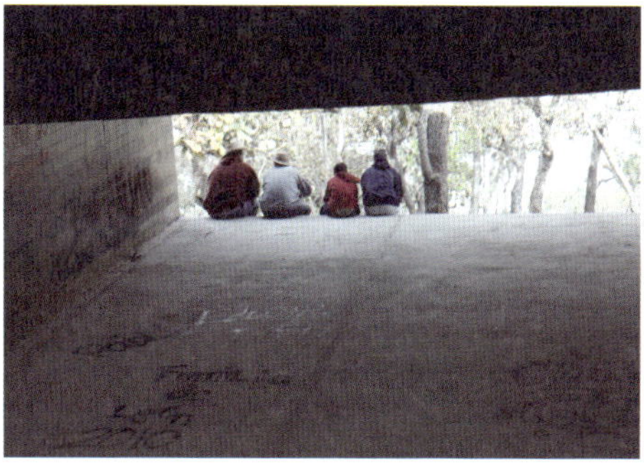
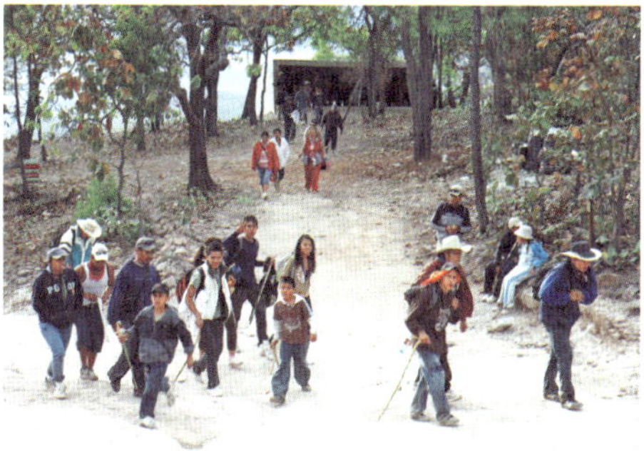

CHAIRLESS FOR VITRA
チェアレス

The Ayoreo Indians from Paraguay developed a principle that was parallel from the western evolution of chairs. Instead of developing an object where the body could rest from the gravitational force, this device uses the force of the body getting tired as an impulse to hold it; the more tired we get, the more we tend to open our legs and the more that force pushes our back to a more comfortable position. The other brilliant thing: the use the ground as part of the furniture. We just learned from those principles set in play and produced the industrial version of it.

パラグアイの先住民アヨレオ族は、西洋人が椅子を考案するのに平行して、ある原理を編み出した。身体を重力から解放して休ませるためのオブジェを開発する代わりに、ここでは人間が姿勢を保とうとする力がしだいに緩んでくることに目をつけた。人間は疲れてくると、脚を伸ばしたくなってくるし、そうなるともっと楽な姿勢を求めて背中を反らせる、ということだ。もうひとつ素敵なところは、地面を家具の一部として利用していること。私たちはこの原理をたまたまある用例から学び、それを製品化しただけである。

Ayoreo indian of Paraguay

Design by: Alejandro Aravena
Collaborator: Víctor Oddó
Design/Manufacturing Period: 2008-2010
Location: made in Campus Vitra, Weil am Rhein, GERMANY

Renzo Piano on Chairless

BANSI BANK
バンシ銀行

The competition asked for an iconic tower for the Bank. We proposed a volume that could be perceived as a narrow element, at the scale of the neighborhood and robust at the metropolitan scale. The subsequent narrow bay was also meant to allow natural cross ventilation and for natural light to reach more area of the plan. Finally we thought of touching the ground, liberating as much green space as possible and keeping the existing shortcuts through the lot.

コンペではバンシ銀行を象徴するタワー案が募られた。私たちは、見た目が薄く、近隣に馴染むスケールで、なおかつ大都市の街並みにも埋もれない力強さを兼ね備えた建物を提案した。当然柱間は狭くなるが、そのぶん風通しと日当たりは良くなる。また接地面を減らすことで、緑地を極力開放し、敷地を貫いていた近道も残した。

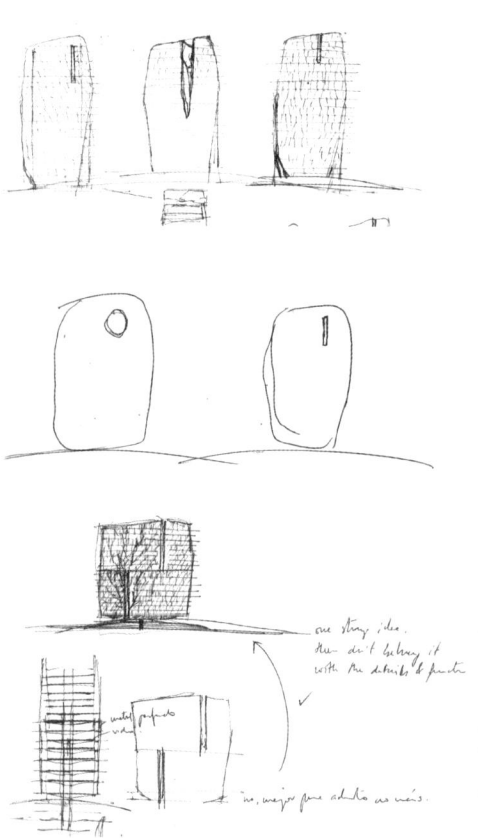

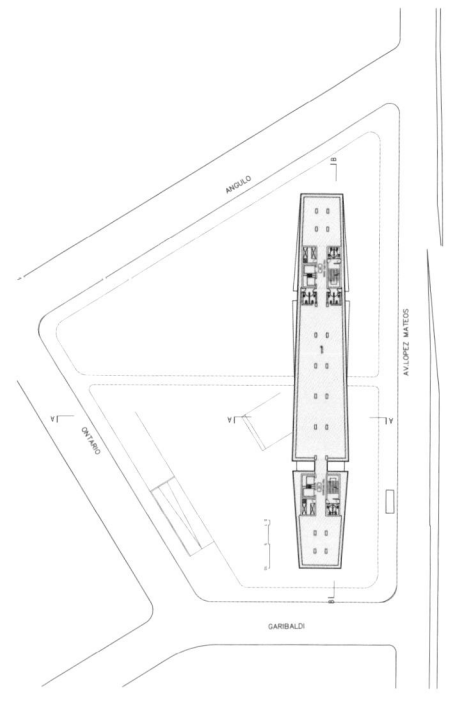

Typical floor

Architect: Alejandro Aravena
Partner Architects: Rebecca Emmons, Víctor Oddó
Collaborator: Agnes Poignant
Design period: 2009
Building Area: 16,000 m²
Location: Guadalajara, MEXICO

Cross section

Long section

83

PLAYA ONDA RESORT
プラヤ・オンダ・リゾート

Intact landscape was an important asset of the operation. We followed the level curves of the terrain, keeping the building at a constant distance from the hillside, close enough to allow for access, and distant enough to allow the nature keep on flowing underneath. Water instead, used the building to travel perpendicular to the slope, accumulating height before being restored back at the bottom of the complex.

ここでは手つかずの風景が貴重な財産となった。建物の配置は、等高線に沿いつつ、山の斜面とは一定の距離をとることで、人が自然にアクセスできる程度に近づけつつ、足下の豊かな自然を邪魔しない程度に遠ざけた。逆に水のほうは建物を利用する。山の水は建物を垂直に伝い落ちてスロープに流れ込み、最後は施設の足下に貯められる。

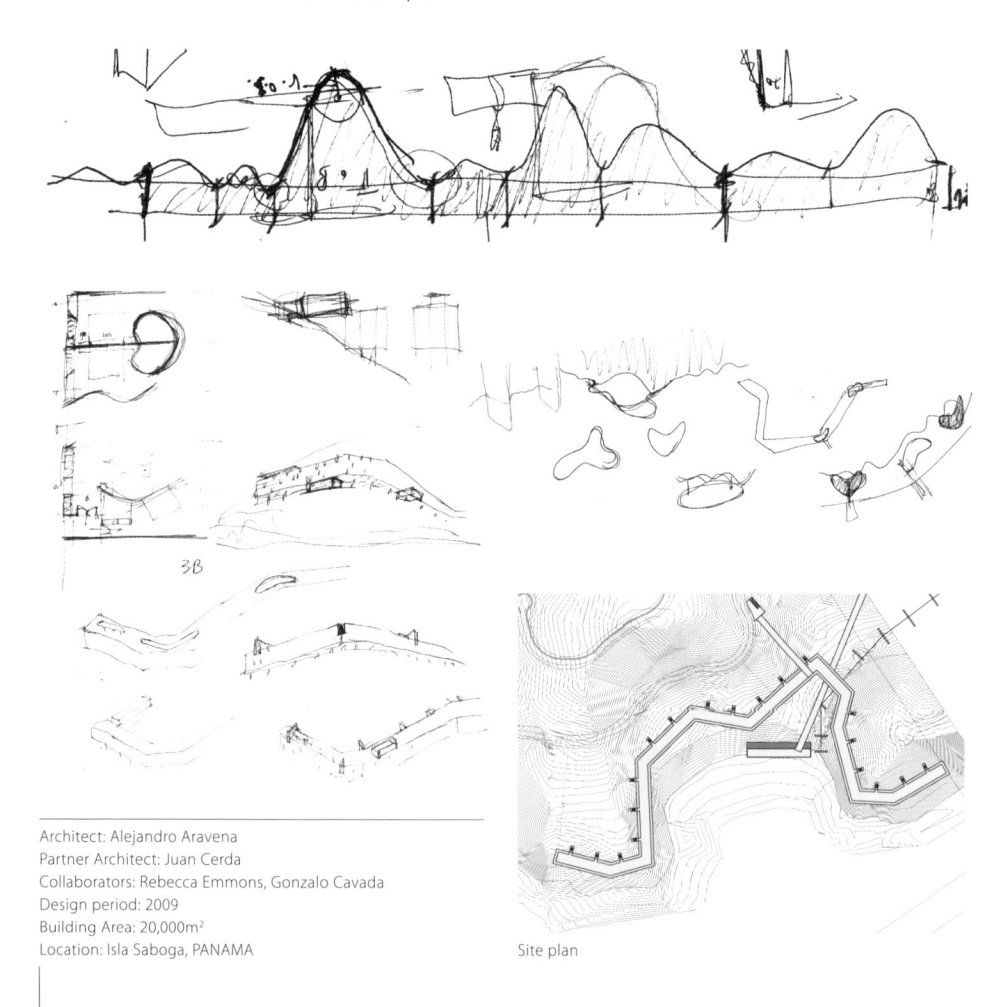

Architect: Alejandro Aravena
Partner Architect: Juan Cerda
Collaborators: Rebecca Emmons, Gonzalo Cavada
Design period: 2009
Building Area: 20,000m²
Location: Isla Saboga, PANAMA

Site plan

Apartment type A

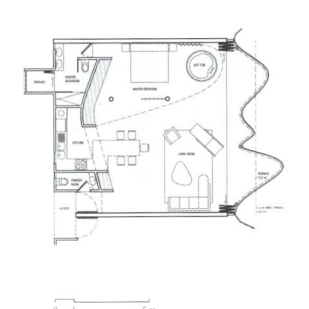

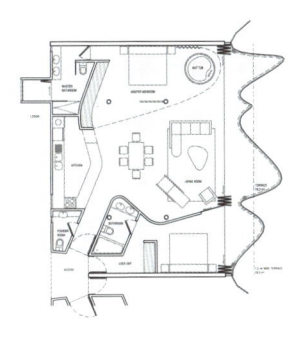

Apartment type B

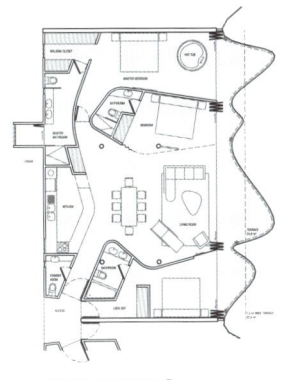

Apartment type C

KUNSTMUSEUM BASEL EXTENSION
バーゼル美術館増築

Museums tend to present a paradox: they are normally very well located, in highly used urban contexts, but programmatically they tend to favor closed introverted boxes. We proposed to have regular hermetic volumes, neutral and flexible for museums standards, resting on top of free bars able to react to the irregularity of the site, permeable, and kind to the pedestrians. We just displaced some monoliths on top to let some controlled natural light in, and also to take advantage of the privileged views over the city and the Rhine River.

美術館というものはどこか自己矛盾的な施設である。せっかく都心の一等地という好立地のわりには、閉じた箱にこもるようにプログラムされている。私たちの提案は、よくある閉じたヴォリューム群に、規範どおりのニュートラルな外観とフレキシブルな構成を与えたものだが、ただしそれらの下にバーを噛ませ、このバーをいびつな敷地に合わせて変則的に配置した。このバーの並んだ地上階は通り抜けが可能であり、歩行者にも優しい。上層のモノリスをいくつかずらして隙間をつくり、そこから館内に少し光を入れたり、館内から街並みやライン川を見晴らせるようにした。

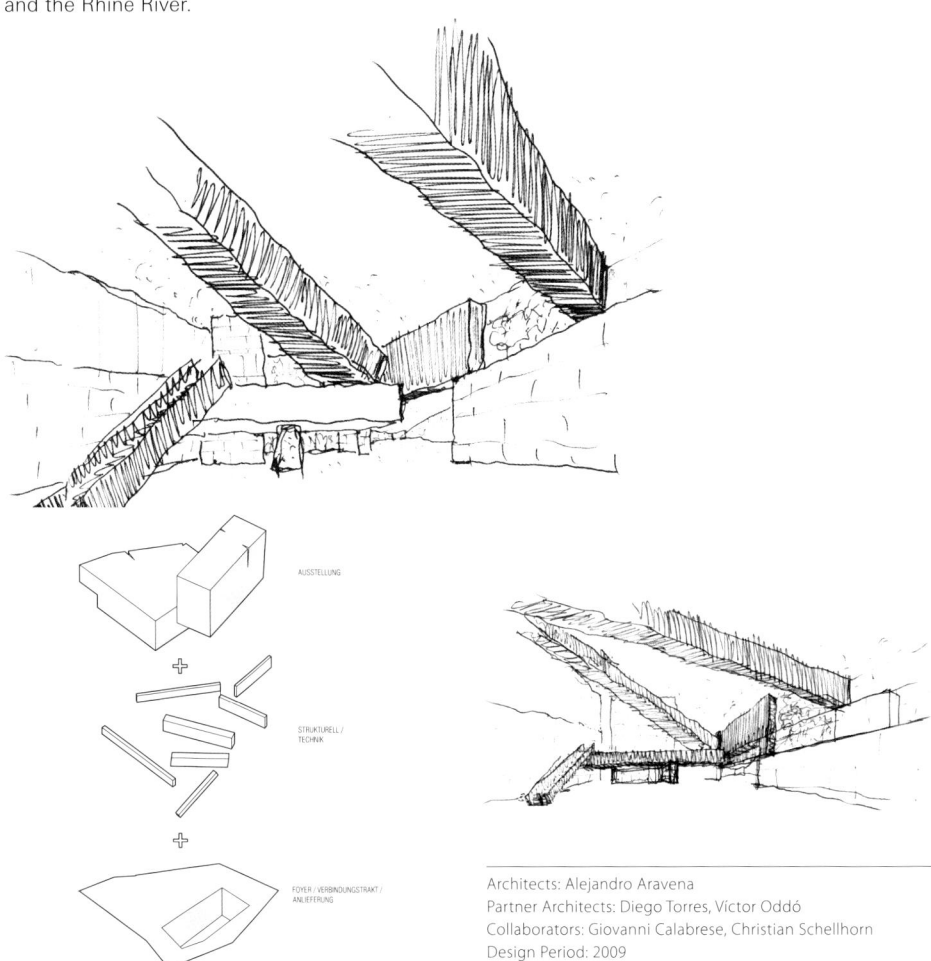

Architectural concept

Architects: Alejandro Aravena
Partner Architects: Diego Torres, Víctor Oddó
Collaborators: Giovanni Calabrese, Christian Schellhorn
Design Period: 2009
Building Area: 8,000m^2
Location: Basel, SWITZERLAND

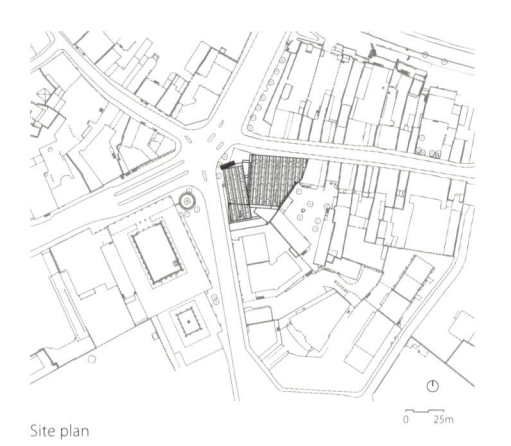

Site plan

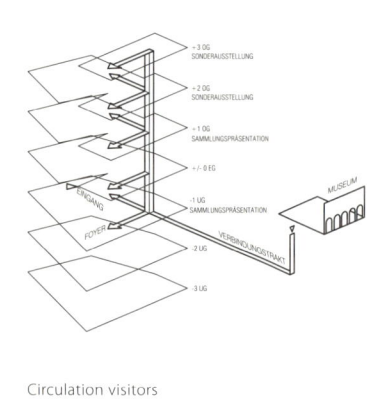

Circulation visitors

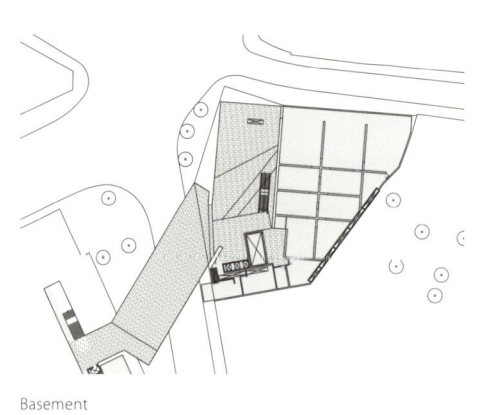

Basement

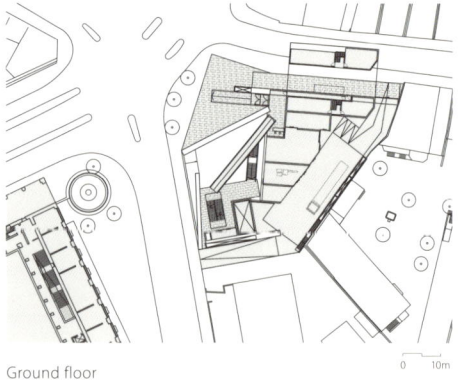

Ground floor

88 | Alejandro Aravena Architects

Second floor

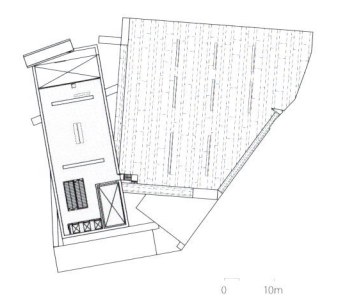

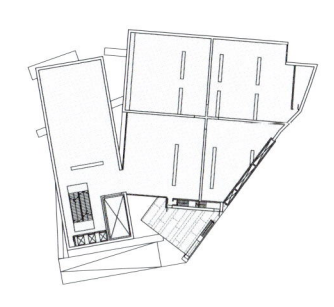

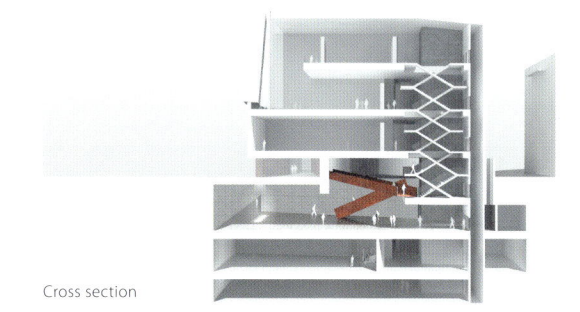

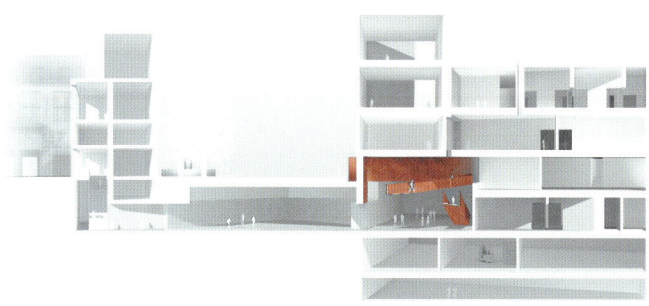

Third floor

Cross section

Long section

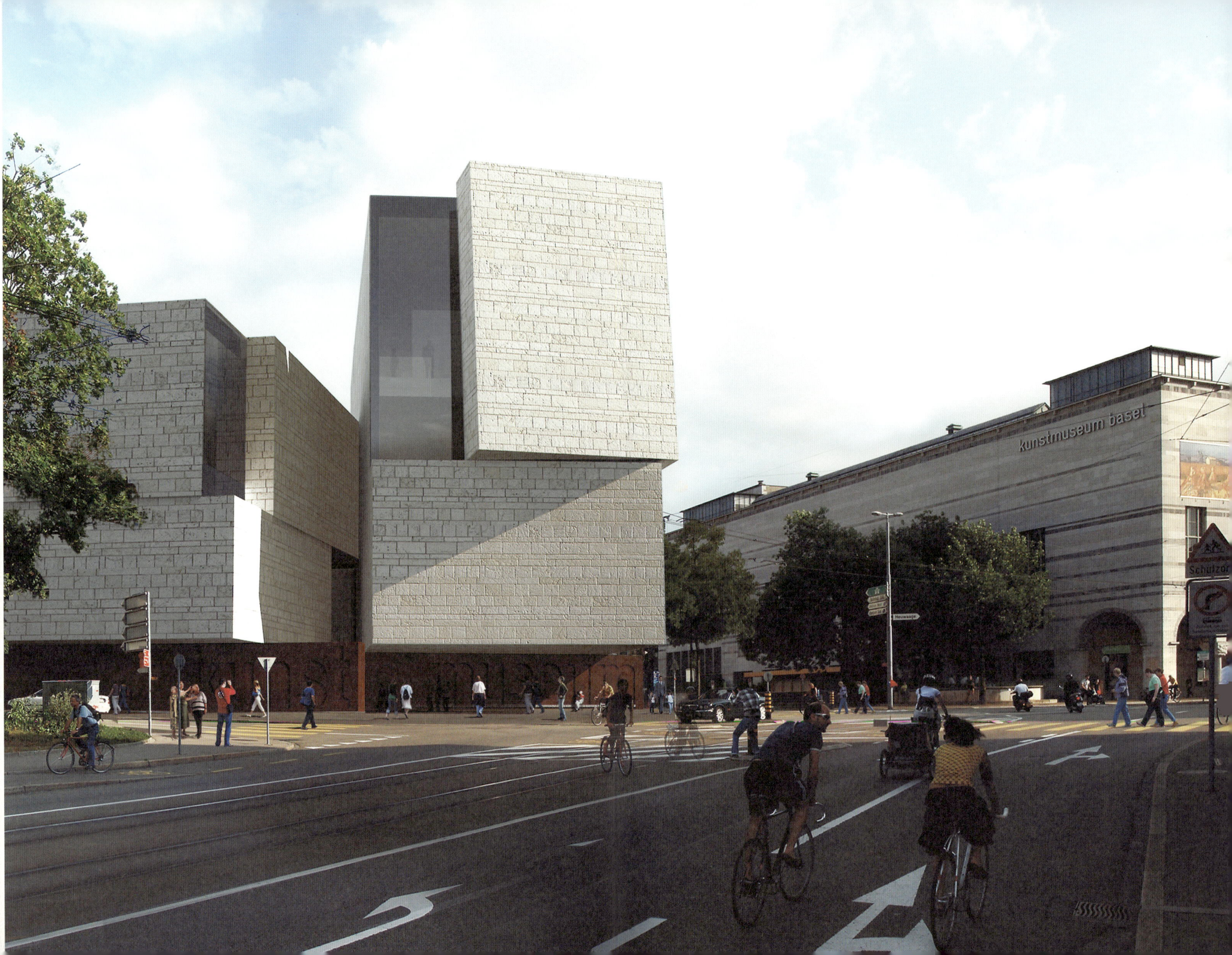
kunstmuseum basel

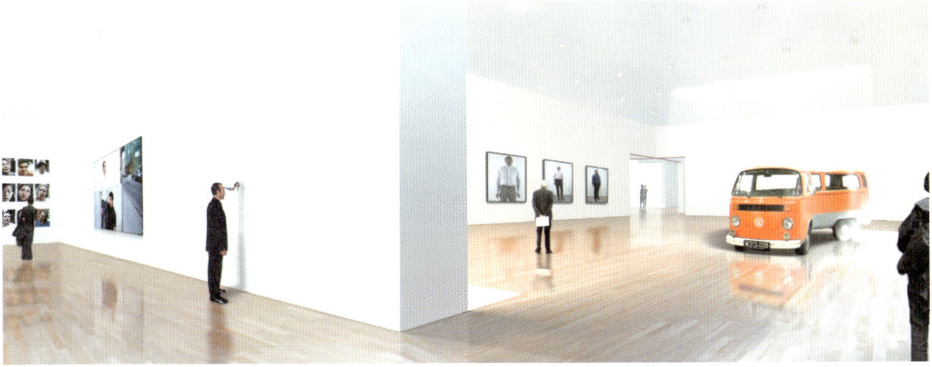

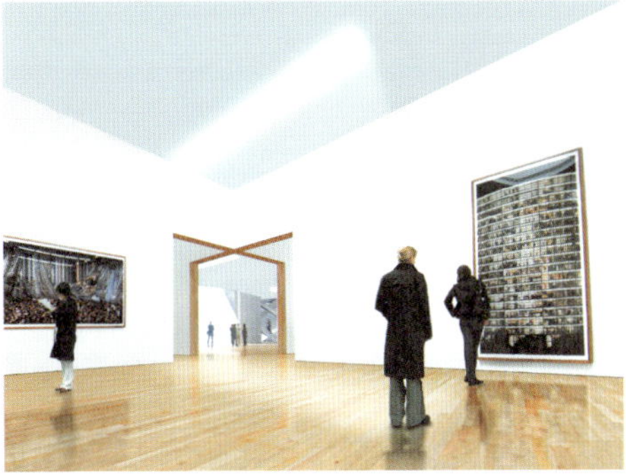

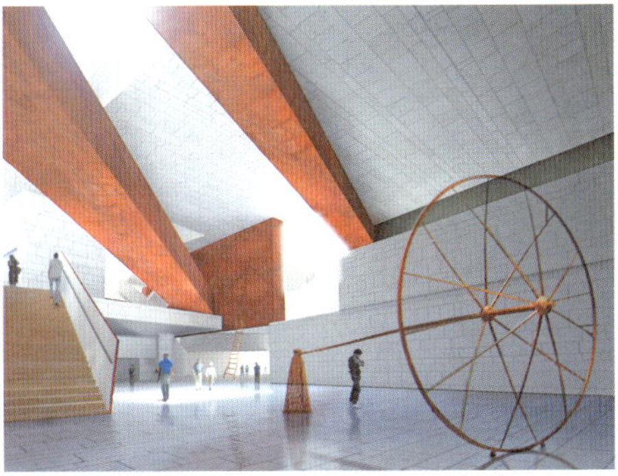

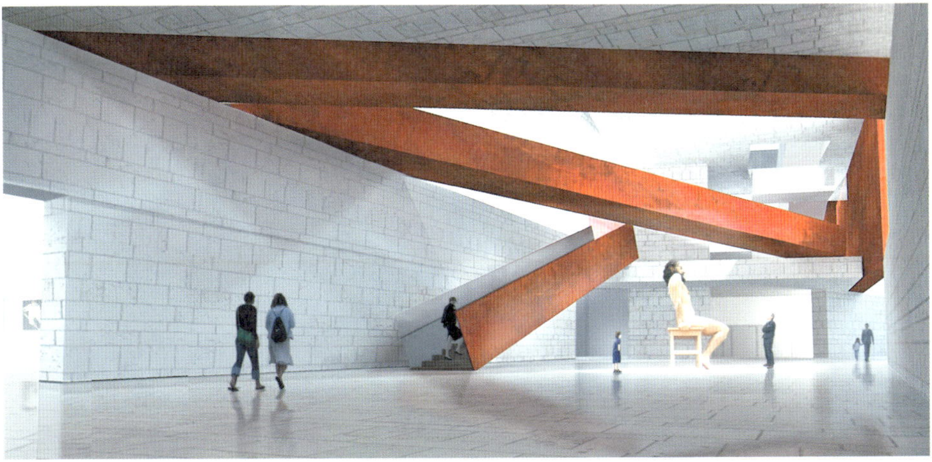

OCEAN WINERY
オーシャン・ワイナリー

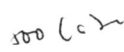

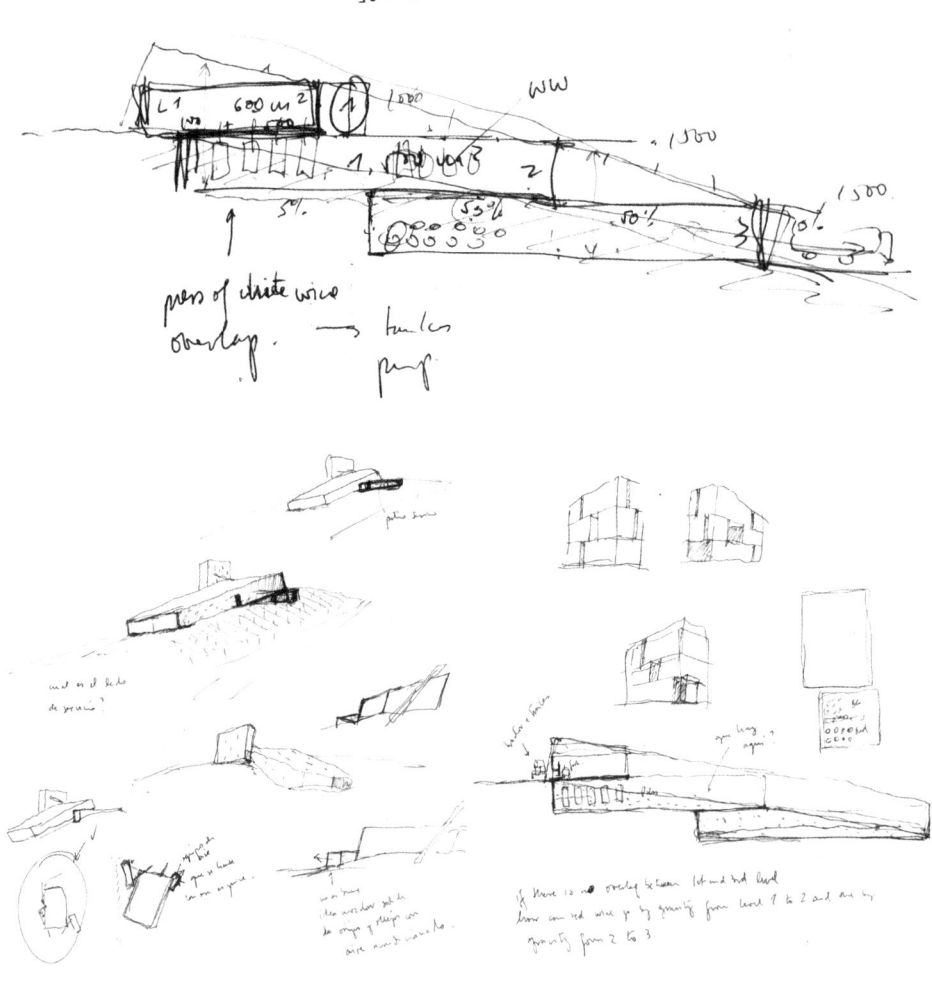

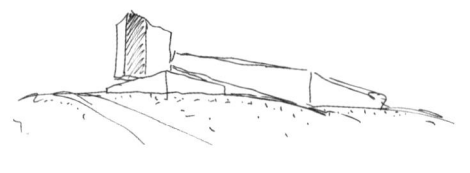

Architect: Alejandro Aravena
Partner Architects: Ricardo Torrejón, Victor Oddó
Collaborator: Gonzalo Cavada
Design Period: 2009
Building Area: 4,200m²
Location: Nierstein, GERMANY

Premium wines are expected to let nature operate with as little intervention of man as possible. This building looked for the right slopes nearby the terroirs in order to let gravity guide the process of winemaking. Actually gravity is the force that keeps all the pieces of the complex together. Primitive compositional principles are adequate when dealing with such old archaic programs like wine making where time is expected to add to the quality of the whole.

高級ワインほど、人間が極力介入せずに自然の営みに委ねてつくられるという。ここではワイン醸造を重力によって行うので、その施設を建てるのに頃合いの斜面を探した。重力はまた、施設が解体しないように各部分をまとめる力でもある。ワイン醸造のような古風なプログラムには、原始的な構造原理で建てるくらいがちょうどいい。時間が全体のクオリティを高めてくれるのだから。

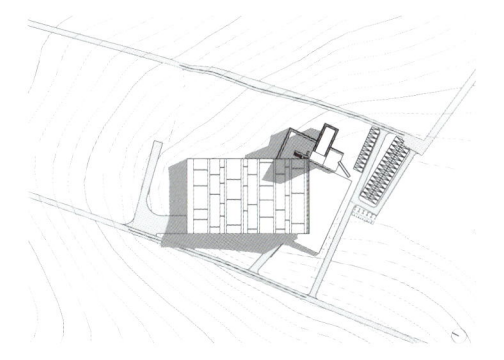

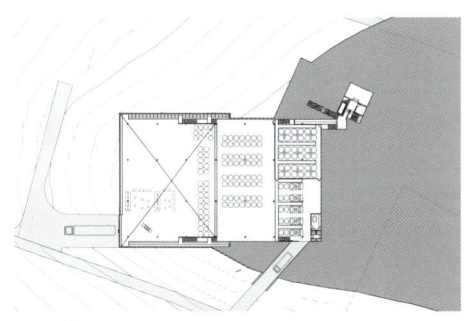

Site plan

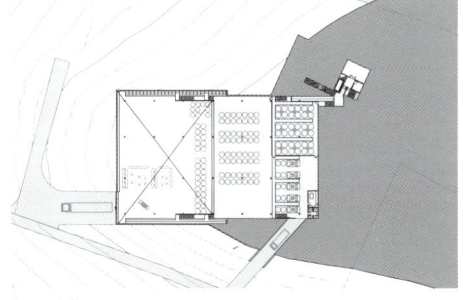

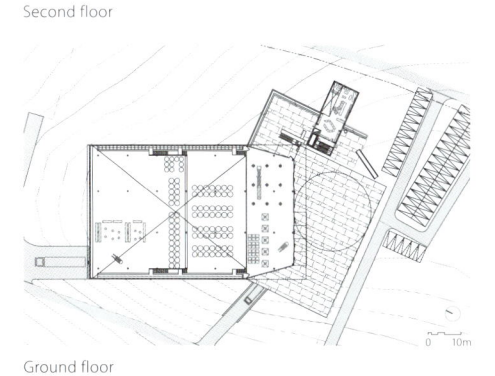

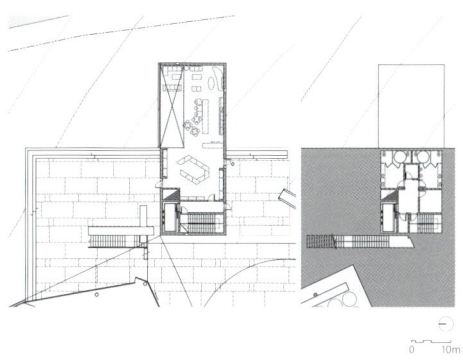

Second floor

Ground floor

Tower ground floor

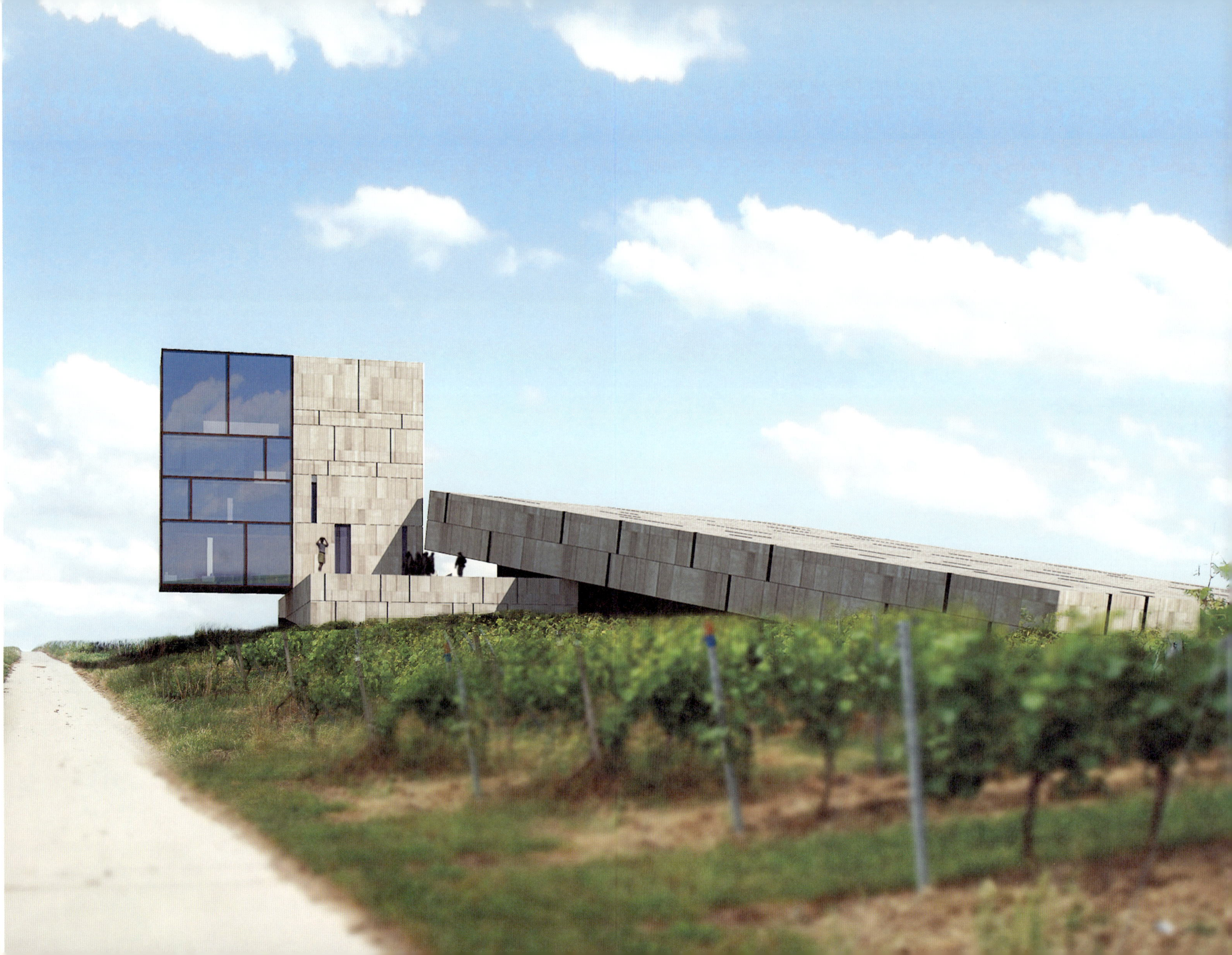

99

MEDELLIN MUSEUM OF MODERN ART
メデジン近代美術館

The museum extension was meant to activate a new area of the city. Colombia has also a great tradition of building in brick. So we proposed a form both archaic and new enough to condense the forces in play and able to bring the skills and knowledge around brick to a new level. The hyperboloid works as an inverted arch in section, the most ancient way for bricks to transform force into form.

この美術館の増築には、メデジン市の新興地域を活性化する狙いがあった。コロンビアには煉瓦建築の偉大な伝統がある。私たちはここに働く種々の力を古くて新しい形態に凝縮し、さらに煉瓦にまつわる技能と知識の水準を引き上げることにした。双曲面の形態は、断面では反転アーチとなる。ちなみに力をフォルムに転じた最古の煉瓦構造がアーチである。

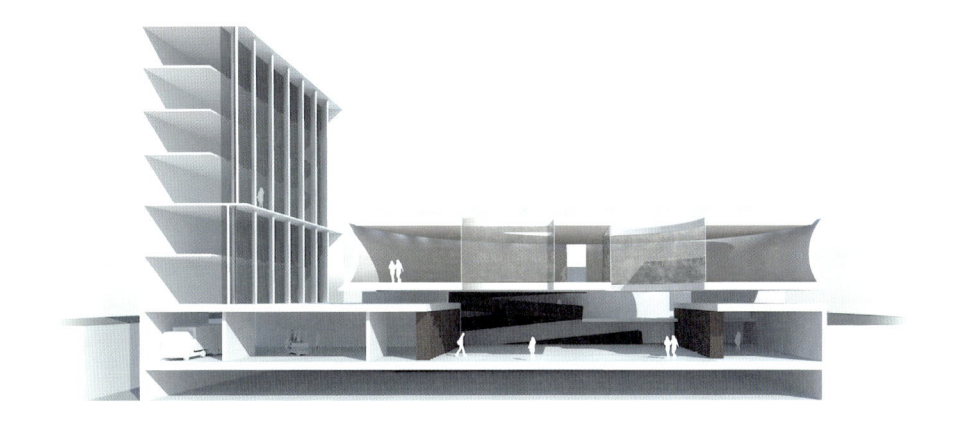

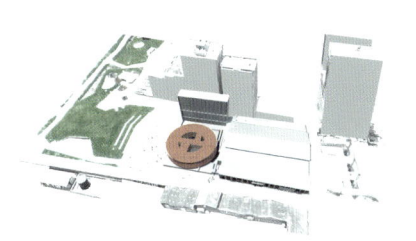

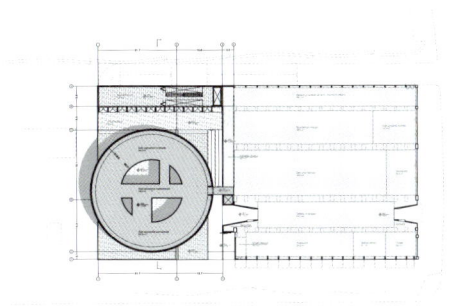

Second floor

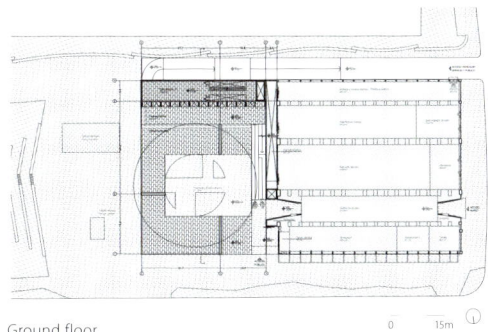

Ground floor 0 15m

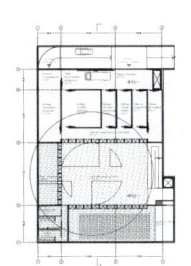

Basement

Architect: Alejandro Aravena
Partner Architects: Juan Ignacio Cerda, Víctor Oddó
Collaborators: Giovanni Calabrese, Elena Chiavi
Design period: 2009-2010
Building Area: 4,300m²
Location: Medellin, COLOMBIA

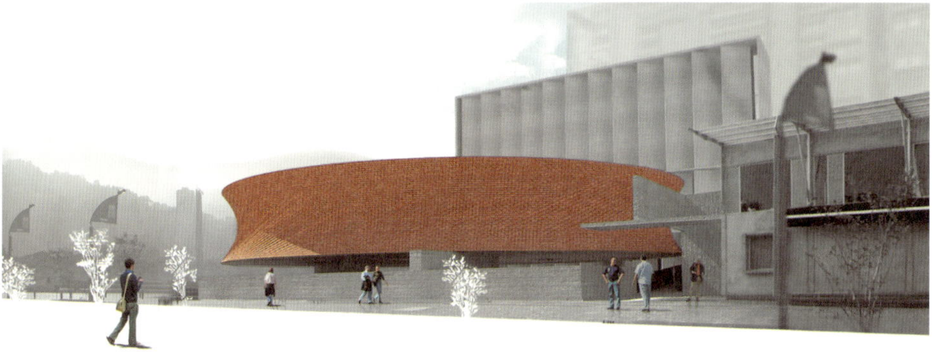

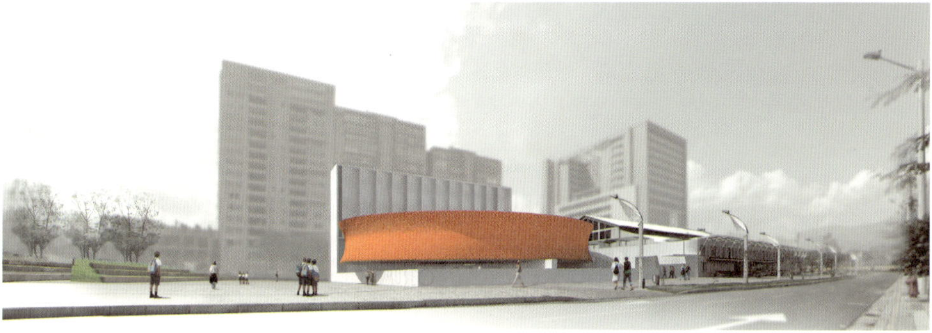

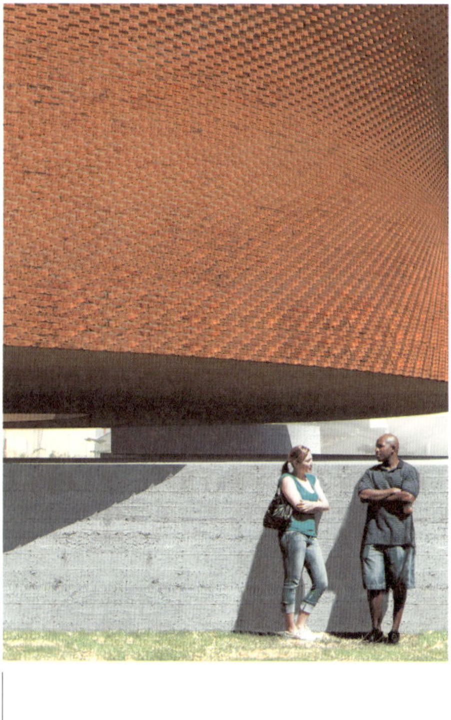

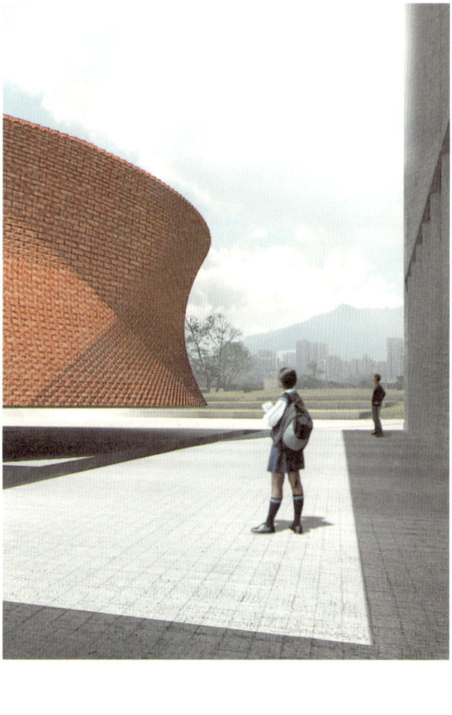

103

ETLIN HOUSE
エトリン邸

As the Sao Paulo house, this project explores the capacity of architecture to dissolve the notion of interior and exterior and become a continuum between outdoor and indoor. Being in a wide-open natural context, we wanted to caliber to extroversion towards views and prevailing winds with the right need of introversion of domestic architecture. On top of the house there is water used for enjoyment in the form of pool and for thermal isolation as a laminar mass, all sustained in a single central column as water tanks do.

「サンパウロの住宅」同様、このプロジェクトでもやはり建築が内と外の概念を打ち消し、屋内と屋外の連続体を出現させる。周囲にはどこまでも自然が広がる。よって屋外の眺望や外気に狙いを定めて開き、と同時に住宅建築に当然求められる内向性も確保する。屋上には水を張り、娯楽用プール兼断熱層とする。以上はちょうど給水塔のように中央の柱1本で支えられる。

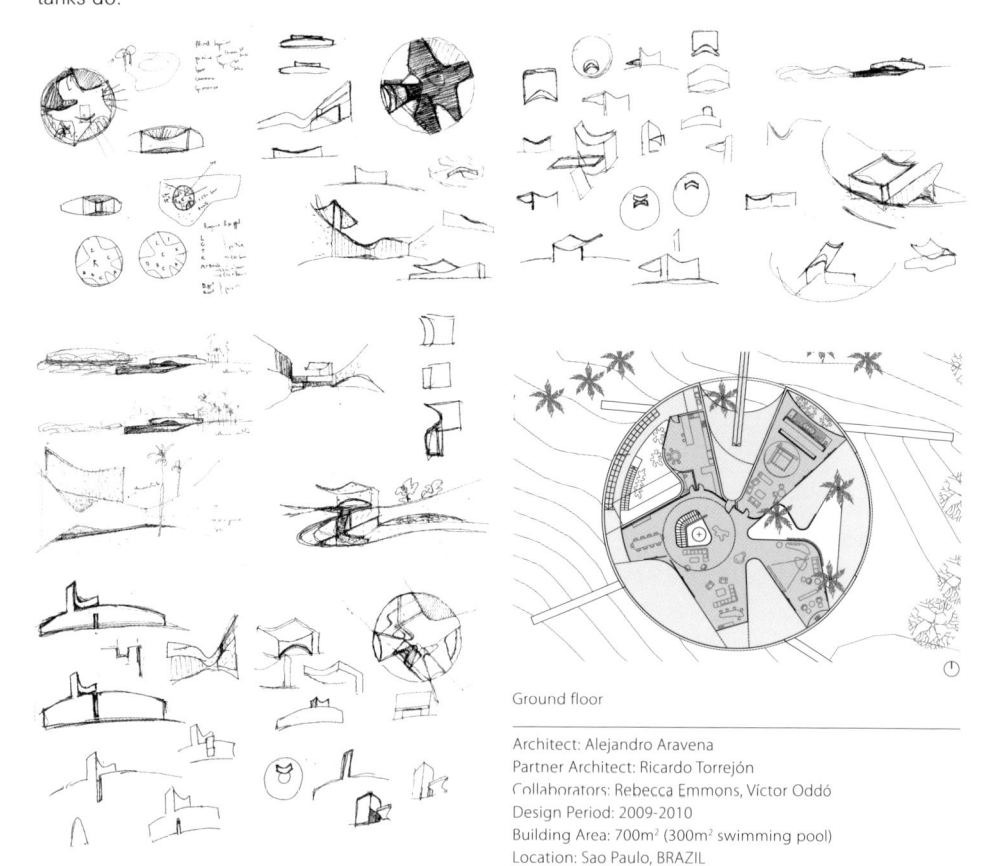

Ground floor

Architect: Alejandro Aravena
Partner Architect: Ricardo Torrejón
Collaborators: Rebecca Emmons, Víctor Oddó
Design Period: 2009-2010
Building Area: 700m² (300m² swimming pool)
Location: Sao Paulo, BRAZIL

Section

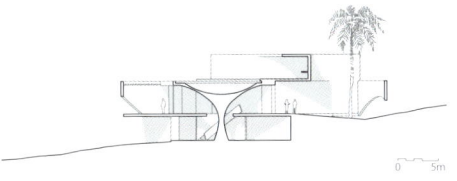

CAREY HOUSE
ケアリー邸

The clients wanted a house that was not a house, meaning that they wanted to be as integrated as possible with gardens outdoors and the spectacular views of the Andes. We thought of a courtyard house following Mies' schemes, but instead of being introverted in a lot, we opened it to perimeter towards geography. This house is mainly structure spanning away from the slope in order to gain the horizontality necessary for inhabitation.

施主が求めたのは住宅らしくない住宅であった。つまりは戸外の庭やアンデス山脈の壮大な眺めとできるだけ一体になりたいということである。であれば、ミースの計画にあったようなコートヤード・ハウスが向いている。ただし内向きの配置ではなく、外の地形に向けて開かれた配置にする。基本的には斜面の上に迫り出した構造によって、居住に必要な水平性を保つ。

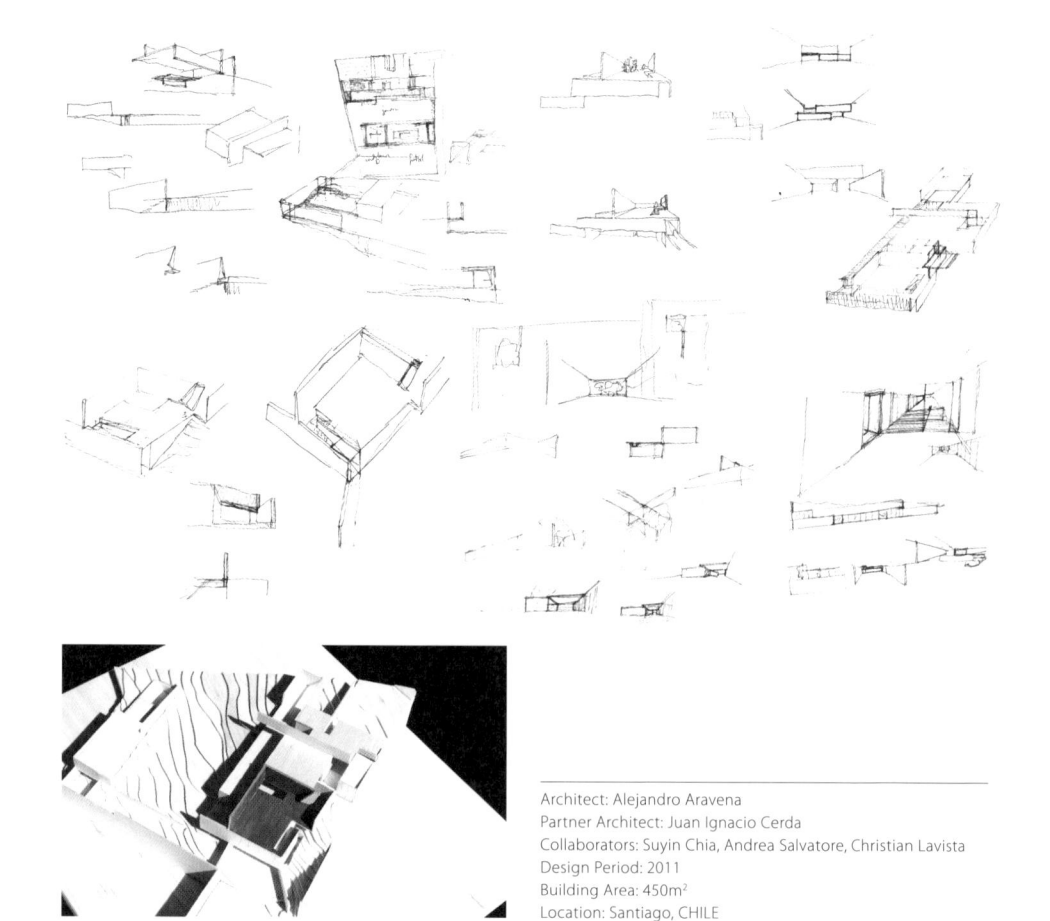

Architect: Alejandro Aravena
Partner Architect: Juan Ignacio Cerda
Collaborators: Suyin Chia, Andrea Salvatore, Christian Lavista
Design Period: 2011
Building Area: 450m²
Location: Santiago, CHILE

Site plan

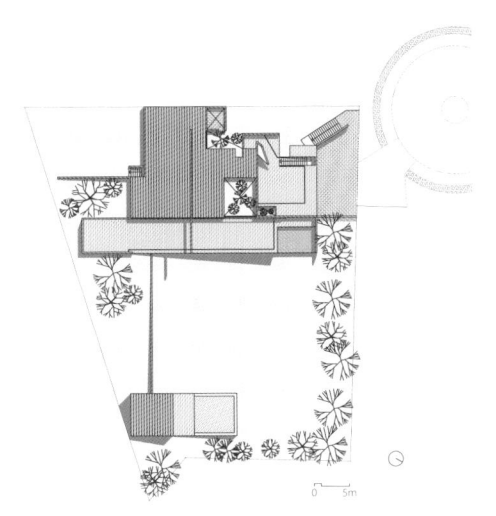

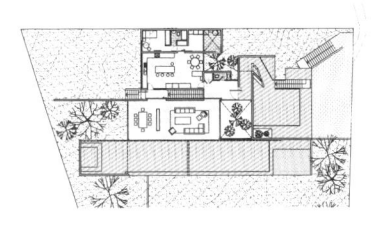

Second floor

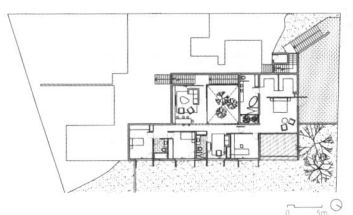

Ground floor

Basement

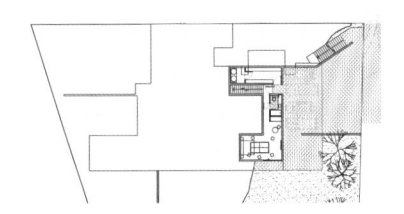

ANACLETO ANGELINI INNOVATION CENTER
アナクレート・アンジェリーニ・イノヴェーション・センター

Innovation and knowledge creation requires increased encounters among people, necessitating openness as a desired attribute for its architecture on the one hand; on the other hand, developments and inventions have to be protected, so security and the ability to close and segregate are appreciated architectural conditions as well. We proposed a rather opaque construction towards the outside, which is also efficient for the Santiago weather and then have a very permeable architecture inside. Having the structure and the shafts on the perimeter of the building inverts the typical curtain-wall building layout and concentrates openings at specific points in the form of elevated squares.

革新と知の創造には、人と人との出会いが不可欠であり、となるとその建築には一方では開放性が求められる。他方、開発や発明は隠密に行われるので、セキュリティや閉鎖性や隔離性もまた建築の条件に含まれる。そこで外部に対しては不透明な建物にした。サンティアゴの気候からしてもこのほうが合理的である。そのうえで内部には透明性の高い建築をつくる。躯体とシャフトを建物の外周に配し、典型的なカーテンウォール・ビルとは配置を逆転させ、また開口部は空中広場のある箇所に限定した。

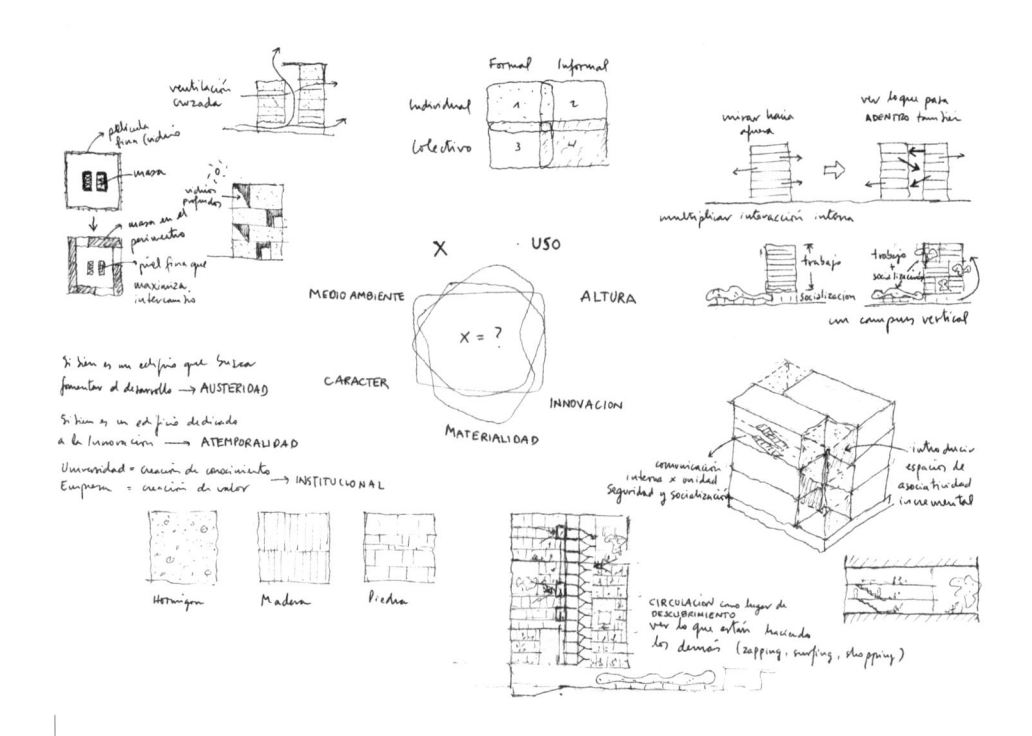

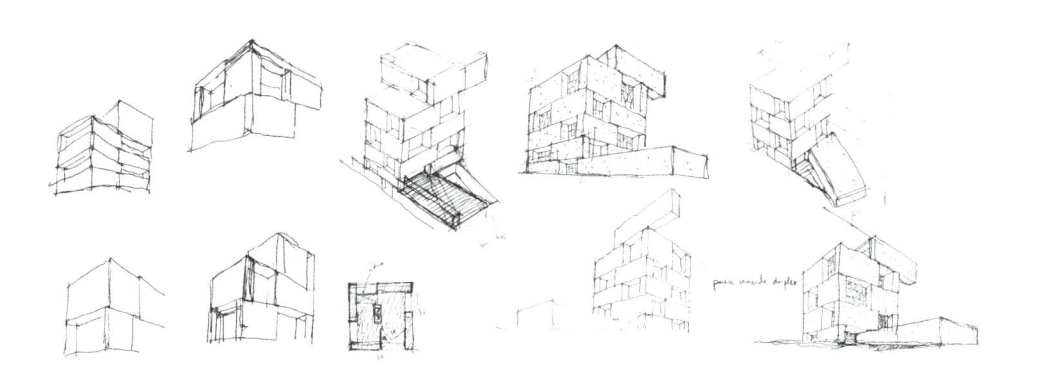

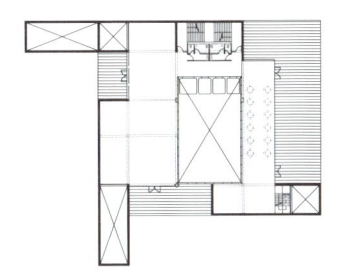

12th, 13th floor

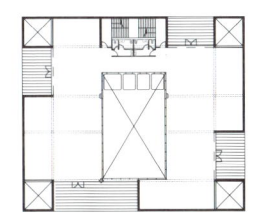

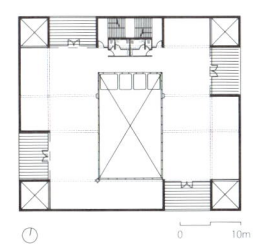

11th floor

2nd, 3rd, 4th, 8th, 9th, 10th floor

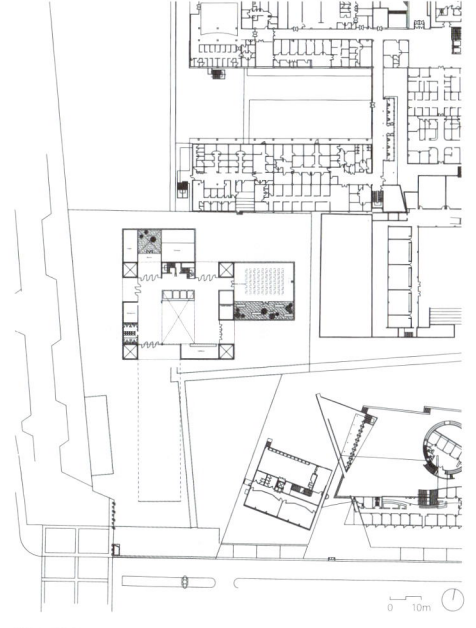

Site plan

Architect: Alejandro Aravena
Partner Architect: Juan Ignacio Cerda
Collaborators: Cristian Irarrazaval, Samuel Goncalves, Alvaro Ascoz, Víctor Oddó
Client: Angelini Group + The Cathoric University of Chile
Design / Construction Period: 2011-2013
Building Area: 9,000m²
Location: The Catholic University of Chile, Santiago, CHILE

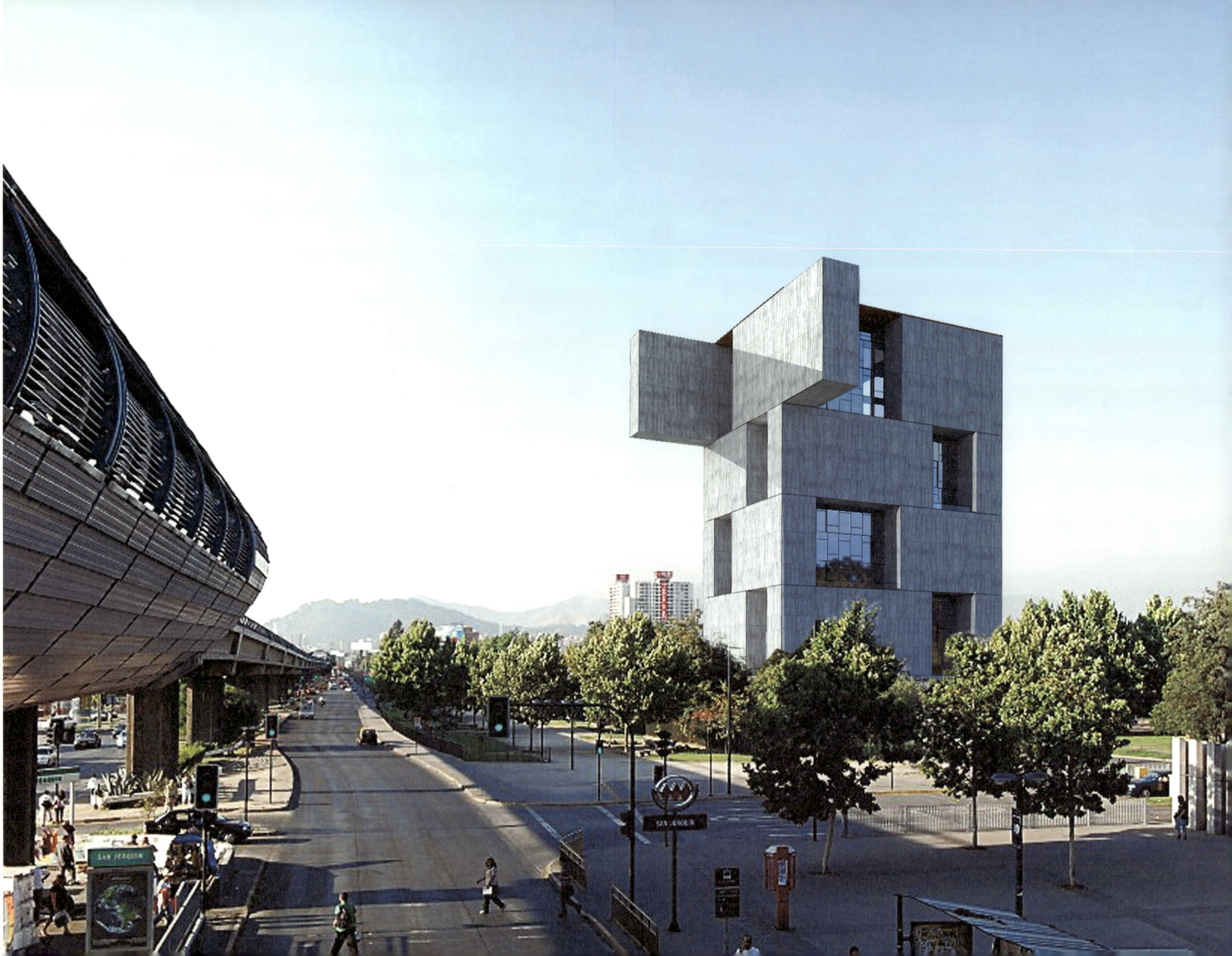
SAN JOAQUIN

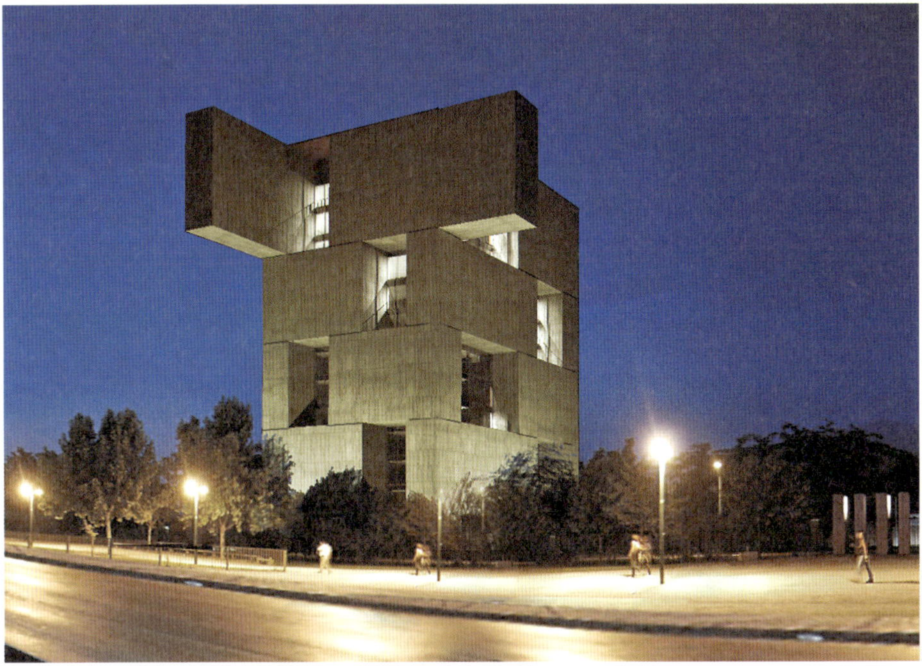

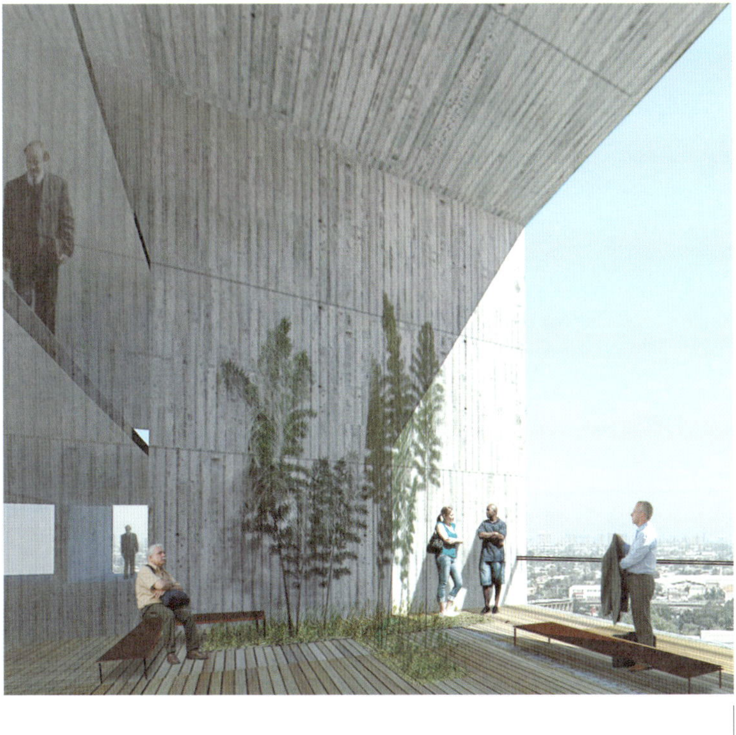

Perspective section

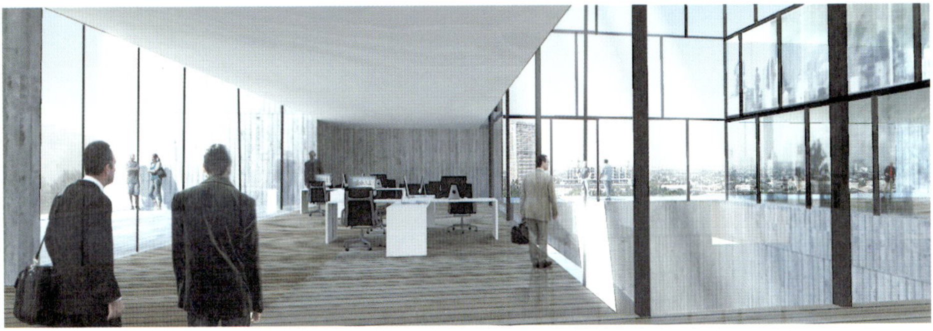

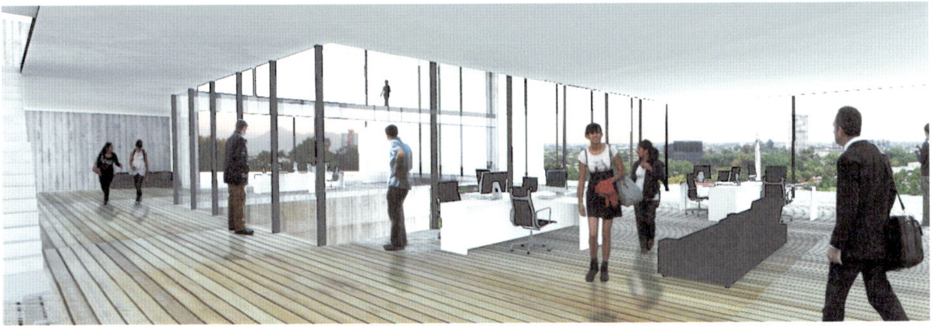

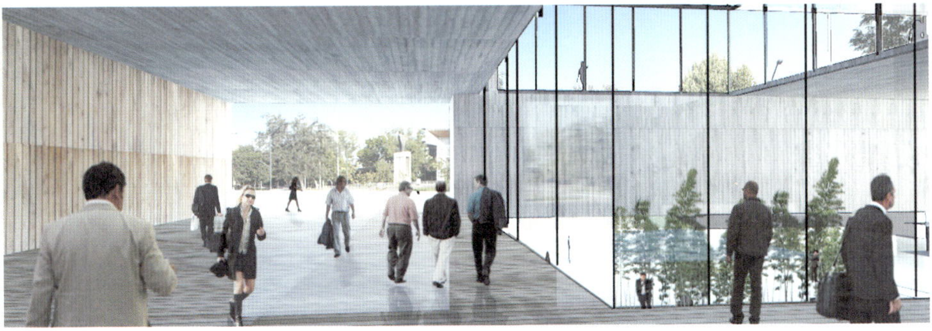

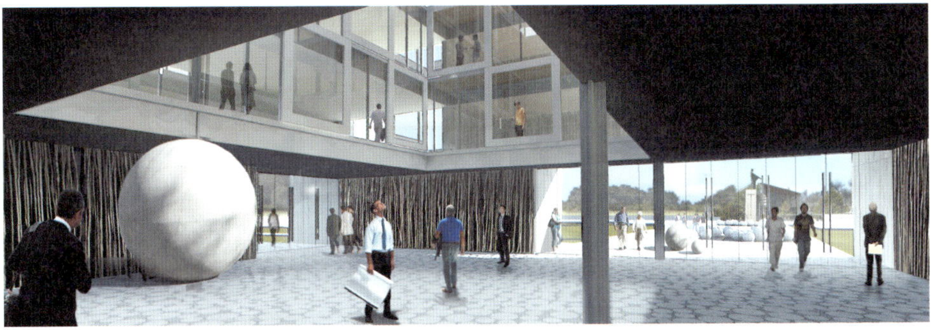

ELEMENTAL

ELEMENTAL

Elemental is a Do Tank, a company working in urban projects of infrastructure, public space, transportation and housing using the city as a shortcut towards equality. It started as a Housing initiative at Harvard University founded by architect Alejandro Aravena and engineer Andres Iacobelli. Over time, it began to work on projects of public space and infrastructure as the Metropolitan Park or more recently in the reconstruction of the entire city of Constitución hit by an 8.8 earthquake and tsunami on February 27th 2010. At present time has as partners the professionals working in the projects, the Catholic University of Chile and the Chilean Oil Company COPEC.

Regarding housing specifically, and in order to have an impact, we decided to accept every single constraint in the current market and policy conditions, no matter how restrictive that was. That policy worked based on the State subsidizing the demand, by giving a voucher to an eligible family who then had to go to the private market to buy solution. The policy was property oriented: owners benefiting from a subsidy became owners of the units. The voucher consisted of a direct subsidy from the state of $7,200 dollars plus family savings of $300 dollars. So with $7,500 we had to buy the land, provide the infrastructure (water, sewage, electricity and streets) and build the house. That amount of money meant in the best of the cases, around thirty-six square meters.

The market responded to those policy conditions of scarcity with two strategies: reducing and displacing. Given that the money was scarce, the market offered tiny houses of thirty-six square meters located where land cost almost nothing, in the outskirts of cities, seg-

エレメンタルは「ドゥ・タンク［行動集団］」として、インフラストラクチャー、公共空間、交通、ハウジングに関する都市プロジェクトを手がけ、都市を社会平等への近道として利用する。当初はハーバード大学で建築家のアレハンドロ・アラヴェナとエンジニアのアンドレス・ヤコベッリが設立したハウジング・イニシアティヴであった。しだいに公共空間やインフラ関連のプロジェクトを手がけるに至り、たとえば「メトロポリタン・パーク」や、最近では2010年2月27日にM8.8の地震と津波に襲われたコンスティトゥシオン市の復興計画も担当している。現在のエレメンタルの共同経営者にはプロジェクトの各担当専門家のほか、チリ・カトリック大学とチリ石油会社COPECが名を連ねている。

特にハウジングについていえば、世の中に一石を投ずるためにも、私たちはそのときどきの市場や政策からいかに厳しい制約を課されようが、そのいっさいを受け入れることにした。その政策とは基本的に国が住宅需要に対して補助金を出すのだが、ただしそれは政府が有資格世帯に証明書を発行し、あとはめいめいが個人取引によって住宅を購入するという仕組みになっている。これは持ち家を奨励する政策であり、だから補助さえ受けられれば家主になれる。この証明書があれば国から補助金7,200ドルと家計貯蓄として300ドルを受け取れる。私たちはこの計7,500ドルで土地を購入し、インフラ（上下水道、電気、道路）を整備し、住宅を建てる。けれどもこの金額では36m²の住戸を建てるのが関の山だ。

こうした国の財政状況を受けて市場はふたつ手を打った。縮小と移動である。金がなければ市場は、郊外のタダも同然の土地に建てられたわずか36m²の狭小住宅しか提供しない。貧しい者ほど都会のあらゆる機会から遠ざけられてしまうのである。

私たちはこの問題をふたつの面から設定し直した。ひとつは、36m²の狭小住宅で完結してしまうのではなく、それを広い住宅の半戸とみなすこと。となると、ではどちらの半戸を我々が担当するのかが鍵となる。公的補助を受ける以上、住人の手に余るほうの半分を

regated from the opportunities that are so valuable for the poor coming to cities.

Our proposal consisted in reframing the problem in two directions: first, we proposed that instead of considering thirty-six square meters as a small house, it was more strategic to consider thirty-six square meters as half of a good house. Once the problem is reframed as doing half of a good house instead of a small one, the key question is: which half do we do? With public funds one should do the half that a family will no be able to do on its own. We identified five design conditions that belonged to that more difficult first half and created an open system that families could complete afterwards themselves.

Our second point was that all of us, when buying a house, expect it to grow its value over time. And we thought there was no reason for a poor family not expect the same with their subsidized units. So we identified a set of design conditions that allowed housing to perform as an investment and not as a mere social expense. If a family then went to a bank to ask for a loan to start a small business or pay for the education of their children, they could use the household as a tool to overcome poverty and not only as a shelter against the weather. The more value the unit gained, the better it could work as an asset able to have a parallel life as capital.

If we had to synthesize our operations, we would say that the equation we are trying to solve is to design low rise, dense enough complexes able to pay for expensive well located land, with no overcrowding and with capacity for each family to grow.

In the following pages there are different designs that try to translate those goals into form.

こちらで引き受けるべきであろう。こちらの担当する半戸には5通りのデザインが考えられた。いずれもオープン・システムとなっているので、残り半分は住人自身が手を入れていけばいい。

いまひとつには、住宅を購入する者なら誰しもその資産価値の上昇を期待するということ。家が貧しいとか、補助金付きの住戸だからといって、同じことを期待していけない謂れはない。そこで私たちはハウジングが社会支出ではなく投資として成立するようなデザインを設定した。たとえばちょっとした商売を始めるとか子供の教育費を支払うために銀行にローンを申し込むにも、この家財を利用して貧困を克服していけばいい。雨露をしのぐだけの家ではないのだから。住戸の価値が上がるほど、生きた財産、すなわち資産になる。

私たちの仕事を総括するなら、それは方程式を解くようなものだと述べておこう。つまり、ある程度高密な低層集合住宅を、地の利が良く地価の高い土地に建てても採算がとれるようにする、ただし過密を避け、各戸が増築できるだけの余地を残すにはどうするか、という方程式である。

こうした目標の具現化に向けて取り組んだ事例を、以下に挙げる。

ELEMENTAL: Projects in the World

- New Orleans, USA
- Monterrey, MX
- Iquique, CL
- Tocopilla, CL
- Antofagasta, CL
- Copiapo, CL
- Valparaiso, CL
- Santiago, CL
- Rancagua, CL
- Constitucion, CL
- Temuco, CL
- Valdivia, CL
- Sao Paulo, BR

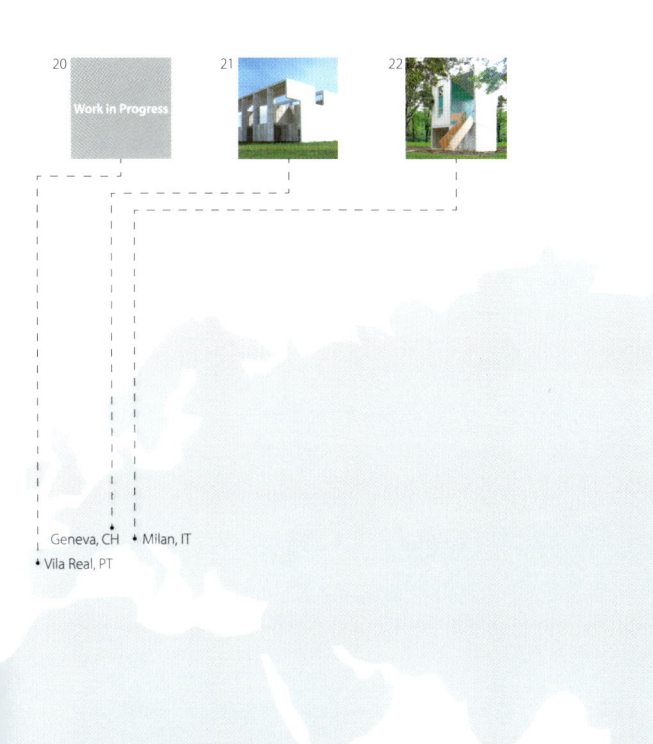

Geneva, CH   Milan, IT
Vila Real, PT

1: Quinta Monroy Housing	p. 122
2: Tocopilla Housing	
3: Antofagasta Housing	
4: Copiapo Housing	
5: Valparaiso Housing	
6: Pudahuel Housing	
7: Barnechea Housing	p. 138
8: Metropolitan Promenada	p. 146
9: Housing Complex Social Centers	p. 136
10: Renca Housing	p. 132
11: Espejo Housing	
12: Pintana Housing	
13: Rancagua Housing	
14: Constitucion Plan for Sustainable Reconstruction	p. 158
15: Temuco Housing	
16: Valdivia Housing	
17: Make it Right Foundation	p. 144
18: Monterrey Las Anacuas Housing	p. 140
19: En Sully Housing	
20: Vila Real Housing	
21: Prefab Concrete Prototype	
22: Vila Real Housing	

QUINTA MONROY HOUSING
キンタ・モンロイの集合住宅

The challenge of our first project was to accommodate a hundred families using a subsidy of $7,500 dollars that in the best of the cases allowed for thirty-six square meters of built space in a 5,000 square meter site, which cost three times what social housing could normally afford. None of the solutions in the market solved the equation. So we thought of a typology that, as buildings, could make a very efficient use of land and as houses allowed for expansion. After a year, each property value was beyond $20,000 dollars. Still, all the families have preferred to stay and keep on improving their homes, instead of selling them.

最初のプロジェクトでは、[一世帯あたり] 補助金7,500ドルで、いかに100世帯分の住戸を建てるかがテーマとなった。既存の5,000m²の敷地は、ソーシャル・ハウジングの相場からすると地価が三倍もする。これでは一戸あたりの建築面積は36m²がせいぜいのところである。だがこの方程式を解くようなものはいっさい市場には出回っていなかった。そこで私たちはあるタイポロジーを考案した。土地を有効利用する建物と、増築可能な住戸を組み合せるのである。1年後には各戸の資産価値が20,000ドルを超えた。今のところ売却された住戸はなく、皆ここに住み続けながら自宅の普請に勤しんでいる。

Original state of Quinta Monroy

Housing typology offered by the market

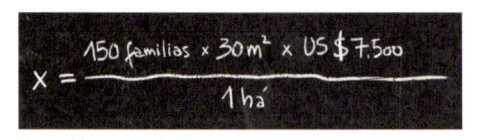

$$X = \frac{150 \; familias \times 30 m^2 \times US\$7.500}{1 \, ha}$$

The problem to resolve

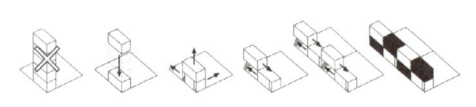

The solution: the Parallel Building

Dec. 2004

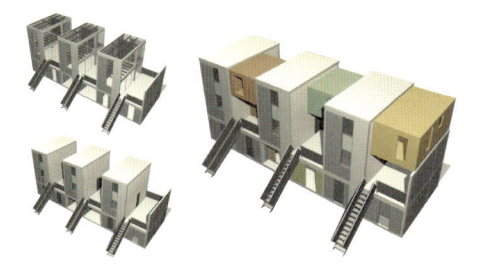

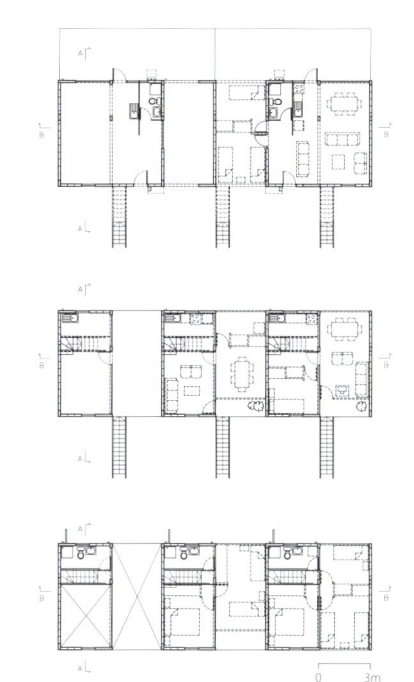

Architect: ELEMENTAL
Team: Alejandro Aravena, Andrés Iacobelli, Alfonso Montero, Tomas Cortese, Emilio de la Cerda
Design/Construction Period: 2003-2004
Building Area: 3,620 m² (93 housing complex)
Initial house: 36m²
Expanded house: 70m²
Initial Apartment: 25m²
Expanded Apartment: 72m²
Density: 162.5 houses/ha
Location: Iquique, CHILE

Aerial view original state

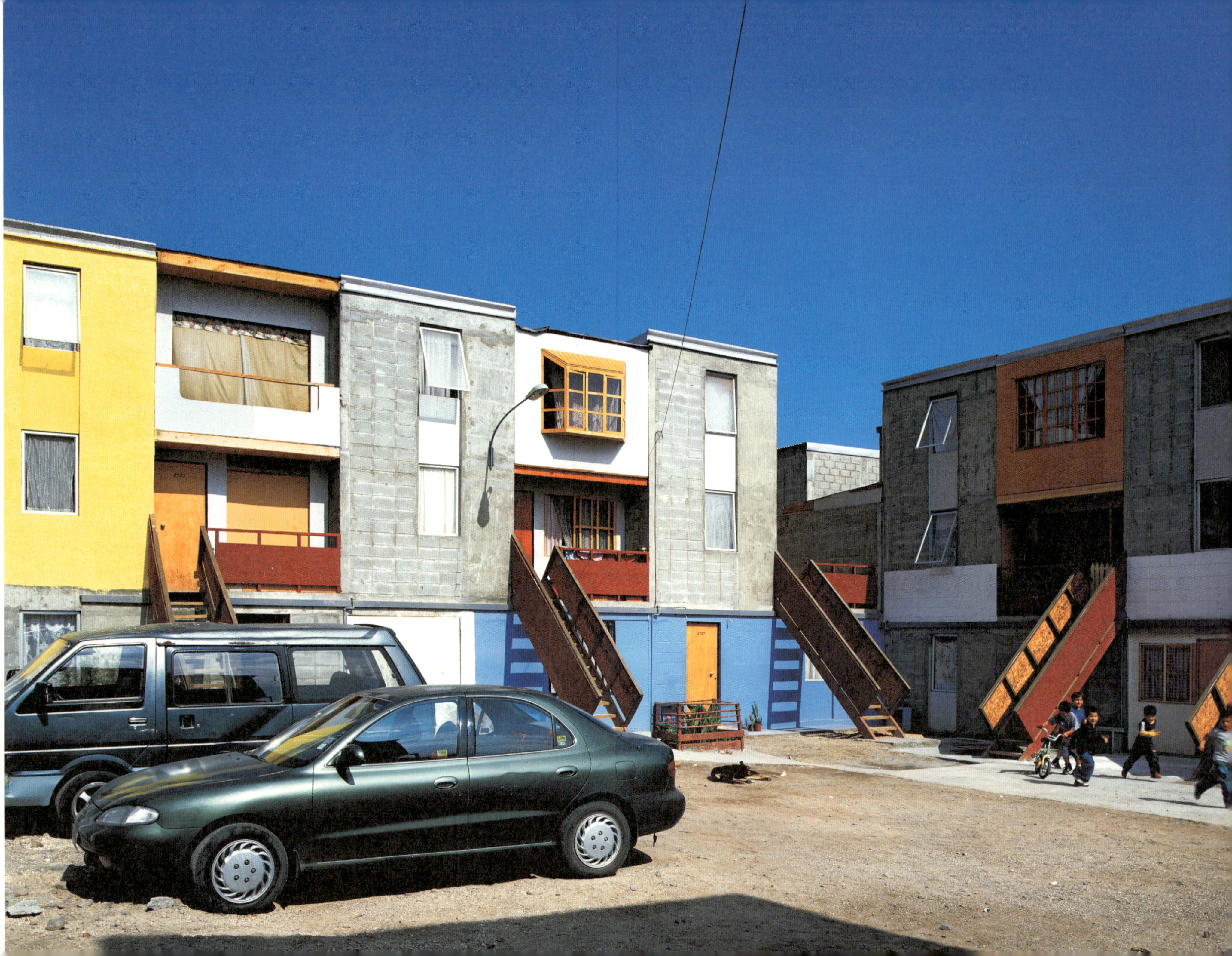

Jul. 2006

Dec. 2004

Jul. 2006

130 | ELEMENTAL

131

RENCA HOUSING
レンカの集合住宅

The aim was to accommodate 170 families in a two-hectare site that used to be a clay quarry and was then used as a debris dump. Families lived across the street so it was desirable to maintain the location. But the cost of meliorating the soil was out of the standard of what social housing could afford. So we developed a dense enough urban layout with all the units still having their own courtyard. Given that in Santiago rains, we had to achieve a waterproof exterior skin. Expansion was then expected to happen inside, in the triple height void of the unit.

170世帯分の住宅を2haの敷地に建てることになった。敷地はかつては粘土採取場であったが、その後はゴミ捨て場になっていた。入居者は通りの向かいに暮らしていたので、いまさら立地を変えるわけにもいかなかった。だが土壌改良にはソーシャル・ハウジングには不釣り合いなほど法外な費用がかかった。そのぶん都市並みに高密な配置にせざるをえなかったが、それでも全戸に専用の中庭を設けることはできた。雨の多いサンティアゴなので、耐水性のある外装にした。したがって増築工事は3層高の吹抜けをそなえた住戸の内部に限られる。

Site plan

Cross section

Long section

Third floor

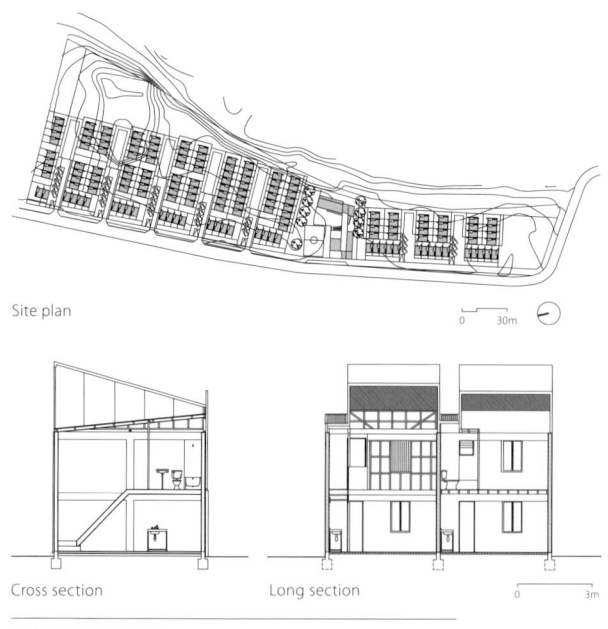

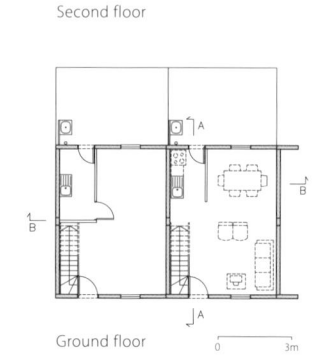

Second floor

Ground floor

Architect: ELEMENTAL
Team: Alejandro Aravena, Tomas Cortese, Juan Cerda
Design/Construction Period: 2004-2007
Building Area: 5,100 m^2 (170 housing complex)
Initial house: 36m^2
Expanded house: 68m^2
Density: 131 houses/ha
Location: Renca, Santiago, CHILE

Community design workshop

Interior of the house, before and after the expansion made for the family

133

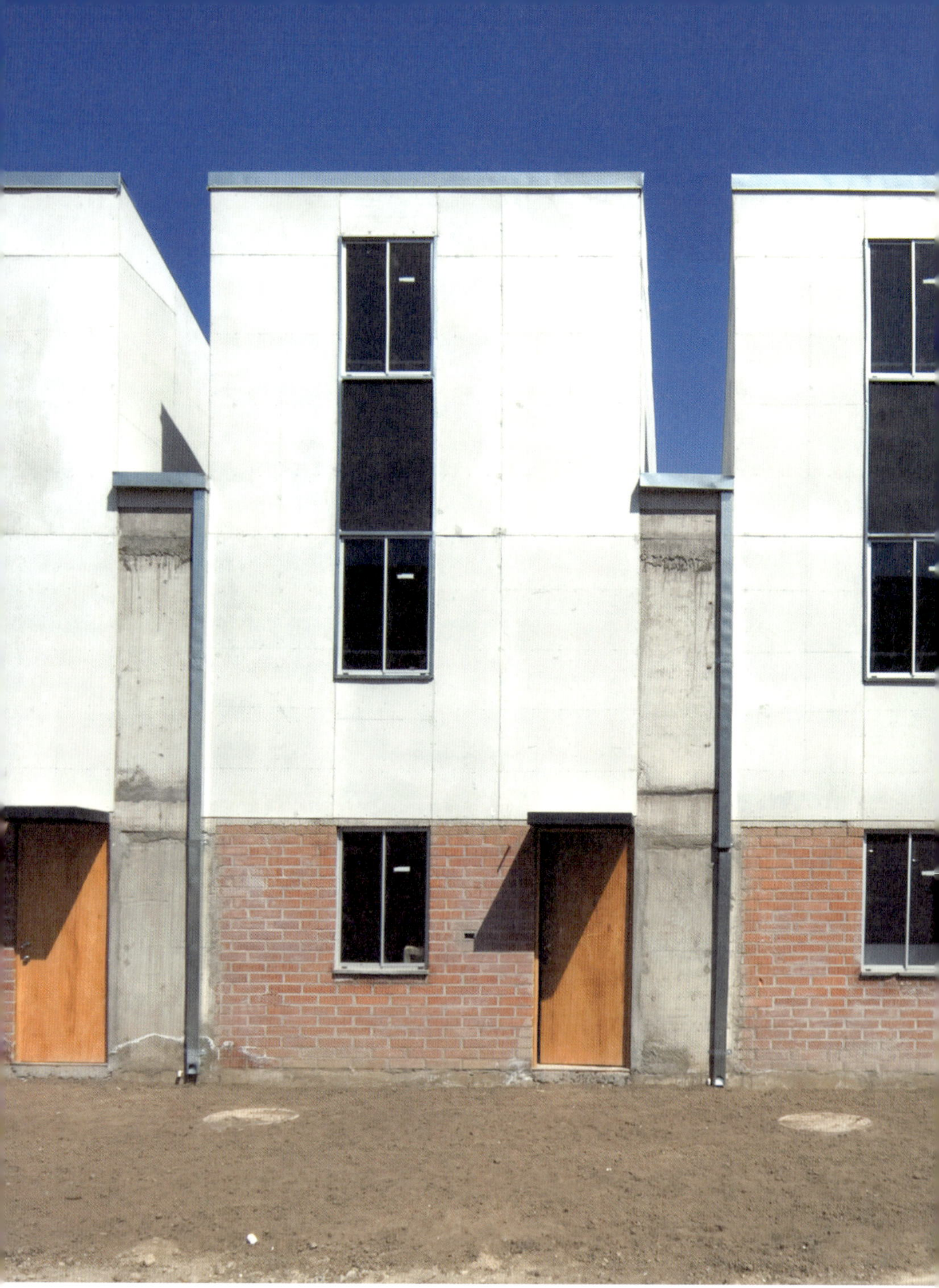

House after self construction expansions 2007-2010

HOUSING COMPLEX SOCIAL CENTERS
集合住宅の集会所

Chilean Housing policy requires that projects consider a social center. Its size varies depending on the number of units of the complex. In order to have a design able to be adjusted to different sizes, we developed a strategy of having a volume that reacted to site and project conditions, and on top of it a sloped box that by resting on one side directly on the ground, gave the building the height of a public building without incurring into excessive costs.

チリの住宅政策では、集合住宅には集会所を併設するよう定められている。集会所の規模は戸数に応じて増減する。私たちはこうした規模の変化に適応するために、敷地やプロジェクトの条件に応じてヴォリュームを伸縮させることにし、さらに別のボックスの一辺のみを地面に固定して、さきのヴォリュームの上に乗り上げるようにして斜めに載せる。こうして高さを稼ぐことで、余分な費用をかけずに公共建築らしさを演出する。

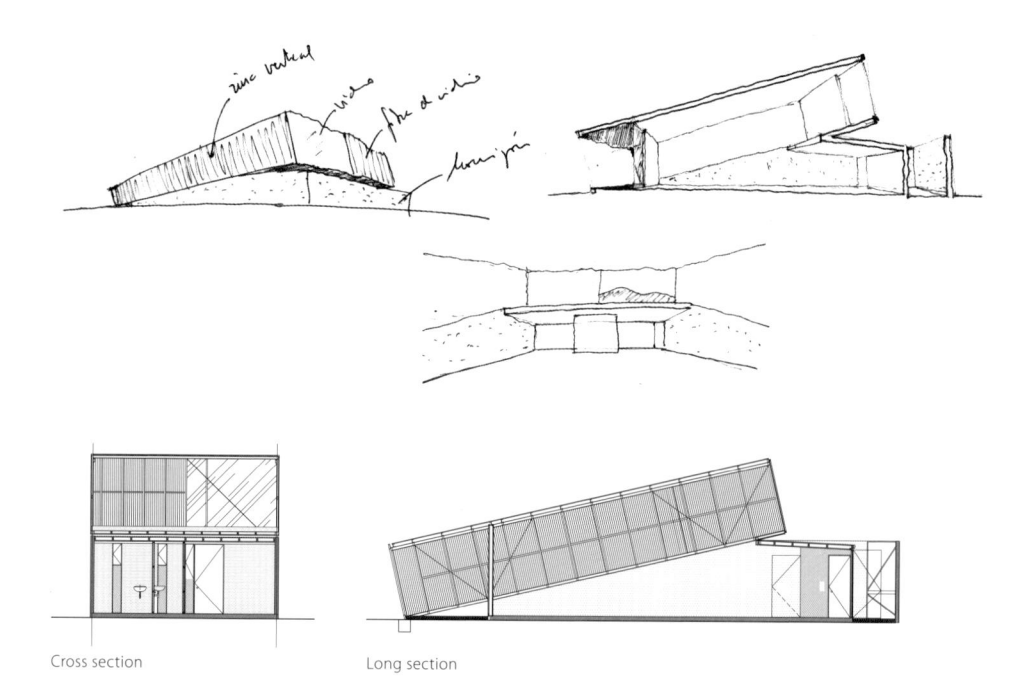

Cross section

Long section

Architect: ELEMENTAL
Team: Alejandro Aravena, Tomas Cortese, Juan Ignacio Cerda
Design/Construction Period: 2005-2010
Building Area: 120-300m²
Location: Temuco/Santiago/Valparaiso, CHILE

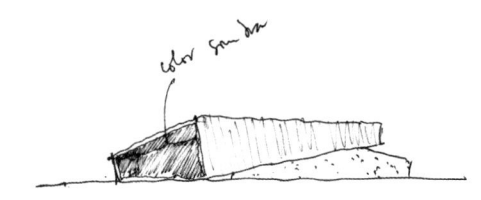

137

BARNECHEA HOUSING
バルネチアの集合住宅

This project is located in the most expensive neighborhood of Santiago. We wanted, with very low budget subsidies, to allow the families to keep on benefiting from the proximity to jobs, education, transportation, health facilities and even recreation and quality public space. Units are arranged around a collective courtyard, a territorial level of association that is somewhere in between the private and the public space, which is crucial in fragile social environments. These 150 units are the first phase of a total of 1,000 families that will be given a solution at the end of the program.

このプロジェクトはサンティアゴ市内でも屈指の高級住宅地にある。わずかな補助金しか出なかったが、それでもせめて住人には近くに職場、学校、交通、医療施設があることの利便性を享受し、娯楽施設や充実した公共空間の恩恵も受けてもらいたかった。住戸は共用の中庭を取り囲むように配置されている。この中庭は住民同士の交流の場であり、開かれても閉じてもいない、いわば半公共空間となっている。脆弱な社会環境ではこうした公私の線引きが難しい。この150戸はまだ序の口にすぎず、ゆくゆくは1,000世帯分の住戸が供給される。

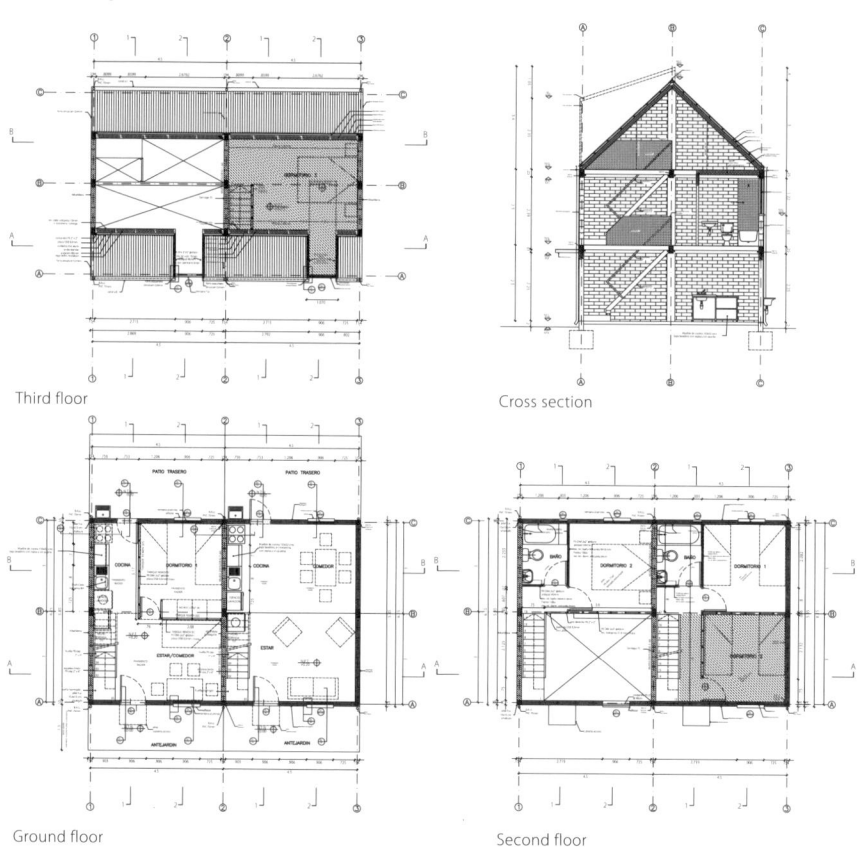

Third floor

Cross section

Ground floor

Second floor

Architect: ELEMENTAL
Team: Alejandro Aravena, Ricardo Torrejón, Juan Ignacio Cerda
Design/Construction Period: 2006-2010
Building Area: 6,600m² (150 housing complex)
Initial house: 44m²
Expanded house: 69m²
Density: 60 houses/ha
Location: Santiago, CHILE

MONTERREY LAS ANACUAS HOUSING
モンテレイの集合住宅 ラス・アナクァス

In the Mexican housing market, the cheapest solution that is offered is about $30,000 dollars. So the poor are not being reached. We developed an improved version of Iquique where houses underneath and duplex apartments on top have an initial cost of $20,000 dollars, but can achieve a middle-income standard of seventy-two square meters after self-built expansions. The efficiency in land use without overcrowding, allowed us to purchase land in a neighborhood where the average cost is $50,000 dollars. We expect the families to benefit from that value gain and from the fact that cost of land expresses close availability of services and opportunities.

メキシコの住宅市場では、住宅の最安値が 30,000 ドルである。貧乏人にはとても手が届かない。私たちはイキケ［キンタ・モンロイ］の改良版を試みた。初期費用 20,000 ドルで下階の住戸と上階のデュプレックスを建設し、ただし住人が自主的に増築すれば中間所得層世帯の平均面積と同等の広さ 72m² を手に入れることができるようにする。過密にならない程度に土地を有効利用することにしたので、幸いにも地価相場が平均 50,000 ドルの地域に土地を購入することができた。住人は資産価値の上昇によって利益を得るだろうし、また地価相応の利便性ゆえに各種公共サービスや機会を享受できるだろう。

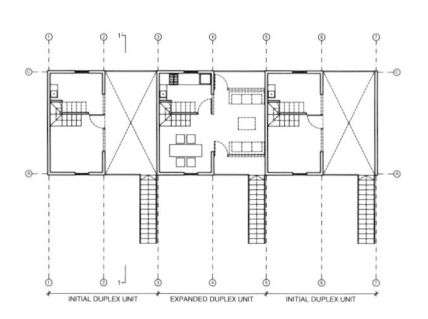

Second floor

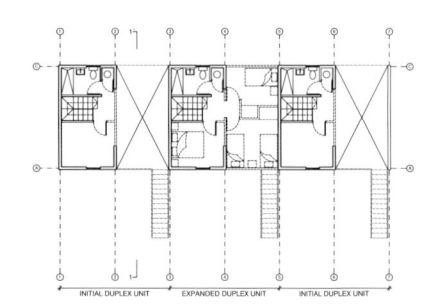

Third floor

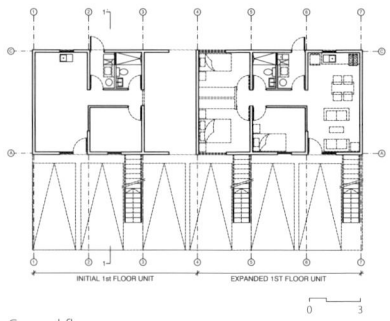

Ground floor

Architect: ELEMENTAL
Team: Alejandro Aravena, Gonzalo Arteaga, Fernando García-Huidobro
Collaborator: Ramiro Ramirez
Design/Construction Period: 2008-2010
Building Area: 2,800 m² (70 housing complex)
Initial house: 40m²
Expanded house: 80m²
Density: 477 hab/ha
Location: Monterrey, MEXICO

141

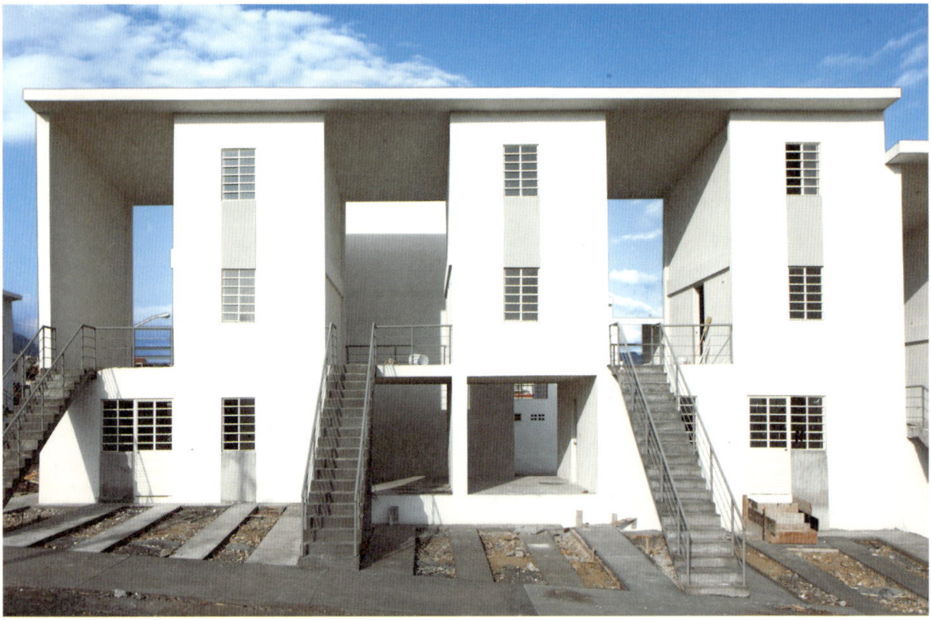

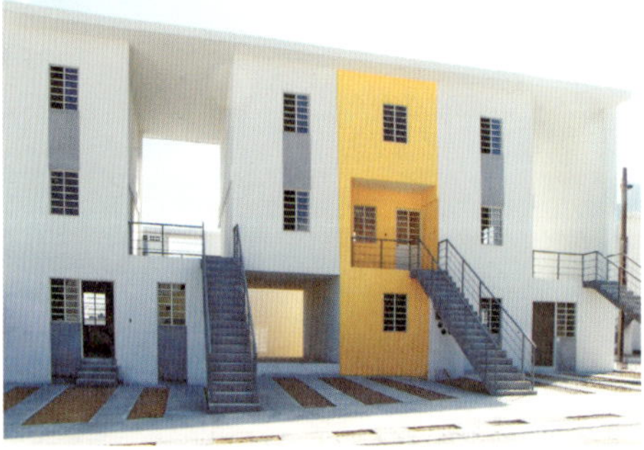

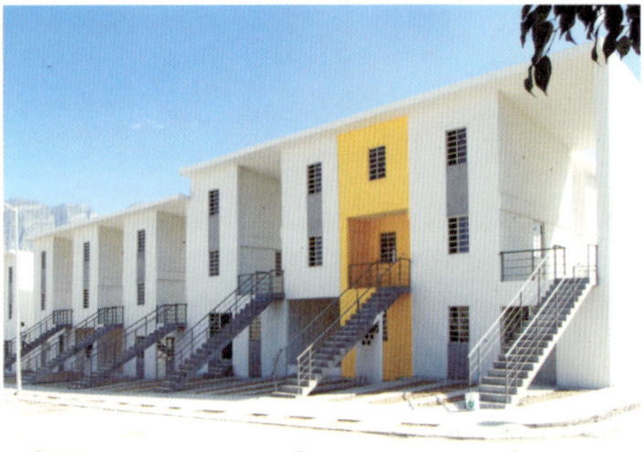

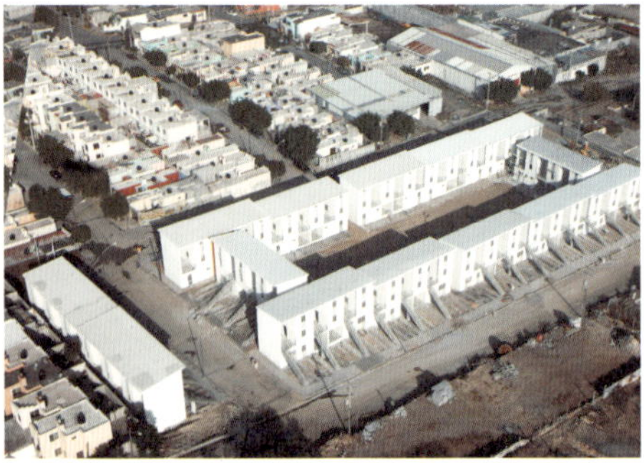

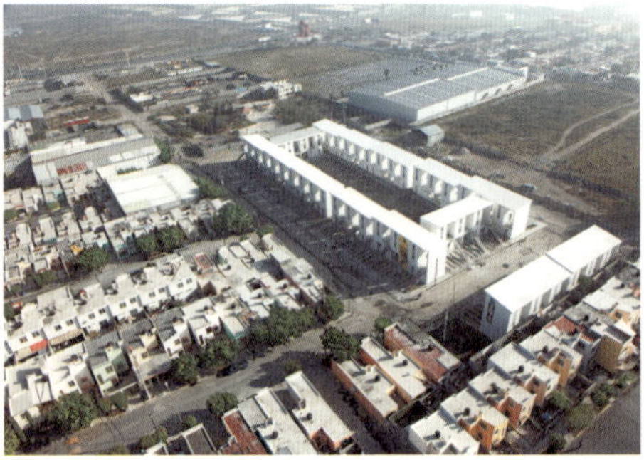

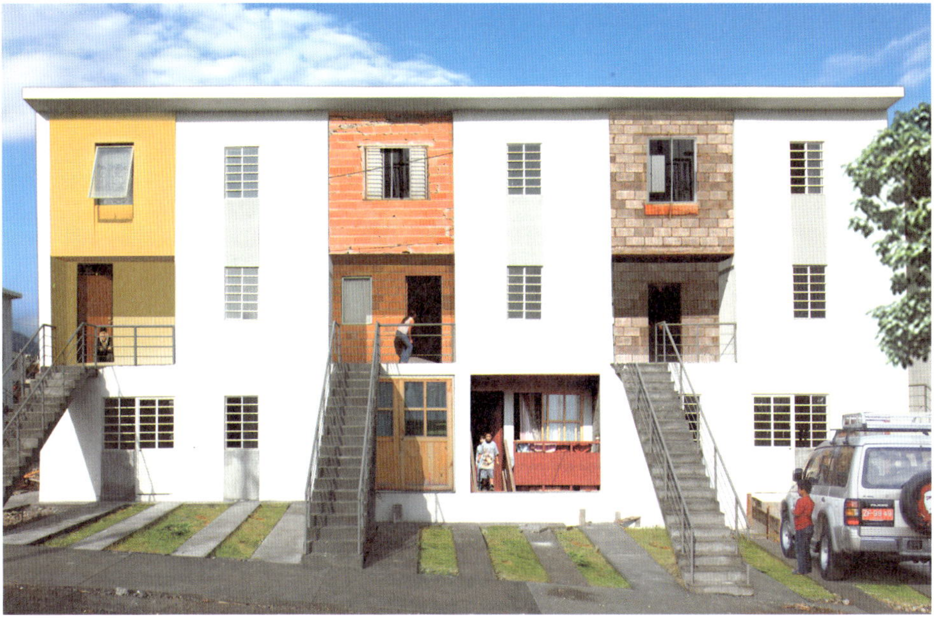

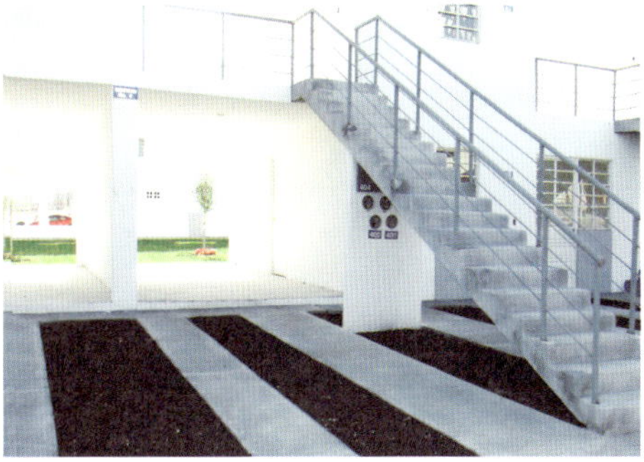

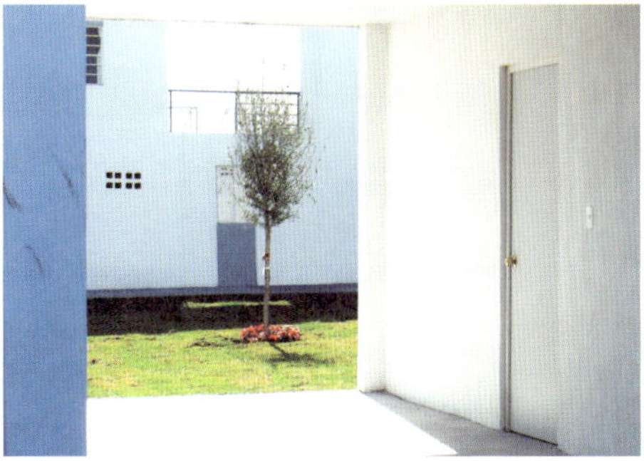

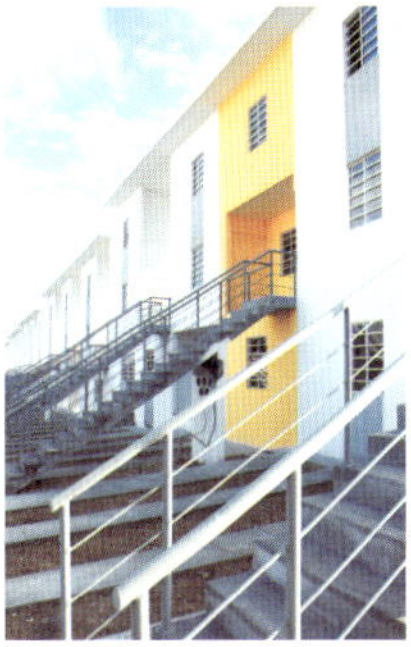

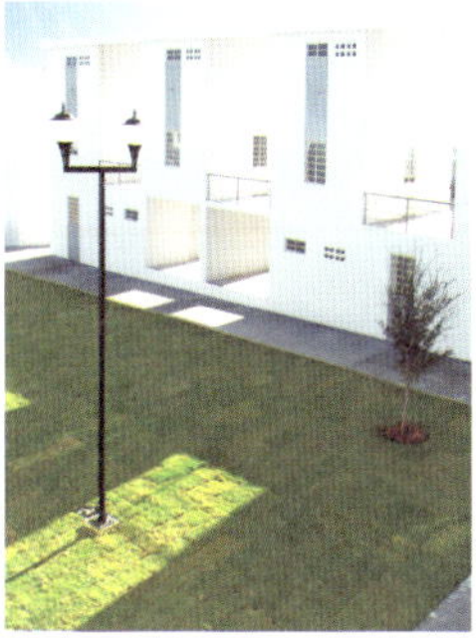

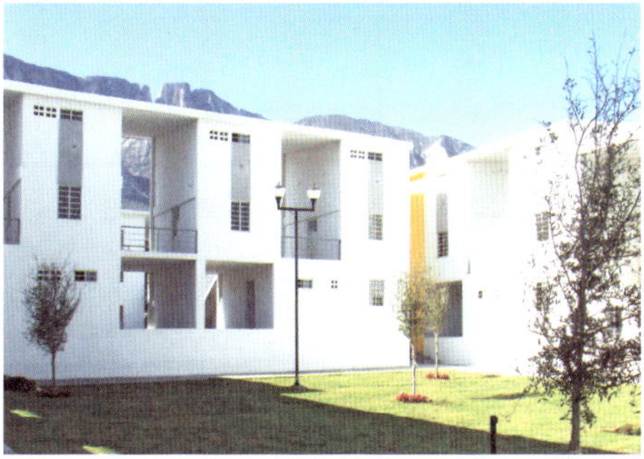

MAKE IT RIGHT FOUNDATION
メイク・イット・ライト財団

Brad Pitt's Foundation, wanted to contribute to the reconstruction of New Orleans after Hurricane Katrina. They called various architects to make proposals of how to rebuild. Due to the lack of money and time, we followed the strategy of doing half of a good house instead of a small one in order to allow future interventions of families.

ブラッド・ピットの主催する財団は、ハリケーン・カトリーナの被災地ニューオーリンズの復興支援にあたっている。同財団は各地の建築家に声をかけ、再建案を募った。時間も資金も不足していたことから、私たちは例によって小さな家ではなく広い家の半分をつくり、残りは住人の介入に委ねることにした。

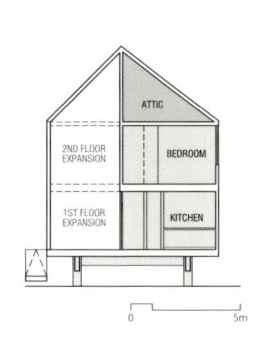

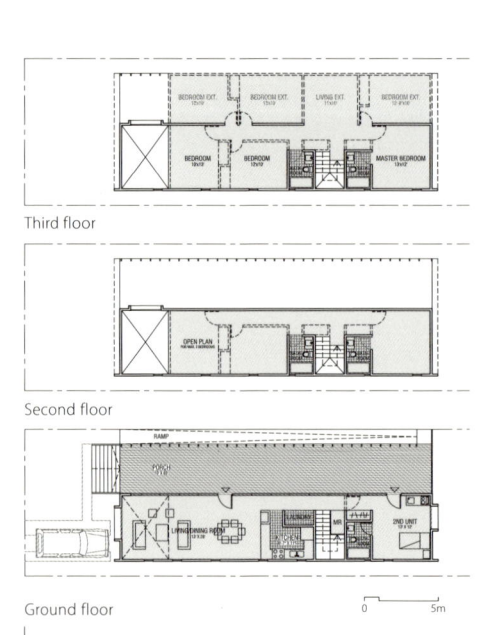

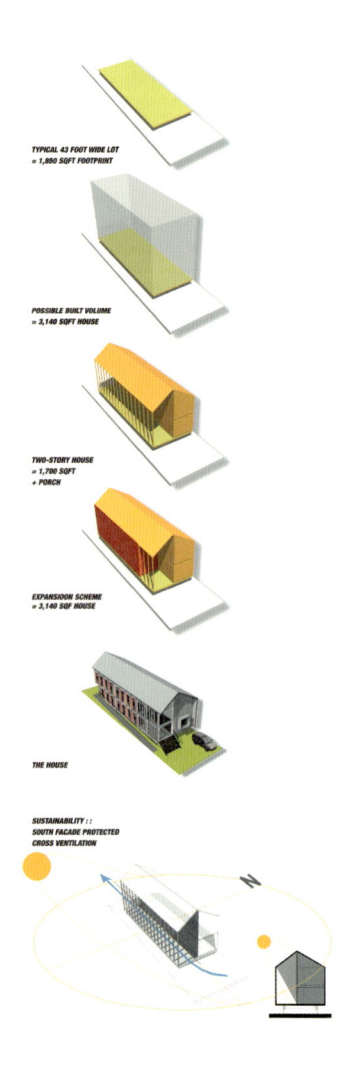

Cross section

Third floor

Second floor

Ground floor

ELEMENTAL

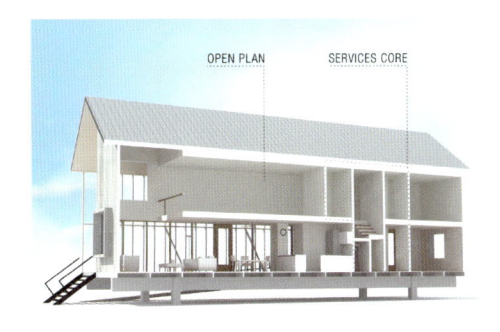

Architect: ELEMENTAL
Team: Alejandro Aravena, Diego Torres, Rebecca Emmons
Design Period: 2009
Initial house: 162m²
Expanded house: 243m²
Location: New Orleans, Louisiana, USA

METROPOLITAN PROMENADE
メトロポリタン・プロムナード

Chile has had an incredible economic growth in the last decade, but the urban standards have not increased proportionally. Santiago for example, has no single place where to go for a long walk. These spaces tend to be associated to the geographical features of cities: rivers, seastrands, hills, but in Santiago, the river has already been used for a highway. The only place left is an old agricultural canal running at the base of the Metropolitan Park, the San Cristobal Hill. It is a ten-kilometer horizontal, continuous path that could be transformed into a pedestrian Promenade. A four-hectare Children's Park on the hillside, besides being a program to celebrate the bicentennial of Chile, can be considered as the initial phase of a promenade that will be completed in the coming years.

チリはここ10年で驚異的な経済成長を遂げたが、これに比例して都市の格も上がるということはなかった。たとえば首都サンティアゴには、長い散歩コースがひとつもない。この種の空間は、都市の地勢（河川、海岸、丘）に絡めて整備されることが多い。ところがサンティアゴ市内の川はすでに高速道路に塞がれている。残るは昔の農業用運河の辺り、すなわちメトロポリタン・パークのあるサンクリストバルの丘の麓のみである。この全長10kmにおよぶ細い歩道を、遊歩道に転用する。丘の斜面には広さ4haの児童公園がチリ建国200年を祝って建設されるが、これは今後整備される遊歩道の第一期工事に相当する。

Master plan

Architect: ELEMENTAL
Team: Alejandro Aravena, Ricardo Torrejón, Víctor Oddó, Juan Cerda, Fernando García-Huidobro, Gabriela Larraín, Rebecca Emmons
Design/Construction Period: 2003-2011
Building Length: 14km
Building Area Children´s Park: 4ha
Location: San Cristobal Hill, Santiago, CHILE

Metropolitan Park, Santiago

Central Park, New York

Original state

Proposal

Original state

Proposal

147

METROPOLITAN PROMENADE

BICENTENNIAL CHILDREN'S PARK
建国200年記念児童公園

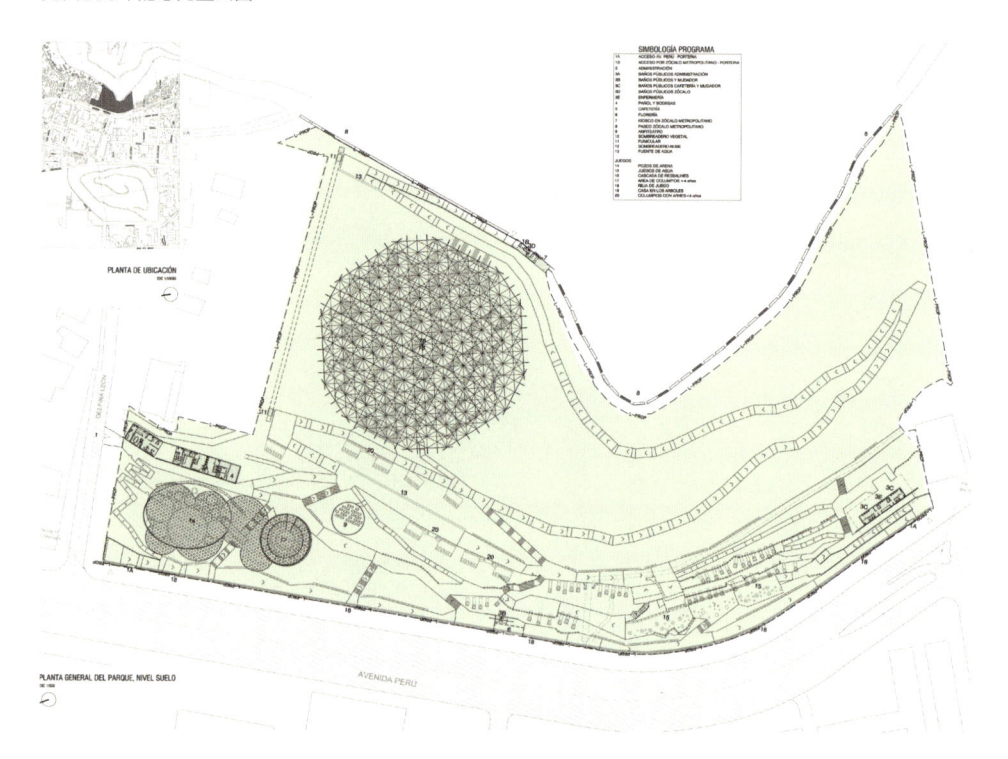

General view project under construction

ESTAMOS EN CHACARILLAS
LLAMAR 90329081
No demoler
FAMILYA ANDRADES SUAREZ

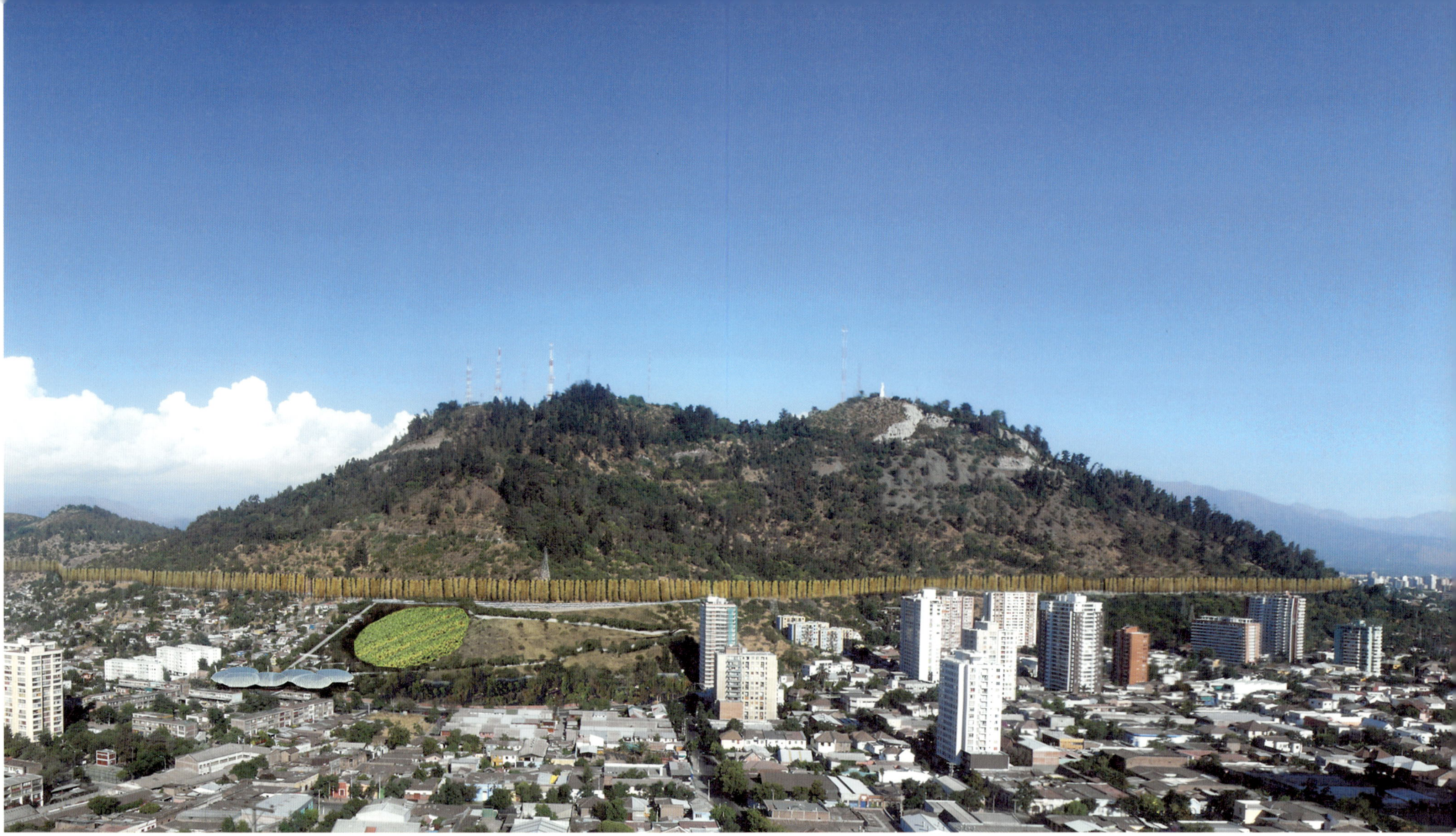

EARTHQUAKE AND TSUNAMI RESPONSE
地震・津波対策

On February 27th 2010, Chile was hit by an 8.8 earthquake and a tsunami just afterwards. We responded to the disaster at three different time periods: one day, ten days and a hundred days.

2010年2月27日、チリはM8.8の大地震に続いて津波に襲われた。私たちは、1日目、10日目、そして100日目というように期限を3つに区切って災害対策を立てた。

EARTHQUAKE AND TSUNAMI RESPONSE

DAY 1: WATER DISTRIBUTION
1日目：水の配給

Day One: The first issue that we wanted to address was to guarantee water availability, because its efficient distribution is necessary to prevent epidemics and allow people to have time left for reconstruction. Given that carrying water is difficult, we proposed to make it roll. The idea transmitted by Youtube and text messages, was to place plastic bottles inside a tire a making it roll, an operation that increases from ten to twenty-five liters the collecting capacity, doable even by children.

1日目：真っ先に対処すべきは、水の確保であった。水を手際よく配給しないと、伝染病が蔓延し、再建を遅らせてしまう。だが水を運搬するだけでも骨が折れるので、水を転がして運ぶことにした。その方法はYoutubeや携帯電話のテキストメッセージを通じて伝えられたように、水を入れたペットボトルをタイヤの内側に詰め込み、そのタイヤを転がすだけである。これなら一度に10ℓどころか25ℓの水を運べるし、子供にも運べる。

DRINK　　**COOK**　　**CLEAN**

Architect: ELEMENTAL
Team: Alejandro Aravena, Víctor Oddó, Juan Cerda
Design/Construction Period: 1 day, March 2010
Location: CHILE

1. FILL THE BOTTLES WITH WATER
2. PLACE THE BOTTLES ON THE WHEEL
3. WHEEL LIFTS
4. ROLL THE WHEEL

http://www.qdrum.co.za/

http://www.hipporoller.org/

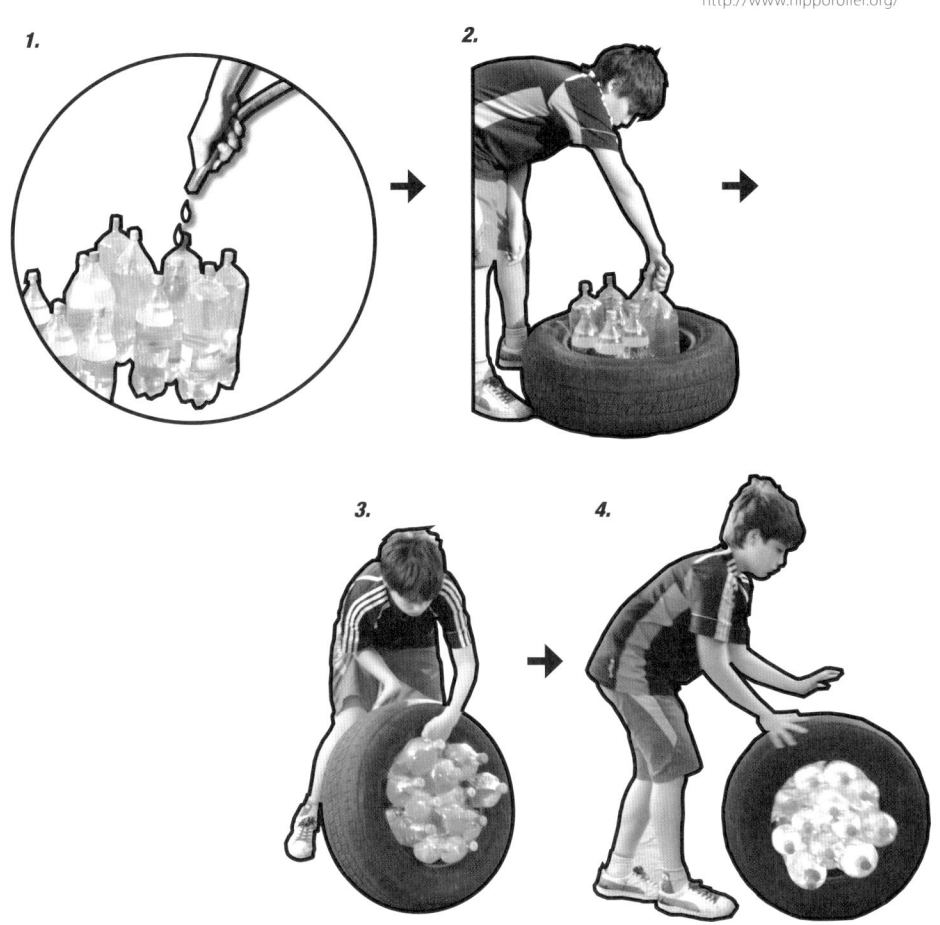

1.

2.

3.

4.

http://www.youtube.com/watch?v=3z-4Djq3leQ

EARTHQUAKE AND TSUNAMI RESPONSE

DAY 10: ELEMENTAL SHELTER
10日目：エレメンタル・シェルター

Day Ten: Emergency requires fast action. But urgency tends to be wrongly associated with delivering disposable solutions. We proposed to frame the problem of emergency shelters as an advance of the definitive reconstruction so that once emergency is over, shelters can be dismantled and become part of final solutions. Shelters seen as a kind of down payment allow for better quality of temporary units, but also make definitive reconstruction easier, since part of the square meters to be delivered, are already in use by the families.

10日目：非常時には迅速な行動が求められる。だが非常時ほどなぜか使い捨ての手段に頼りがちである。私たちは緊急シェルターという問題を、将来の再建への布石ととらえることにした。平常に戻ったときに、シェルターを解体してその部材を恒久的な建物に再利用すればいい。シェルターを一種の頭金とみなせば、良質の仮設住宅が可能になるだけでなく、将来の建設も容易になる。なぜならすでに住宅の一部が現地に調達されており、実際に使われ始めているからだ。

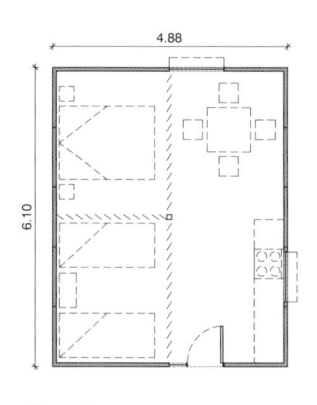

Ground floor

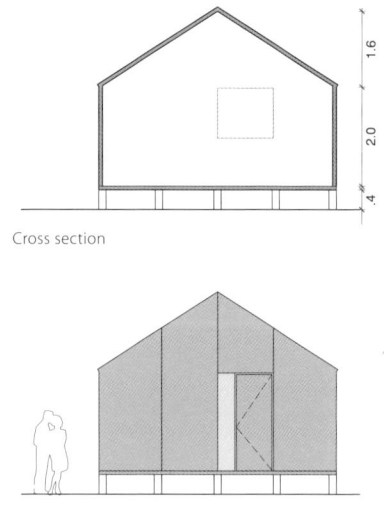

Cross section

Elevation

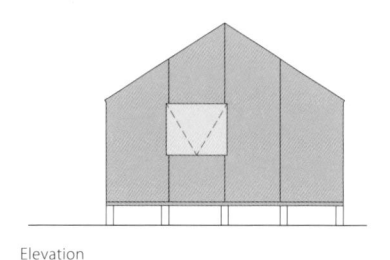

Elevation

Architect: ELEMENTAL
Team: Alejandro Aravena, Víctor Oddó, Juan Cerda, Fernando García-Huidobro
Collaborators: Julieta Scarafia, Eduardo Guiot
Design/Construction Period: 10 days, March 2010
Building Area: 30m²
Location: CHILE

Built in 24 hours

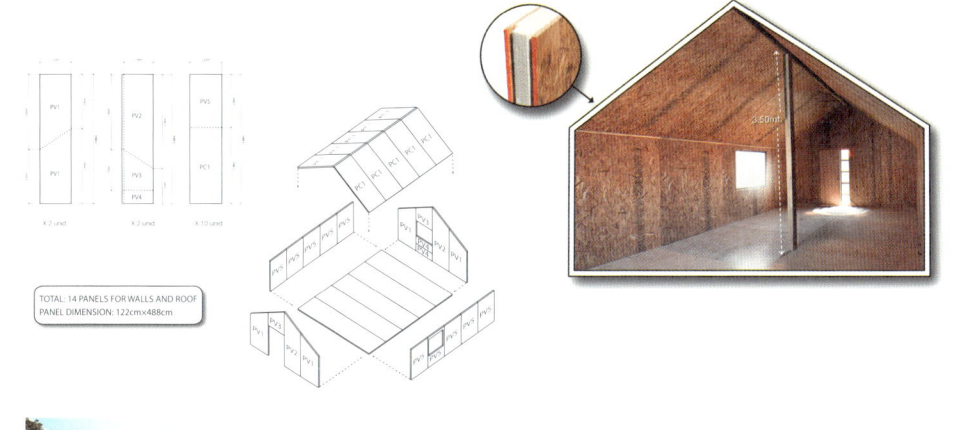

TOTAL: 14 PANELS FOR WALLS AND ROOF
PANEL DIMENSION: 122cm×488cm

Emergency housing complex in Constitucion

EARTHQUAKE AND TSUNAMI RESPONSE

DAY 100: CONSTITUCION PLAN FOR SUSTAINABLE RECONSTRUCTION

100日目：コンスティトゥシオン市のサステイナブルな復興計画

Day Hundred: Chile resisted the earthquake well, but was not prepared against the tsunami. Our cities lacked not only effective evacuation plans, but mainly did not have an urban DNA able to resist the impact of waves. We were asked to do the masterplan to rebuild the city of Constitucion and we were given a hundred days to do all the designs from tsunami mitigation to housing, from public buildings to energy and economic reactivation. Being a coastal country, we cannot afford to simply abandon risky areas. Evidence shows that infrastructure is useless to resist the energy of displaced water. So we proposed a threefold strategy: first, an alert and evacuation plan to reach within fifteen minutes a safe zone on the hillsides. Second, a coastal forest able to produce enough friction to reduce the energy of the waves instead of trying to resist them; the topography underneath had to be rough and bumpy for further rubbing against waves momentum, minimizing the area with prohibition of use and inhabitation. And third, a conditioned building zone with collapsible enclosures in the lower levels. By introducing a forest in between the city and the sea, we are responding against geographical threats with geographical answers. We have now 1000 days to implement this all.

100日目：チリの国土は大地震を耐え抜いたが、津波対策までは手が回らなかった。どの都市も避難計画に不備があったうえに、そもそも津波に耐えられるようなDNAが都市にそなわっていなかったからであろう。私たちはコンスティトゥシオン市の依頼を受け、同市再建に向けマスタープランを作成することになった。期限100日で、津波対策からハウジングに至るまで、公共建築からエネルギー復旧や経済復興に至るまで、すべてのデザインを仕上げなければならない。チリは沿岸国なので、危険地域を単に避けるわけにもいかない。今回の災害により、インフラは津波の威力にはとても敵わないことが立証された。そこで私たちは三段構えの防御策を立てた。その1：市民を高台の安全圏に15分以内に退避させる警報発令・避難計画を立てる。その2：津波に抵抗するのではなく、海岸林によって摩擦を起こして津波の勢いを殺ぐ。また地表面には凹凸や起伏をつけて摩擦を増やし、一帯を利用・居住禁止区域に指定する。その3：条件付き建築区域を設け、域内の建物についてはいざという時に低層階の壁が外れるよう設計しておく。都市と海の間に森林を挿入することで、地理的な脅威に対し地理的な解答をもって応ずるわけである。以上すべてを実現するのに、残された時間は1000日となった。

Architect: ELEMENTAL
Partner Institutions: MINVU, ARUP, Municipality of Constitucion, Fundación Chile, Arauco
Design/Construction Period: 100 days, 2010–20XX (Under Construction)
Building Area: city of 35,000 inhabitants
Location: Constitución, CHILE

Masterplan for Reconstruction

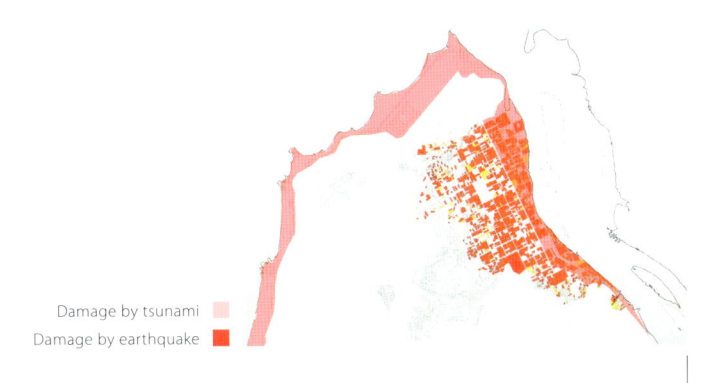

Damage by tsunami
Damage by earthquake

PROJECT CHART

PRES CONSTITUCIÓN

1. **INFRASTRUCTURE**
   - 1.1. Transportation Plan
   - 1.2. Rain Water Plan
   - 1.3. Anti-Tsunami Plan

2. **PUBLIC SPACES AND FACILITIES**
   - 2.1. River Edge
   - 2.2. Coastal Edge
   - 2.3. Downtown

3. **HOUSING**
   - 3.1. Typology Catalogue
   - 3.2. Pilot Projects

4. **ECONOMIC DIVERSIFICATION**
   - 4.1. Tourism
   - 4.2. Wood Cluster

5. **ENERGY**
   - 5.1. Heat Recovery
   - 5.2. Resource Management
   - 5.3. Passive Solar Housing

Damage by earthquake

Damage by tsunami

2.1. RIVER EDGE
Park open to the river
Productive and public programs
Total Cost: US$ 4.6 MM*

2.2. COASTAL EDGE
Seaside walkway
Recreational facilities
Elimination of plant odors
Total Cost: US$ 10.3 MM

2.3. DOWNTOWN
Consolidation of plazas
Pedestrian and commerical circuit
Reconstruction of iconic buildings
Total Cost: US$ 12.9 MM

RIVER PARK

TOURIST SQUARE

FIRE STATION

RIVER MARKET

SCHOOL ENRIQUE DONN

CULTURAL CENTER

*cost of mitigating park included in 1.3 Mitigation

PRES proposal

PRES proposal

Damage by earthquake and tsunami

PRES response

Interview with Alejandro Aravena

Interviewer: **Ken Tadashi Oshima**
Born in 1965. Associate Professor, University of Washington, Seattle/Architectural Historian

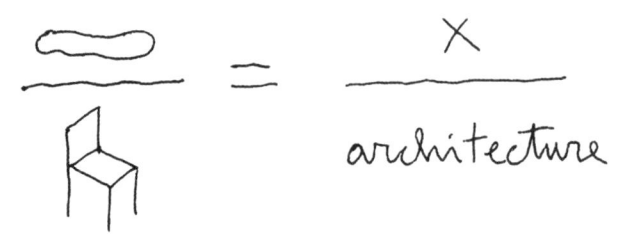

$$\frac{\text{cloth}}{\text{chair}} = \frac{x}{\text{architecture}}$$

———To help us understand your work and design process, could you begin by discussing the intriguing equation illustrated on the cover of your Electa monograph?

Well, this equation expresses an approach to design, which is about framing the question in the right way. Actually, we spend a lot of time designing the question and not just the solution. I could use a photograph of this book to describe our approach, which at first glance shows a Paraguayan Indian sitting on the floor. If one looks more carefully he is using a chair. I think that photograph is extremely relevant because when we normally think of the most typical design for a chair, we think of legs and a seat and a back (points to drawing of typical chair). In a way, these Indians from Paraguay framed the problem of how to design a chair in such a radical way that we would liken our practice to follow the same approach.

There are three things that could be said about this Indian and this particular design of a chair. The first one is that this man has no money, so the only thing he can afford is this modest piece of cloth as a chair. So design under scarcity of means is relevant. This is pretty much the case in the entire world. Half of the population of the world is under the line of poverty, so to learn how to design under scarcity is relevant. That's one thing.

The second thing is that even if this man had more money, a different design for a chair makes no sense because this man is a nomad. Only a foldable, easy to carry piece of cloth is the right design for him, and in a way what we can learn from that, is that design has to be precise.

アレハンドロ・アラヴェナ　インタヴュー

インタヴュアー：**ケン・タダシ・オオシマ**
1965年生まれ。ワシントン大学准教授・建築史家

———まずは仕事の進め方について伺いますが、エレクタ社から出たこのモノグラフの表紙になぜか方程式が描かれています、これはどういう意味でしょう。

この方程式はいわばデザインへのアプローチであり、ここで問いを正しく設定するわけです。私たちは解を出す前の問いの設定にもたっぷり時間をかけます。せっかくですからこのモノグラフに収められた写真を使って説明しましょう。パラグアイの先住民が地面に腰を下ろしているだけの写真です。ところがよく見ると、彼は椅子を使っている。もうそのものずばりです。ふつう椅子といえば、（典型的な椅子の図を指して）脚があって座面があって背もたれがあって、というふうに思い浮かべる。ところがこのパラグアイの先住民は、こんなふうにも椅子をデザインできるのだと、問いの枠組みを変えてくれた。それで私たちもこのアプローチに倣うことにしました。

この先住民とその独特な椅子のデザインから、三つのことがいえます。第一に、この男性には金がない。だから布きれを椅子として使うほかない。デザインに金はいらない、ということです。これについては、ほぼ万国共通でしょう。世界人口の半数が貧困線以下の生活水準にある以上、その貧しさとデザインを両立できるだけの術を身につけておいたほうがいい。以上が第一の点。

第二に、この男性は仮に金をもっていたとしても、別の椅子を欲しがらないだろう。それは彼が遊牧民だから。折りたためて、携帯しやすい布きれのほうが、彼にとっては使い勝手の良い椅子なのです。ここから得

Finally, it represents a kind of limit in that you cannot keep taking things out – you cannot keep reducing the answer because the noun "chair" would disappear and what would remain is only the verb "to sit." Somehow we as architects do work with that ultimate limit where we still find a noun. So in a way, we want to touch that limit just before only the verb "to sit" would remain. We want to arrive at that moment just before there is no noun anymore, which is the moment when a problem is irreducible.

So, in the equation, one could say that this piece of cloth (points at sketch of "chair-less" on cover of book) is to a chair as X is to architecture. And we're always trying to find the most relevant, the most precise, and the most irreducible value for X.

In a way, this equation, that was a proposal of how to approach a project, was brought then to the industrial version of this design, which was developed together with Vitra. Somehow here, we're not starting from the noun, "chair." The question is not, "How to design a chair?" The question is, "How do we sit?" So, we do start with verbs, with situations, because in the end that's what we work for, for life – studying, working, eating, and living. For that verb, we try to find the most relevant, precise and irreducible noun, which is Architecture. In this case, it was the design of a chair, a foldable chair, which is "chair-less." But in general, I would say that it is about the approach, so that for any type of building – be it housing or a city, be it institutional or corporate –, we spend time framing the question in the right way. Find the most irreducible, precise and relevant value starting from the situation, and the verb is what we try to do.

It is true that our practice has two different extremes that might be seen and perceived as if they're opposites. I will explain why they are not opposites. On the one hand, there are institutional buildings or buildings that are trying to be cutting edge or state of the art. In these cases, to do an irreducible project is a choice. We would like to see our process of design as a filter against arbitrariness, as a process where everything that is not strictly necessary has been taken out. Everything that is not the case is eliminated, and what you get is just the ultimate synthesis for the design. On the other end, we work in social housing, or in public projects. Particularly in the case of Chile, it is about dealing with scarcity. In those

られる教訓は、デザインに妥当性を欠いてはならない、ということです。

第三に、物事にはもうこれ以上は削れないという限界――解を徹底的に削ぎ落としてゆくと、とどのつまりは動詞の「座る」だけになり、名詞の「椅子」が消えてしまう臨界――がある。どうも我々建築家は、この名詞が残るすれすれのところで作業をやめがちです。むしろ私たちは、動詞の「座る」しか残らないぎりぎりの状態まで突き詰めてゆきたい。名詞が消える寸前まで追っていくと、これ以上の単純化が不可能な瞬間が訪れます。

この方程式では、布きれ（モノグラフ表紙の「チェアレス」のスケッチを指して）と椅子の関係は、Xと建築の関係に相応しています。私たちはこのXに値するもの、すなわち最も適切、妥当にして単純であるものをたえず探求していきます。

この方程式によってアプローチの仕方が決まると、つぎはデザインの製品化に取りかかります。これについてはヴィトラ社と共同で行いました。ともかくここでは名詞の「椅子」を出発点としなかった。問題は「椅子をどうデザインするか」ではなく「人はどう座るか」。動詞、つまり人がどういう状態にあるかを思い浮かべるのも、私たちの仕事がしょせん人間の生活――学んで働いて食べて暮らす――に根ざしているためです。この動詞「座る」に対して、なにがいちばん適切かつ妥当で単純な名詞かと考えると、それは＜建築＞なんです。この場合は椅子、折畳み椅子、それも「椅子いらず（チェアレス）」の椅子のデザインでした。ただしこのアプローチはどんなタイプの建物――集合住宅であれ都市であれ、公共施設、企業建築であれ――が相手でも変わらないので、いつだって問いの設定には時間をかけます。まずは状況や動詞を想定して、そこから極力単純かつ適切かつ妥当な値を出す、それが私たちの方針です。

たしかに、うちの仕事にはふたつの極があって、見方によっては両者は正反対にも映る。なぜまったくの正反対でないかは、いま説明します。一方の極には、公共施設や最先端・最新系の建物がある。こうした建物に対して単純化を図るも図らないも、設計者の自由です。私たちは、できることならデザインを通じて恣意性を取り除いていきたい。どうしても必要なもの以外、よけいなものは残らず排除する。そうして究極のも

cases, being irreducible is not a choice, but a must. From social housing we learn how to use scarcity as a tool to arrive to the core of things. While doing cutting edge architecture we train our muscles to use design's power of synthesis. Social Housing is not only an ethical question, it is a difficult problem; it requires professional quality more than professional charity. In the state of the art architecture we train our design skills to deal with complexity without reducing it. So it's a cross pollination and feeding from one practice to the other, and I would say that in a way expresses the strategic work that we try to put forward.

———So that clearly shows an elemental process that I can see relates to the firm name "Elemental," and you as an individual working within that framework. But what is that precise relationship between you as an individual, and your firm, Elemental, and that idea of the firm name expressing that design process?

I would say that when this firm Elemental initially started, we wanted to change the approach of design to social housing, which is always seen as something negative or what you have to do because you don't have enough means and enough resources. Somehow, an elementary project is something that you would like to do no matter how many resources you've got. So this capacity of filtering what is superfluous is a desirable thing, and we wanted to enter social housing not by complaining or dreaming what we cannot do, but by really appreciating the need of answering with what is strictly the case and going straight to the core, one shot and no chance for mistake nor for two hits – just one.

It started as an academic initiative at Harvard University back in the year 2000. What we wanted to do in the beginning was to meliorate the quality of social housing because not many architects were working there. We thought, if we eventually had a point – it was not guaranteed – but if we eventually had a point, if we succeed in making a contribution, well that might positively affect a huge amount of people. We're talking in the case of Chile, of 60 percent of what's been built, using some kind of subsidy. So if you're able to improve one millimeter it's going to be multiplied by hundreds of thousands of units per year. Not too many people were working in that field, so we thought it was strategic to spend time thinking about the question in this particular field. On the other hand we knew that in

のだけをデザインに取り込む。他方の極にある仕事が、ソーシャル・ハウジングや公共プロジェクトです。ことにここチリでは、なにをするにも事欠きます。この場合、好きで単純化を図るのではなく、そうせざるをえない。ソーシャル・ハウジングから学んだことは、金がないほうが物事の核心に迫れるということです。かたや最先端建築を手がけることで、種々の要素を統合するデザイン力が鍛えられます。ソーシャル・ハウジングは単に倫理的な問題ではなく、難しい問題だけに、ここでは職業的な善意以上に才能が問われます。だから最先端建築では、単純化を図らずに複雑なものは複雑なまま扱うことで、その方面のデザイン力を鍛える。異種交配というか、一方の仕事で得た経験を他方の仕事にフィードバックする。これが私たちのめざす戦略的な機能です。

────なるほど、そうした基本プロセスを、事務所「エレメンタル」とその一員であられるご自身も踏襲している。ところで事務所では具体的にどのような立場におられるのですか。事務所名はこのデザイン・プロセスにちなんでつけられたのでしょうか。

　そもそもエレメンタルを立ち上げたのは、ソーシャル・ハウジングの設計を別の角度からアプローチしようと思ったからなんです。やれ資金不足だのやれ資源不足だのといって不承不承それを引き受けるのではなく。私たちは、資金の多寡にかかわらず、とりあえずはなにか基本的なプロジェクトに取り組んでみたかった。となると、さっそく取捨選択の能力が求められる。それからソーシャル・ハウジングに携わる以上、あれがないこれがないと不平不満を言い立てるのではなく、とにかく状況に即して答えを出していこう、一発で問題の核心に迫ろう、と肝に銘じた。二度目はないのだから、失敗は許されない。一度限りです。

　エレメンタルは、ハーバード大学のアカデミック・イニシアティヴという位置づけで2000年に始動しました。そして手始めにソーシャル・ハウジングの質の向上に取り組むことにしました。建築家があまり目を向けない分野ですから。その時に思ったのは、仮にこの試みに手応えがあったら──その保証はなかった──、仮に自分たちがそこにいくらかでも与することができれば、その効果はとてつもなく大勢におよぶであろう、と。たとえばチリではこれまで総棟数の6割がなんらかの補助金を受けて建てられています。ということは仮に1mmでも改善できれば、年間

order to have an impact, we had to follow every single rule that the market was following, accepting all the policies. So the will of reality, and deep pragmatism were at the base of this initiative. Once you think that your contributions are going to come in a built form, not on paper, not in an exhibition, not on screens, but by building with a certain scale, if you accept market conditions, it's not about one unit, it's at least about a hundred units. Once you go for that, you have to build a structure to be able to operate within a reality that in a way required from us, not just time in the design of the project, but also in how we organize ourselves in order to be able to act within reality.

So, what started as an academic initiative, by 2005 became a company, a for-profit company with social interests. The for-profit condition is crucial in order to be sustainable. You can't depend on charity. Actually, the question of social housing is so difficult that if there's something that is needed, it's professional **quality**, not professional **charity**. Quality has to be paid. What we've identified as one of the missing links in the entire chain of delivering quality, was the availability of skilled professional work in every single step – from design to building to social working and politics in that chain. If you want it to be of excellence, you have to pay for that. So that's why at the very beginning, we identified that for-profit was key to make it sustainable and to be able to capture professional quality.

We just wanted to use that quality in projects that have a public impact and a social relevance. With time, Elemental became a company of such a scale that I ended up merging my own professional practice as an architect with Elemental, which is a company that provides services of architecture. I pay Elemental a fee for developing my projects, as any other client would do to hire Elemental services. And being a company with shares and partners and a board, that fee has to be very transparent. It was a natural joint venture between my own practice and Elemental. Elemental actually is a company whose partners are the Chilean oil company, COPEC, the Catholic University and the professionals that came up with this idea ten years ago. So at this moment in time, not just the design for social housing requires some level of innovation, but also the way and the strategy of how to work, as the organization and management of our work as well.

———What were some of the political and economic conditions that

その何十万倍もの規模で改善が見込めます。この分野は手薄になっていただけに、これは時間をかけて検討するに値するテーマだと踏んだわけです。反面、これを波及させるには、市場の法則に忠実に従い、なおかつ政策にも同調しないといけない。結局このイニシアティヴを支えたのは、冷徹な現実とプラグマティズムです。そしていよいよ自分の働きが、一定の規模をもった建物として実現することになる。つまり紙の上でも展覧会でも映像でもなく、それも1戸どころか少なくとも100戸あまりの集合住宅として実現させるには、市場条件を満たすことです。いったん覚悟を決めたら、現実と闘いながら建てていかなければならない。一定の時間内に設計するのはもちろんのこと、どんな状況にも対処できるよう体制を整えておく必要もある。

このアカデミック・イニシアティヴが、2005年には法人化され、営利事業として社会利益を追求することになった。あえて営利事業にしたのは、慈善事業では長続きしないからです。だいいちソーシャル・ハウジングは決して生やさしい問題ではないので、職業的な善意ではどうにもならない。必要なのは、プロの仕事なんです。そのプロの仕事にはきちんと対価が支払われないといけない。ソーシャル・ハウジングの価値連鎖図にことごとく欠けていたのは、プロの仕事です。設計にせよ施工にせよ、社会福祉、政治にせよ、どこにもプロが介入していない。タダで良い仕事はできません。それで私たちは最初から、長続きさせるには営利事業にしてプロの仕事をするしかない、と悟ったのです。

ただしこのプロのクオリティにこだわるのは、公共性・社会性の高いプロジェクトに限りました。しだいにエレメンタルは大所帯になり、各種の建築サーヴィスを提供するまでになり、ついに私自身も建築家としてここに合流するに至った。この私も自分のプロジェクトをエレメンタルに担当してもらう際には、正規の料金を支払います。エレメンタルは共同経営者と取締役会を擁する株式会社である以上、収支は透明でないといけません。私の事務所とエレメンタルが合弁したのはしぜんの成り行きでした。それこそエレメンタルの共同経営者には、チリの石油会社COPECとチリ・カトリック大学、さらに10年前にこの事業を発案した専門家らが名を連ねています。この時代、一定の革新性が求められるのは、なにもソーシャル・ハウジングのデザインに限らず、組織体制や経営戦略だってそうです。

you drew from, allowing this to happen? Was that a big change from previous decades?

Well, I think I need to speak a little bit of the context of Chile in order to understand what our contribution was, and also about the conditions we ourselves thought this aim of doing better use of public resources was. I said, "we want to build, not just to discuss"; that's why we call Elemental a "do-tank", and one of the conditions was to accept the policy as it was. Another condition was that we were not going to start from ourselves. It's not asking yourself, "Well, what would be good social housing?" We went out to the people that have the problem and asked them if we could be of any help or if there was a niche where we could apply our knowledge, or to be honest, our ignorance. I mean, when we started, I didn't have a clue what a subsidy was. So it's not that I knew about that, but exactly the opposite. I just wanted to overcome a kind of self-embarrassment because I felt really bad being an architect, not knowing how to say something smart about social housing, which was the rule, not the exception in Chile.

What is mainly done in Chile is housing units with extremely limited resources. So starting from outside, from those who had the problem, meant that we met the Minister of Housing back in 2001, and he said that there was a new policy about to start, for which the market was not getting any solution. So there was the need for new knowledge. There was a new question but not enough knowledge, so innovation was a natural consequence and we thought that the place where such a contribution to knowledge should happen is in a University. That's why we started. The particular condition of the housing policy that we accepted, was a subsidy of 7,500 dollars with which we had to buy the land, provide infrastructure, and build the housing units. That, in the best of the cases, meant about 30 square meters. The policy asked in those 30 square meters to build a bathroom, a kitchen, a living room, a dining room and one bedroom. We thought that if you frame the problem in that way, then we're never going to produce any good. It all started when I was invited to teach at Harvard GSD and in Cambridge I met who ended being my partner Andres Iacobelli, who is a transport engineer whom was doing his Master's in Public Policy at the Kennedy School of Government. We came with this idea of reframing the problem of social housing, accepting all those conditions of the policies and the market. I would say that the biggest shifts

――――それを後押しするような政治経済情勢があったということですか。10年以上前と比べてそんなに様変わりしたのでしょうか。

ここでチリの国内事情について少しお話しておきましょう。でないと、私たちの果たした役割も、私たちが公共材の活用を考えるに至った経緯も見えてこないでしょうから。私はこう言ったんです、「ただ口で議論するよりも、実際に建てようじゃないか」。エレメンタルを「ドゥ・タンク［行動集団］」と呼ぶ所以です。その条件のひとつが、現行の政策をそのまま受け入れること。もうひとつは、こちらから発案しないこと。「いったいソーシャル・ハウジングとはどうあるべきか」を自問しないということです。こちらから悩みを抱える人びとのもとへ出向いて行って、なにか手助けできることはないかと訊いて回った。あるいは自分たちの知識を生かせるようなすき間市場(ニッチ)がないだろうか、といえば聞こえはいいけれど、本心はこれまで自分たちの見過ごしてきたものを誰かに教えてもらおう、ということです。当初は補助金のなんたるかも、てんでわかっていなかった。自分の得意分野どころか、不得意分野だった。建築家のくせに、ソーシャル・ハウジングについて気の利いたことのひとつも言えず、そんな己の不明を恥じていました。チリではソーシャル・ハウジングは珍しいものでも何でもありませんでしたから。

チリではソーシャル・ハウジング、それもごく低廉なもののほうが一般的です。さて、私たちがこののけ者にされた悩める人びとの力になろうと住宅担当大臣に面会を求めたのが2001年。聞くと、ちょうどこれから政策が変わるという。でも市場はまだそれには対応していない。つまり、誰かが知恵を出すのを皆が待っている。新しい問題が浮上したけれども、それに応えるだけの知恵がなかったので、どこかで新機軸を打ち出さなければならない。その新機軸を考案するなら大学しかありません。それが事の発端です。当時の住宅政策の規定によると、補助金7,500ドルで土地の購入からインフラ整備、住宅建設に至るまでをすべてまかなわなければならない。それだとせいぜい1戸あたりの面積が30m^{2}にしかならない。そこに浴室も台所も、居間、食堂、寝室もぜんぶ収めろという。これを、どう収めるかの問題ととらえてしまうと、ろくなものはできません。そんなときに、私はハーバードGSD（デザイン大学院）の客員教授に喚ばれ、このケンブリッジで将来のパートナーとなる輸送工学の専門家アンドレス・ヤコベッリに出会ったのです。当時彼はケネ

in the frame of the question were two:

First, what the market does with such a scarce amount of money is to pick a middle-income standard house and reduce it, squeezing it up to 30 square meters because you don't have enough money. It then places it where land costs nothing, in the periphery of cities. That's pretty much the case in Latin America. You have huge amounts of poverty belts far away from opportunities. Where units stand at a cost of 7,000 dollars per unit. So you save in land, and you save in size. If you want to make them better, the intuitive solution tends to be, let's make them bigger. To our understanding, that would have been to answer right, the wrong question. So the first shift was, if there's not enough money, instead of considering 30 or 40 square meters as a small house, why don't we think of 30 or 40 square meters as half of a good house. When you frame the problem of having a limited amount of resources as doing half of a good house instead of a small house, the key question is, "which half do we do?" We thought that with public money, we had to focus on everything that families could not do on their own, and do it in a good way. Allowing families' capacity of building their own environment, which is the case in Latin America to achieve a middle-income standard, once they apply their own capacity of self building. So half of a good house instead of a small one. And that's how we came with the idea to do the half that families cannot do on their own. So that was the first change in the framing of the question.

Second, all of us when buying a house, expect it to grow its value over time. In social housing that was not the case. It looked more like buying cars than houses. I mean, because of where they were, far away from opportunities, at the outskirt of cities, a process of deterioration, of decreasing its value, is what happened. In the case of Chile, we're talking about a policy, which gives you a subsidy, and once you receive the subsidy to purchase a house, you become the owner of the house. So what you're doing is to trespass public money to a family asset. If you're a poor family, you would like that that transfer of money from public to private gain value over time, so that it works as an investment and not as a social expense. So we worked in identifying a set of design conditions that can make that public money gain value over time and perform as an investment and not as a social expense. In that sense, we had to redefine the notion of what does it mean quality. So instead of a bigger house, quality for us was redefined as a unit capable of gaining value

ディ行政大学院の博士課程で社会政策を専攻していました。その彼と一緒に、政策や市場の条件にはとことん従ってみてはどうかというふうに、ソーシャル・ハウジングの問題を一から設定し直してみたのです。すると、問題の枠組みを大きく変える契機がふたつありました。

ひとつには、市場が資金不足にどう対処するかです。なにしろ建設費が足りないので、中間所得層向けの標準住宅を土台に、その面積をどんどん切り詰めて［1戸あたり］30m^2 にまで絞り、それを郊外のタダも同然の土地に建てるのが市場のやり方です。ラテンアメリカでは珍しくないことです。運に見離された貧困層が圧倒的多数を占めている。1戸あたりの建設費はわずか7,000ドル。だから土地代も面積も切り詰める。この改善策として直観的にひらめいたのが、面積を広げることでした。不合理な問いに対して、合理的な解をもって応ずるわけです。発想の転換その1は、金がなければ1戸あたりを30〜40m^2 とする代わりに、その30〜40m^2 を広い家の半戸分ととらえてみるというもの。限られた予算しかないのなら、なにも狭い住宅にこだわらずとも、広い住居の半分というふうに発想を転換させればいい。いちばんの問題は、「どちらの半分をこちらで用意するか」。公金を使うなら、住人が自力でできないことはすべてこちらで引き受け、引き受けるからには最善を尽くすことにしました。住環境を整えることに関しては住人自身の手に委ねる。ラテンアメリカの貧困層はセルフ・ビルドに慣れていて、その気になれば彼らは中間所得層並みの住環境を手に入れます。そういうことも念頭に置いて、住人の手に余るほうの半戸をこちらで用意することにしました。以上が最初の契機です。

第二の契機は、住宅の購入にあたってその資産価値の上昇を願わない人はいない、という事実。けれどもソーシャル・ハウジングに対しては誰もそんな期待をしない。住宅というより自動車を購入する感覚に近い。不遇の人々の暮らすその郊外の家々は、劣化が進み、資産価値は目減りする一方です。ところでチリでは、政府が補助金を出してくれる。その補助金を使って住宅を購入すれば、家主になれる。公金を横領して蓄財しているようなものです。もしも自分が貧しかったら、もらった公金を元手に儲けたいと思うものです。となると、公金が社会支出ではなく投資に回ることになる。では、どんなデザインなら、このように公金が社会支出にではなく、ゆくゆくは資産価値の上昇に結びつくか。それには

over time.

These two shifts, half of a good house instead of a small one, and a unit able to gain value over time, had to be achieved through design. We're not working in this as policy makers or economists. Of course, the problem is so complex that you have to talk the language of economy, of financing, of policy, of even the social conditions. Actually the social aspect is crucial. Half of our projects are not built by ourselves, I mean, they're going to be built by families. So you better engage with the families, talk to them, split tasks – who's going to do what. In that complexity, I guess architecture has a big say because it can synthesize complexity without reducing it, organize information so that we can move towards a proposal and not just a diagnosis. But we are here as designers.

> ———So in buying these houses rather than renting the houses, the families really feel the investment in their whole future. They really have this kind of social dimension of building their lives rather than just…

Yes. This is pretty much the case in Latin America in general, that housing policies are property oriented; beneficiaries of subsidies become owners of the units. If you design them in the right way, eventually you can allow the housing units become an asset able to have a parallel life as capital and therefore work as a family investment. Unfortunately, merely enlarging the house does not necessarily guarantee a value gain. Evidence shows just the contrary. If design is not strategic, the capacity of families of adding on their own to a design that was not conceived as an incremental design actually deteriorates the neighborhood. So there are some specific design conditions where families' capacity of self-building can mean adding value instead of deteriorating neighborhoods. In Latin America what we have in general are these property oriented policies and a culture of self-construction that was developed spontaneously as a response to subsidies that can not pay for a big enough house. We accepted those policies and we just tried to use the force of the self-construction culture in a positive sense.

> ———This design thinking is so basic and commonsensical in many ways and really inspirational to both architects and the population at large. Was this thinking very different from what you were taught in

クオリティの概念を改めないといけない。つまりクオリティとは、広い家ではなく、資産価値の上がるような住戸を指すのです。

以上ふたつの発想の転換から生まれた、狭い住戸ではなく広い住居の半分でありながら、なおかつ資産価値の上がる住戸は、デザインしだいで実現可能です。私たちの立場は、政策立案者でも経済学者でもありません。たしかに難しい問題ではあるので、こちらも経済用語だとか、金融用語、政治用語、社会用語を使う場面も生じてきます。それこそ社会的側面は絶対に無視できない。プロジェクトの半分は、私たちではなく住人自らが建設するので、彼らともうまくつきあいつつ、彼我の間で役割分担もしなくてはならない。そうした難しい状況下でものをいうのが、やはり建築です。建築は複雑なものを複雑なまま取り込み、情報を整理してくれる。おかげで分析から一気に提案にこぎつけられる。だいいち私たちの立場はデザイナーですから。

─── 賃貸ではなく分譲住宅なら、住人も将来への投資と思うことができますね。それに住人に人生設計をさせるという社会的側面も……

ええ、というのもラテンアメリカ諸国は総じて持ち家政策に傾いていますから。補助金受給者を家主にするというふうに。デザイン次第では、住戸も資本に匹敵するだけの財産になり得るので、庶民にとっては投資の対象になる。あいにく家を広くしたからといって、必ずしも資産価値が上がるわけではありません。事実はその逆です。そこまで見込んでデザインされていないと、住人が手を加えたせいでかえって景観を損ねかねない。そうならずに住人のセルフ・ビルド程度でそれなりの付加価値がつくように、デザインでお膳立てしておく必要があります。ラテンアメリカの国には総じて、こうした持ち家政策と、補助金では十分な広さの家が買えないことから生じた自力建設の文化があります。私たちはこの住宅政策を受け入れ、あとはこの自力建設の文化に乗じただけです。

─── それがデザインの基本であり常識というものでしょうね。世の建築家のみならず一般の人たちにも聞かせたいお話でした。けれど大学では、およそそのようにはデザインを教わらなかったでしょう？ そもそも建築に対する興味の抱き方からして、他人とは異なっていたのでしょうね。

Architecture school as to the nature of design? In looking back at your own background, how might this relate to you becoming interested in architecture?

Now that you mention it, I think yes. Social housing is particularly raw to see. Actually, it applies to architecture in general, but in social housing again, it's not a choice. You start from outside architecture. I mean you start from policy, from market, from families, users, owners … So in general, I would say, we are forced to use a basic language. I would add that we are forced to use a common language – common in the sense of a shared language and in the sense of an ordinary language. You better explain your ideas in a very simple way. Otherwise, economists, policy makers, families are not going to get what you're talking about. And you need them as partners because it's a very complex problem. So you start from outside architecture, and then go through architecture to give an answer. I mean you use the tools of architecture, which are very powerful because of design's power of synthesis.

Once you're finished, the work's success is verified outside architecture again. Value gain for example. That's something that's a very objective thing that not only architects can appreciate. Actually it's a very, again, common language. Quality of a neighborhood, satisfaction with where you're living – are you happy in your house or not? All this is very basic, common language. I would say that we as architects are not trained in starting from outside architecture, going through architecture, and then going back at the end of the process to the society at large as an approach. I think we're trained to start from within architecture, using architectural language that only other architects understand. We are trained to work so that other architects admire us, and then it's very fine if you're published in architectural magazines and that might lead to a kind of endogamic relationship. That notion of creativity as a practice that creates its own world and set of rules is very dangerous because the price you can pay is irrelevance. Nobody cares about what architects do, only other architects.

To put it in a slightly different way, only if you're working with not enough knowledge or in an unfriendly or uncomfortable field, you are forced to be creative. Social housing was particularly challenging in that sense, because it is the ultimate

そう、たぶんね。だいたいソーシャル・ハウジングはまだまだ未熟な分野です。まあ建築にしても未熟な分野ですが、そのなかでもソーシャル・ハウジングはひどく後れをとっている。まずは建築以外のことから手を着けることになる。政策や市場を調査し、住人や家主のもとへ出向き……。だから平易な言葉で話さざるをえない。共通言語──誰にでも通じるふつうの言葉──を使わざるをえない。こちらの考えを極力かみ砕いて説明する。でないと経済学者にも政策立案者にも住人にも話は通じません。この人たちの協力なしには、早晩行き詰まってしまいますから。こうして外堀を埋めてからやっと、肝心の建築に取りかかることができる。ここで建築という強力なツールを登場させて、デザインによって複数の事象を統合していきます。

さて仕事が完了しても、その成否はまたしても建築の外部からしか判断できません。たとえば価値の増加。これこそが究極の目標であり、建築家のみならず誰もがそれを望んでいる。しかもこれは共通言語でもある。たとえば、近隣のクオリティ、満足のゆく住まい──住まい手は幸せかどうか。いずれも平易な共通言語です。ところが我々建築家は、この外堀を埋めてから建築に取りかかり、最後にいま一度社会に目を向けるというアプローチには慣れていません。むしろ建築を起点に物事を考え、同業者にしか通じない専門用語を使うよう訓練されている。同業者の賞賛を浴びたい、あわよくば建築雑誌に掲載されたい、というのが本心です。これでは馴れ合いになってしまう。独創性を追求するあまりに、独自の世界やルールをつくってしまうのは非常に危険です。はたしてそれで報われるだろうか。建築家の仕事なんて同業者以外だれも見向きもしてくれません。

少し見方を変えると、知識がないほうが、あるいは不慣れな分野のほうがかえって、人は独創的にならざるをえないんです。その点、ソーシャル・ハウジングはじつにやりがいがありました。己の独創性を徹底的に試されますから。いたって平易な言葉を使ってこちらの難解な理を通さなければならないわけですから。その理が通ってはじめて己の務めを果たしたことになる。逆に難しい言葉で語る人は、己の非力をはぐらかしているにすぎません。ちなみに私のパートナーはエンジニアであり、建築の「け」の字も知らない──至極まっとうな──人間ですが、その彼

test for verifying if you are being creative: you have to talk in an extremely simple way and still able to communicate that you have a point that was not obvious. Only then you might think you have a contribution. If you have to talk in a very complicated way, then you're just disguising the fact that you're not making any contribution. Actually, my partner, being an engineer and not having a clue what architecture is – which is very healthy – says that architects work in the following way: we are confronted with reality that is complex, we try to reduce that complexity and then give a complicated answer to make as if we are dealing with complexity. Engineers do just the opposite: they start from the complexity of reality, keep that complexity intact, and because of it, try to give the most simple answer for that. I would say that only if you are able to bring new light to a problem that was unable to keep on moving forward, by giving the most simple possible answer, only then you might have a point. If you need a very complicated language to explain what you are doing that's just a kind of smoke cloud, to disguise the fact that you're not being creative enough.

———In your efforts to transform the architectural profession by beginning with education, how did you frame the studio problem at the Harvard Graduate School of Design?

I would say that it was mainly about establishing the constraints and the restrictions. Normally it's thought that universities and academia lacks reality or it has a certain distance with reality. That is true, and it is necessary. Because it is not about transforming universities into a professional office. I mean, you need distance with reality to have the big picture and actually reframe problems, which is exactly what we did with Elemental: looking at the problem at large and reframing the question. So it is not about going into reality knowing exactly the cost per square meter – you have to have a notion, but that is not the point. The biggest bridge and link with reality is to identify the constraints and the restrictions, which are normally left out, because it is believed that only that way creativity will happen. It's just the contrary. Only if you have constraints and restrictions, you have to be creative. Only if there are rules you do have freedom. So I think, and that was very clear in my partner's approach as an engineer, we have to start from constraints. Make an explicit declaration of every single constraint. You might not have a clue what the answer is, but at least have a notion of the equation that

にいわせれば、建築家は複雑な現実に直面すると、それをいったん簡略にしておいて、そのくせ複雑な問題を扱っているとばかりにわざわざ込み入った解を出してくる。エンジニアはその逆です。彼らは複雑な現実を複雑なまま扱いながら、なるたけ単純明快な解を引き出してくる。たとえ難題に行き詰まっても、解を極力単純化するようにすれば、問題の糸口は必ず見えてくるもので、そうしたらしめたもの。逆に難解な専門用語を用いないと説明できないようでは、相手を煙に巻くだけ、はったりにすぎません。

——— 建築家という職業を、まずは教育を通じて変えていくためにも、たとえばハーバードGSDのスタジオではどんな課題を出しましたか。

もっぱら制約と規制を課すことですかね。大学や学究的な世界はとかくリアリティが欠如しているだの、浮世離れしているだのと言われがちです。たしかにそのとおりですが、しかしそれも必要なんです。大学を事務所にして商売をするわけではありませんから。むしろ現実とは一定の距離をとったほうが、大局的な見方ができるし、問いを設定し直すこともできる。それこそエレメンタルが問題を俯瞰し、問いを設定し直したように。平米単価がいくらいくら、といった実務には立ち入らない——そうした概念は必要だけれども、それが狙いではない。現実を最も意識させられるのは、制約と規制の存在です。このふたつはふつう、独創性を阻むからという理由で無いものとして扱われます。でも本当はその逆で、制約や規制があったほうが、人は独創性を発揮させるというもの。ルールがあって、はじめて自由も生まれる。そのことを痛感したのも、例のエンジニアであるパートナーが必ず制約から手を着けるんです。彼は制約を片っ端から書き出していく。その時点では、どんな解に行き着くのかまるで見当もつかないけれど、少なくとも方程式を立てることはできる。といっても、建築は科学ではありません。方程式とはいえ、解がひとつとは限らない。ではなぜ方程式を立てるかというと、問題の所在をはっきりさせるため、また仕事の成否を事後的に検証するためです。それで私は制約にこだわるんです。ハーバードで開いたワークショップは、その名も「3,200ドル」。理念はどうでもいい——大事なのは制約と規制です。もちろん建築ツールやデザイン・スキルも動員する。しかしその前に「この金額をなにに使うか」を決めることが、現実とつきあううえでは最も手堅い方法です。私たちは制約を外すことは絶対にしませ

you're dealing with is. That doesn't mean that architecture is a science. By talking of an equation, it's not that you have one single answer. The notion of an equation is because you can be very clear about what you're trying to solve, and verify afterwards if you're being successful or not. So I would say that it was about constraints. The title of a workshop at Harvard was "3,200 dollars." That was the title of the studio. I am not interested in ideas – I'm interested in the constraints and the restrictions. Of course you need all the architectural tools and design skills. But it is by framing the problem as "what are we going to do with that amount of money," what establishes the most strongest and most healthy link with reality. We never left any constraint out. Actually, we went for them, to charge the question.

———— What did some of the enlightening results that the students come up?

Well I have to say that this didn't just happen at first. I mean, at the beginning I myself was completely wrong. And I remember after the first half of the studio of social housing, I realized that I was framing the problem in the wrong direction. And just after a review, Hashim Sarkis, a Aga Khan professor at the GSD, came and said, "How much money did you say you have?" 7,500 dollars. "And how many families are you dealing with?" 100 families. "What's the best 750,000 dollar building that you can do?" It was a punch in the face. What we were doing was trying to make the best possible 7,500 dollar units, and then multiply it a hundred times.

In Sarkis' question was the shift that led to the right design. The shift from the unit to the entire big picture of the project was such a major one, that it was obvious that I was framing the question in the wrong way. I apologized with the students and said, "sorry, what we have done so far, it's useless. Throw it away to the trash. Mistakes are never a complete waist of time, but we will have to start all over from scratch." Of course then you have brilliant students that within the right questions are able to produce many alternatives, many tests. I can't remember a specific example, or it would be hard to explain it with words. I could show you an image, and it's kind of self-explanatory. Almost every single student that worked within the right set of rules was able to give an enlightening answer. But

ん。それどころか制約に真っ向から挑みました。

——学生の案に、はっとさせられるようなものはありましたか。

あいにく初めのうちはさっぱり成果が上がりませんでした。これについては私自身に非があります。スタジオ前期にソーシャル・ハウジングを取り上げたんですが、終わってみて初めて自分の問題設定がまずかったと反省した次第です。その講評会の直後にGSDアガ・カーン教授のハシム・サルキスが「予算はいくらなの？」と訊いてきた。7,500ドル。「何世帯で？」100世帯。「総工費75万ドルの建物としたら、なにができる？」顔面に一発食らいましたよ。私たちは1戸あたりの予算7,500ドル内でどれだけのことができるか、それを100倍にしたらどうなるか、というふうにしか考えていなかった。

サルキス教授の問いが正しい道に導いてくれたおかげで、個別の住戸からプロジェクトの全体像へと頭を切り替えることができました。明らかに自分の問題設定が間違っていたので、学生に詫びました、「悪いけど、これはボツ、ゴミ箱行きだ。でも間違えたからといってまるまる時間を無駄にしたとは思わないで、気を取り直してまた一から始めよう」。優秀な学生もいますから、問いさえ適確に設定すれば良い反応が返ってきます。具体例はいまちょっと思い浮かばないというか、言葉では説明しにくいので、図をご覧いただければ一目瞭然です。ルールさえきちんと決めれば、学生はほぼひとり残らず与件に従って、鋭い解答を出してくる。最初のつまずきは私のせいです。ただ先述したように私の強みは、知識があることではなく、ないことなんです。むしろ無知な人間のほうが、周りが行き詰まっているときにもとぼけた質問をして、それで突破口が開かれることもままあります。私もこのことをきっかけに、開き直りました。そのうちに「もしも……だったら？」と平気で訊けるようにもなった。思い込みは禁物ですね。

——GSDのアカデミックな世界に一時引きこもったあとでは、また違った目で母国チリをご覧になったのではありませんか。外国帰りの目には、チリの建築が新鮮に映ったとか。ハウジング・イニシアティヴを通じて新たな問題意識が芽生えたとか。

the problem at the beginning was myself. As I said, my biggest asset in the beginning was not my knowledge, but my ignorance. Eventually, not always, eventually if you're ignorant, particularly in working in very charged questions, you're able to ask those stupid questions that allow you to move forward. In this case, I learned how to do stupid questions afterwards. So over time, I was very rigorous with my own ignorance, trying to keep that capacity of asking things like, "what if?" and not take anything for granted.

————Did having this academic distance teaching at the GSD give you new insights in coming back to Chile? In other words, did you see the practice of architecture here in Chile with fresh eyes? Building on the whole housing initiative, did new, broader questions arise?

I would say that the fact of being invited to teach at Harvard was already a learning process. I mean, in that context you ask yourself, "What can I say here that is useful? Do I know about something that others don't, so that I can be a voice that contributes to the discussion instead of just repeating to prove that I'm able to talk the language of the others as well?" I thought that one of the few things where I might have a say was dealing with scarcity, coming from a country like Chile.

Again, with a little bit of context, Chile is a country of 15 million people, so one tenth of Japan. We're living in a piece of land that is twice as big as Japan, and the average income is about 10,000 dollars, which grew radically in the last ten years. We're now on the threshold from going from underdeveloped to become eventually in a decade or two decades, in a developed country, which for a Latin American country, it's a big success. But still we are a country that in general terms is a poor country. Or a country where scarcity is something that, even if you're not aware of it, is the DNA of what you're doing every day. So my thought was that by going to Harvard, dealing with scarcity was a kind of advantage that I could have. It was not guaranteed, but it was a potential.

So scarcity at the time for me was important, not because it was something to deal with the humanitarian issues or ethical questions or social housing. I don't think I'm a particularly good person – I'm just an average person. But at the beginning I thought that scarcity is a filter against arbitrariness. And I had a problem in gen-

もとよりハーバードへ赴任したこと自体が、私には良い勉強になりました。あそこでは日々自問していましたよ、「なにか気の利いたことを言わないと。どうにか耳新しいことを言って議論の輪に加わらないと、ただの英語が話せる外国人になってしまう」。そしてチリ出身の自分になにか言うべきことがあるとすれば、たぶん貧困に関することだろう、と思い至りました。

ここで再びチリに関して若干補足をすると、チリの人口は 1,500 万人、つまり日本の人口の十分の一です。国土は日本の倍の広さで、国民の平均所得はここ 10 年で激増したので 1 万ドル前後。チリは今後 10 年、20 年以内に発展途上国から先進国の仲間入りをするはずで、そうなるとラテンアメリカの中では大出世です。それでも世界的にみればまだまだ貧しい方です。あるいは貧しさが、我々の DNA には刷り込まれているのかもしれない。ハーバードで貧困問題を扱えるのも、そんなチリ人であればこそ。成功する保証はないけれど、見込みはありました。

こうして貧困が当時の私のテーマになりました。とはいえそれは決して人道的・倫理的な観点からでも、ソーシャル・ハウジングに引き寄せるためでもなかった。私は自分を善人だとは思っていない――ごく平均的な人間です。ともかくこのころの私にとって、貧困とは恣意性を濾過するためのフィルターだったのです。それに私には、いわゆる建築とうまくつきあう自信がなかった。なにしろ建築家個人の創作テーマといった話にはついていけなかったし、だいいち興味も持てなかったので。むしろ建築によってどれだけ問いの価値を高められるか、またなぜそうなるかをきちんと説明しないといけないと思った。予算難なら、自分がそうすることの理由も根拠も逐一述べなければなりません。そのほうが健全ですよね。

ところで、2000 年にハーバードで最初に受け持ったスタジオ名が「otherwise［さもなければ］」の名詞形、「Otherwise-ness［そうでないこと］」でした。建築というものは常に、こうもできるし、ああもできるということを指摘するためです。はたしてあれよりこれがいい、と言い切ることができるのか。エンジニアなら、このほうがいいと言い切ることもできる。でも我々には両者の違いしか言えない。どちらがいいとは断言できません。でも資金や資源が乏しいほど、断言しやすくなってくる。な

eral with architecture, with the capacity of answering questions that come from the creative personal agenda of the architect, which is always not interesting. I was trying to identify the capacity of architecture to add value to a given problem and explain that very clearly. If you're dealing with scarcity of means, you always have to give a lot of reasons why you're doing what you're doing. And that was healthy in principle.

Actually the title of the first studio I taught at Harvard back in 2000 was "Otherwise-ness." "Otherwise-ness," a noun coming from "otherwise", was an attempt to reveal that in architecture you can always do things this way, or *otherwise*. Is one better than the other way? Hard to say. An engineer can say this is better than the otherwise. We just say it's different. We never say it's better. When dealing with scarcity, that eventually is a possibility; you have to prove that what you're doing is better than doing it otherwise. So the first studio I taught was on emergency housing: there's no time and there's no money for answering *otherwise*. To answer with what is the case, period. From emergency housing to social housing there was just a small step. And all the amount of information that we needed to swallow was what explained that small step that for us was a huge one.

So that was our approach to design; we didn't say, "Poor us, that come from a third world country far away." It was a fact, a filter against arbitrariness. I don't judge that. It's a fact. Simultaneously it was a pragmatic approach that tries to identify things that you can do, that at other places can't be done naturally. When we did the Siamese Towers, the plate and the platform was very rough and primitive. I was very aware and conscious that our luxury in Chile is that I can afford to be raw and primitive and tough. In the U.S. I would be sued if somebody stumbles in that type of platform, but here I can be that direct, and that is our luxury. And eventually by going out you realize all these good things without judging them. You just accept them as facts.

——— I believe that project would be very expensive to construct in Japan with its labor intensive construction. On the other hand, the lines might be more perfectly aligned.

Alejandro: In Chile to achieve perfection it is extremely expensive, and to break

ぜその方法がほかより良いかを証明しないといけませんから。スタジオでは緊急避難所を最初の課題に取り上げました。避難所なので、別の選択肢を考えるだけの経済的余裕も時間もありません。当然その答は、しかじかの状況なので、こうなった、以上。避難所からソーシャル・ハウジングへの移行は無理がないように思えました。ところが、ソーシャル・ハウジングに関する情報量は桁違いでした。

私たちはこのようにデザインにアプローチしていきました。決して「第三世界からはるばるやってきて、このざまだ」というふうに卑屈にはなりませんでした。それは事実であって、思い込みはいけない。良い悪いではなく、単に事実は事実。と同時に、なにがここでできて、よそではできないかを知ることで、割り切ることもできます。「シャム・タワー」を手がけたときも、その基礎部分とデッキがやけに無骨でプリミティヴな仕上がりになりました。でも無骨だろうとプリミティヴだろうと粗野だろうと平気でいられるのが、チリという国の豊かさだと痛感したのです。仮にこれが米国なら、誰かがデッキに躓いただけで訴えられますが、この国では遠慮はいらない。これは贅沢なことです。だから外国へ行くと、その是非はともかく自国の良さに気づく。そういう国なんだと。

───仮にこれが日本なら手をかけるぶん建設費も高くつくでしょうね。施工精度もぐっと上がるでしょうけれど。

チリでは完成度を上げようとすると、とても高くつきます。あえて慣例に逆らうのは、逃げを打つようなものです。どう転ぶかわからなくても平気なら、かまいません。でもこの国にはこの国なりの法体系があるし、なんというか、プリミティヴであることを許容する文化がある。かたや先進国世界では、なにかにつけ完璧であることが求められる。スケッチがいい例です。つまり完璧に仕上げようとすると、勢いが削がれてしまう。スケッチにはなにかが生まれ出る力、そしてひらめきがある。己に与えられた状況をあるがままに受け入れようということです。もちろん私たちは各地で仕事をするようになりましたから、チリ式のやり方をそのままよそに持ち込むことはしません。その場の状況くらいは読んで理解に努めます。キーワードは、状況を読む、ですね。ちなみに英語の「Intelligence［知性］」は、その語源からすると「行間を読む」という意味になります。ラテン語の「Intellegere」は「Inter-［〜の間］」と「legere the rules systematically is actually a way to disguise mistakes. And if you're okay with uncertainty, then it's fine. But then there's an entire legal system, a culture of where that level of, I would call it primitiveness, is possible. In the developed world, you're required to be perfect for many reasons. Sometimes it's as in a sketch, I mean, by doing perfect things, you loose power, that power of things coming into being and the way they are thought, as in a sketch. So accept the nature of things where you are. Of course now we're practicing in different places, we're not necessarily trying to bring in what we're doing in Chile to other places. We just read the situations and try to understand. I think that's the key word, to *read* the situations. Actually *intelligence* etymologically means "to read in between." Inter leggere, means that you read in between the lines, and if you're intelligent, that's what you're doing – you're reading in between the lines of reality. And I would say that the real difference of architecture comes from the fact that, more than talent, it requires intelligence. Then of course, everything has to be translated in design, which is a non-verbal operation. It's a kind of unspeakable certainty. While the starting point and the way it's verified requires, I would say, intelligence more than talent.

————To what extent is that culturally based? In receiving the Silver Lion of the Venice Biennale and joining the jury for the Pritzker Prize, you do see things from a more international perspective, and are in a position to see differences. Has that perspective at least between Chile and the States, changed or expanded your perspective or the scope of your work?

I would say that first of all, that there's a movement in two different directions. On the one hand, you gain perspective, it's true, in that you're more capable of being precise in identifying the big picture. Simultaneously, you have to take care of the detail. I mean, big picture with the capacity of managing the detail. I'm not talking about the detail of construction. I'm talking about specifically how you transform reading reality into *operating* reality. So a project is to organize information in the direction of the proposals. Big picture and attention to the detail, is the parallel movement that you're creating a kind of voltaic arc. That's one thing. The other thing is that you gain speed in reading differences and acknowledging what's the core, the strength of the places. But to tell the truth, more than being

［読む］」に分解されますから。その知性があるということは、現実からなにかを推論するということです。よって建築の良否は、才能ではなく知性で決まる。その知性を頼りに、建築家はあらゆる事象をデザインに置き換えていく。デザインは、いわば非言語的な操作であり、言葉では言い表せない確信です。そのためにもまずは才能ありきではなく、知性ありきなのです。

────その土地の文化に根ざすというのは、どの程度のことなのでしょうか。それこそヴェネチア・ビエンナーレでは銀獅子賞を受賞なさり、さらにプリツカー賞の審査員も務められたのなら、国際的な視点をお持ちでしょうし、国ごとの違いもご存じでしょう。少なくともチリと米国の二国をご覧になって、物の見方が変わったとか、仕事の領域が広がったといったことはありませんか。

とりあえず、そのことは大きくふたつの方向に働いた、といっておきます。ひとつには、たしかに視野は広がりました。おかげで物事を大局的かつ正確にとらえられるようになった。と同時に、ディテールにも目を配らなくてはならない。つまり全体像を描きつつ、そのディテールもうまく収めるということです。ディテールといっても、建物のディテールのことではありません。具体的には、読み取った現実をいかに機能する現実に変換していくかということです。プロジェクトでは、情報を整理して提案にまとめていかねばなりません。全体像を描きつつディテールを詰める、というように、このふたつの作業をちょうど電弧（アーク）を描くように並行に進めます。以上がひとつ。いまひとつには、差異を読み取ったり、場のもつ力や核心を見極めたりするスピードが上がりました。ただ本当のことを言うと、おそらく自分が思う以上に迷いがなくなりましたね。物事を俯瞰しつつ、細部にも目を配り、状況を読み取り、デザインという非言語的な確信として解答を出せるようになってきました。

────ところで今年はいよいよ日本で個展が開かれます。こうした発想が、日本でどんなふうに解釈され、どんな反響を生むのか、楽しみですね。

ええ、まあ。以前、日本とチリとの違いについて話したことがあります。違いは国土面積と人口──チリのほうが国土が広く、たとえば都市の外側には、未踏の地がまだいくらでも残されている。なにもない、ただた

aware of what I'm gaining, I'm just trying to be as rigorous as I can, and in looking at the big picture, paying attention to the detail, reading the situation, and giving the answer in the form of design, which is an unspeakable certainty.

>———It will be very interesting, to see the exhibition open in Japan in this coming year. That's one very specific connection illustrating how these ideas can expand or be translated or work in many different ways.

Yeah, somehow, I talked before about the differences between Japan and Chile, which is the size of land and people – bigger land here than in Japan, so if you move out of the cities you find huge amounts of land that has never been touched. So empty spaces, emptiness, I would say is something that strikes you, and nature, untouched nature. But ten times less people, so less critical mass. Those are the differences. But even though we're at geographical antipodes, I mean exactly 12 hours away from each other, when there's summer here, it's winter, it couldn't be more different.

Still we do share the fact that we're both islands. Japan, it is an island in fact. Chile is also a kind of island. We do have the Andes, a big wall that separates us from the South American continent. We have the driest desert in the world towards North, then we have the ice in the South, and then the Pacific Ocean, so in a way we're an island too.

And I guess that we share, I would say maybe two things. A certain shyness – I would say that people in Chile are shy and just work quietly. Chile in a way is a country that works. It's a cold country, people pay taxes, you concentrate on what you're doing... We're still Latin, and eventually that might be the difference between Japanese culture, but we're not just a typical Latin country. You might have perceived that during this stay. We were concentrated and patient in a way. So I would say that despite our differences, there's something that you feel that you're connected with. Particularly, I think that we as architects have learned a lot from Japanese architecture. Despite the high-tech, there's a certain rigor and appreciation of quality of things that are well done. And that's something that is desirable in architectural practice everywhere. That's a kind of universal value.

だ空虚な空間が。その光景は一度見たら忘れられないはずです。そしてここには手つかずの自然がある。人口は［日本の］十分の一しかいませんから、すかすかです。以上が両国の違いです。チリと日本は互いに地球の表と裏にあり、時差でいえばきっかり12時間離れているので、日本の夏はこちらの冬。こんなに遠い国はありません。

でもどちらも島国です。日本は現に島国ですが、チリも島国のようなものです。まず残りの南米大陸とはアンデス山脈という高い壁に隔てられている。北には世界で最も乾燥した砂漠があり、南には氷河が、［西には］太平洋が迫っている。島国も同然に孤立しています。

日本との共通点はふたつあります。ひとつには、おとなしい国民性——チリ人は内気で、黙々と働く。いまひとつは、勤勉な国民性。チリは寒い国で、国民は税金をきちんと収め、よく働く……。それでもラテン系なので、文化的には日本とは異なります。ただ我々チリ人は典型的なラテン系ともちょっと違う。今回こちらに滞在なさって、そう思われたでしょう？　チリ人は勤勉で辛抱強い。チリと日本には違いもたくさんあるけれど、どこか相通ずるところもある。特に我々建築家は、日本建築に多くを学んでいます。日本といえばハイテクですが、それはともかく日本人は目が利く、良いものを良いと認める感性をもっている。そういう資質は、建築の仕事に役立つし、普遍的な価値でもあります。

————今後も建築の仕事を続けていかれるわけですが、当面の課題はなんですか。

先のことはなにも考えていません。なるようにしかならないので。毎朝事務所に着くと、たいてい難題が待ち構えている。4ヵ月前にマグニチュード8.8の地震に見舞われて以来、私たちは都市再建の仕事にかかりきりです。はたして90日間でどこまで復興できるか。こんな大仕事を引き受けることになるとは思ってもみませんでした。ある日突然舞い込んだこの仕事に対し、私たちは例によって冷静に状況を読み取っていった。すぐに問題の所在を突き止め、知恵を出すことができた。これに限らず、私たちは来る日も来る日も新たな難問を突き付けられています。そのたびに、私たちは問いを設定し直す。それ以外には、抽象的な言い方になりますが、建築以外の問題、すなわち社会の関心が集まる問

———In thinking about the continuing challenges of the profession of architecture and yourself, what are your priorities?

I don't think we have a plan in terms of what's next. It just tends to happen. We arrive, we enter the office every day, and we're given questions that are challenging. We had an earthquake; 8.8 on the Richter scale four months ago, and we have been working intensively in the reconstruction of an entire city. How to do an entire city in 90 days? It's a challenge we never thought we could have dealt with. It arrived, and we were just trying to be, again, prepared to read the situation in a strategic way so that we understand that challenge and transform that into new knowledge. I would say that every single day, there's that kind of new challenge that arrives as a question. Eventually we have to build that new question from the project that arrives. That's one thing, but in more abstract and general terms, I would say that the capacity of starting from problems that are non-architectural issues that interest the society at large, and translating and operating them by the specific knowledge of architecture, which is the strategic use of form, is the kind of challenges that we will be facing more and more.

Poverty doesn't belong to architecture. I mean space eventually belongs to architecture, but poverty does not. So that's outside architecture. And we would like to have a say in poverty by being architects. So like that, development, or inclusiveness in the cities, or pollution – Santiago has a major conflict with pollution. Can we as designers do something with pollution? If you ask me today, I have no idea, but I'm sure that if you begin to swallow huge amounts of information, since it's a complex problem that will be a problem of public health, it's a problem of policy, it's a problem of financing, it's a problem of environment, and it's a problem of weather, eventually design can synthesize that complexity and give a clue how to move forward. And I would say that in general, our challenges will come from those non-architectural issues treated through the lens of architecture, which is its power of synthesis and strategic use of form.

July 28, 2010 @ ELEMENTAL, Santiago, Chile

題から手をつけるようにして、それを建築という専門知識を介して変換・操作する、すなわち形態を武器にするわけです。この種の仕事は、今後ますます増えるでしょうね。

貧困と建築は別物です。空間は最終的には建築に帰せられるけれども、貧困は別です。貧困は建築の外にある。私たちは建築家として、貧困について言いたいことを言う。同様に、都市開発についても、都市の包括性についても、あるいは（サンティアゴで大論争中の）環境汚染についても口を出す。我々デザイナーが、環境汚染に対してなにができるか。今いきなりそれを訊かれても返答に窮しますが、仮に膨大な量の情報を吸収して、公衆衛生の問題であるとか、政策、金融、環境、気候問題といった複雑な事柄いっさいをデザインに取り込めば、方向性は見えてくるでしょう。ともあれ、今後も建築以外の分野から課題を与えられることになるでしょうね。それを私たちは建築というレンズを介して観察し、処理する。建築には物事を統合する力、そして形態という名の武器がありますから。

　　　　　　　　　　　2010年7月28日　チリ、サンティアゴのエレメンタルの事務所にて

ELEME

Biography

Alejandro Aravena
アレハンドロ・アラヴェナ

Born in 1967. After studying at the Catholic University of Chile, Aravena established his own firm in 1994. From 2000 to 2005, he served as a visiting professor at Harvard University Graduate School of Design, and is currently a professor at Catholic University. He has been a jury member for the Pritzker Prize since 2009, and was named an International Fellow of the Royal Institute of British Architects in 2010. Among the honors he has received are the Erich Schelling Foundation Architecture Medal in 2006, the Silver Lion for Promising Young Architect at the 11th Venice Biennale in 2008, the Avonni Prize and the Marcus Prize for Architecture in 2009, and the Brit Insurance Design Award (architecture category) in 2010. He was also selected as one of the 20 most outstanding young architects by the British magazine *Icon* in 2008, and has also delivered lectures throughout the world.

Since 2006, Aravena has served as Executive Director of ELEMENTAL S.A. A for profit company with social interests working in projects of infrastructure, transportation, public space and housing, partnering with the Catholic University of Chile and COPEC (Chilean Oil Company).

1967年生まれ。チリ・カトリック大学で学び、1994年に自身の設計事務所を開設。2000～05年ハーバード大学大学院客員教授、現在チリ・カトリック大学教授。2009年～プリツカー賞審査員。2010年～王立英国建築家協会国外会員。主な受賞は、2006年エーリヒ・シェリング建築賞、2008年第11回ヴェネチア・ビエンナーレ建築展銀獅子賞、2009年マーカス建築賞、アヴォニ賞、2010年ブリット・インシュアランス・デザイン賞（建築部門）など。2008年英国『icon』誌上で若手建築家20傑のひとりに選ばれた。また世界各地で講演活動も行っている。

2006年よりエレメンタルの取締役。エレメンタルはチリ・カトリック大学およびチリの石油会社COPECの共同出資により設立された営利会社として、インフラ・交通・公共空間およびハウジングなど社会性の高いプロジェクトに携わる。

Bibliography

PUBLICATIONS BY ALEJANDRO ARAVENA

2007
Alejandro Aravena / progettare e costruire (Milan, Italy: Mondadori Electa).
Foco 76 (Chile), no.4.

2006
Foco 76 (Chile), no.2.
Foco 76 (Chile), no.1.

2003
Material de arquitectura [Architecture material] (Santiago, Chile: Ediciones ARQ).

2002
El Lugar de la Arquitectura [The Place of Architecture] (Santiago, Chile: Ediciones ARQ).
"Un ensayo de 'realismo ascético.' Iglesia del monasterio de Las Condes, Santiago de Chile [A test of "ascetic realism." Church of the Las Condes monastery, Santiago, Chile]." *Casabella* (Milan, Italy), no. 706–707.

1999
Alejandro Aravena, Fernando Pérez Oyarzún and José Quintanilla, *Los Hechos de la Arquitectura [The Facts of Architecture]* (Santiago, Chile: Ediciones ARQ).
"CTRLZ." *ARQ* (Santiago, Chile: Ediciones ARQ), no. 41.

1998
"Un taller fresco [A fresh workshop]." *ARQ* (Santiago, Chile: Ediciones ARQ), no. 39.

1997
"Robinson nell'Isla Grande de Chiloé, with Giovanna Crespi." *Casabella* (Milan, Italy), no. 650.

1994
"Alhambra." *ARQ* (Santiago, Chile), n. 27.
"Simposio de Siracusa [Syracuse Symposium]." *ARQ* (Santiago, Chile: Ediciones ARQ), n. 26.
"Geografía artificial y cuerpo en un mover de pesos." *ARQ* (Santiago, Chile: Ediciones ARQ), no. 21.

1993
"Del magno templo griego [About the great Greek temple]." 1.2 (Santiago, Chile)

1992
Amereida Poesía y Arquitectura: Alberto Cruz-Godofredo Iommi [Amereida Poetry and Architecture] (Santiago, Chile: Ediciones ARQ).
"Vence Prize." *ARQ* (Santiago, Chile: Ediciones ARQ), no. 20.

PUBLICATIONS ON ALEJANDRO ARAVENA (2008–)

2011
"Los+Creativos de Chile: Señor Creatividad, Alejandro Aravena." *SABADO* (Santiago, Chile), no. 659: 3, 18–23.
"Alejandro Aravena." *PEN* (Tokyo, Japan: Hankyu Communications), no. 292: 55.
"Alejandro Aravena. Desarrollo y Sustentabilidad: Desafíos de Chile para Convivir con La Urbanización." *ESTRATEGIA* (Santiago, Chile), no. 5,766: 28.

"St. Edward's Residence Hall." *LOTUS Internacional* (Milan, Italy), no. 145: 16–23.
"Alejandro Aravena: Todas las ciudades costeras debieran llenarse de bosques." *Qué Pasa* (Santiago, Chile), no. 2081: 26– 33.
"Quinta Monroy/Torres Siamesas/St. Edward's University New Residence and Dining Hall" *Catálogo de Arquitectura Chilena, de la II^a Bienal de Arquitectura Latinoamericana, Pamplona 2011* (Santiago, Chile), 6–7, 24–25, 56–57.
"Innovación Social: Soluciones habitacionales de alto estándar y bajo costo." *Innovación en Chile, Una Nueva Cultura para el País* (Santiago, Chile), 9.
"Los pies en el suelo, Alejandro Aravena, la realidad de América/Alejandro Aravena. Dignidad Urbana. Colonia Lo Barnechea, Santiago de Chile." *Arquitectura Viva* (Madrid, Spain), no. 133: 28–35, 110.
"Alejandro Aravena Architects/Ruta del Peregrino." *Abitare* (Milan, Italy), no. 509: 28, 59.
"Elemental Iquique." *Edilizia Residenziale Innovativa, Progettare l'Housing contemporaneo* (Dogana, San marino), no. 1: 96–98.
"New postures-new seats. Alejandro Aravena: Chairless." *INVENTARIO, Tutto è Progetto* (Milan, Italy), no. 2: 88.
"Et Lukket Kapittel?" *arkitektur* (Stockholm, Sweden), 48–59.
"Elemental, Quinta Monroy Housing Project, Iquique, Chile 2003–2005." *a+u* (Tokyo, Japan: A+U Publishing), no. 485: 42–43.
"Acupuncture. Transforming Santiago." *'scape* (Wageningen, the Netherlands), no. 1-2011: 4, 38–43.
"Alejandro Aravena: La escasez es la gran escuela para la arquitectura en Chile." *Pensamiento Propio 8, La Otra Fiesta* (Santiago, Chile), 12–41, 113.
Marc Kristal, "Siamese Towers, Santiago, Chile, Alejandro Aravena, 2005." *Immaterial World, Transparency in Architecture* (New York, USA: The Monacelli Press), 10–17.

2010
"Pontificia Universidad Católica de Chile, Centro de Innovación Metodológica y Tecnológica para mejorar la calidad de los procesos de enseñanza-aprendizaje en la Universidad." *Nueva Arquitectura para el Aprendizaje* (Chile), 120–123, 206.
"Aravena Rehace Constitución/En busca de lo elemental." *ARQ* (Buenos Aires, Argentina), no. 430: Portada, 16 20.
"Four Flat Pillars." *ICON MAGAZINE* (Loughton, UK), no. 88: 131–138.
"AA Alejandro Aravena: The good half house." *DESIGN INDABA* (Cape Town, South Africa), no. 12: 70–77.
"Aravena Social Club." *A&B Architektura & Biznes* (Kraków, Poland), no. 219: 74–79.
"Quinta Monroy Housing." *Small Scale Big Change, New Architectures of Social Engagement* (New York, USA: MoMA), 83–92.
"A dónde va la Arquitectura?" *Revista de Arquitectura y Diseño, AYD* (Barcelona, Spain), no. 118.
"Elemental. Crosses Lookout Point." *a+u* (Tokyo, Japan: A+U Publishing), no. 480: 35.
"Elemental Quinta Monroy." *LOTUS Internacional* (Milan, Italy), no. 143: 102–107.
"Escenario Ampliado, proyecto de Vivienda Social Monterrey." *Zona de Proyecto, Patagonia* (Buenos Aires, Argentina), no. 16: 98–103.
"Alejandro Aravena Arquitecto. Elemental Sostenible." *Esquire* (Madrid, Spain), no. 30: 48.
"Alejandro Aravena: The One Who Changes Social Housing Construction." *Urban Environment Design* (Beijing, China), no. 42: 206–279.
"Quinta Monroy, Elemental." *VIVIENDA TOTAL, Alternativas a la Dispersión Urbana* (Barcelona, Spain: Actar), 246–251.
"Temblor Austral. Lecciones del sismo de Chile. Alejandro Aravena." *Arquitectura Viva* (Madrid, Spain), no. 129: 112.
"Alejandro Aravena, Torres Siamesas." *LOTUS Internacional* (Milan, Italy), no. 140: 80–83.
"Processo al Design 2, Design Trial 2 (La sedia Chairless di Alejandro Aravena per Vitra)." *Abitare* (Milan, Italy), no. 505: 140–145.
"The Interview: Being Alejandro Aravena." *MONUMENT* (Melbourne, Australia), no. 98: Portada, 32–36.
"Alejandro Aravena, Innovador y Jugado." *In Vitro* (Santiago, Chile), no. 72: 46–51.
"Alejandro Aravena A LA VENA." *ED* (Chile), no. 182: 158–164.
"Alejandro Aravena, Ricardo Torrejón. Residenze St. Edward's University, Austin, Texas, USA." *Construire in Laterizio* (Roma, Italia), no. 135: 9, 14.
"Alejandro Aravena Interviews nArchitects." *Praxis* (Columbus, USA), no. 11+12: 28–41.
"MOS Interviews Alejandro Aravena." *Praxis* (Columbus, USA), no. 11+12: 16–27.
"Monterrey." *A Arkitekten* (Danmark), no. 112: 1.
"Alejandro Aravena, Elemental Iquique." *A Arkitekten* (Danmark), no. 112: 22–23.
"Klovede Teglsten I Austin." *A Arkitekten* (Danmark), no. 112: 70.
"Descadeirados." *REVISTA GLOSS* (Brasil), no. 3: 28.
"Alejandro Aravena." *ARQUITECTURA: MAS POR MENOS* (Spain), 34–41.
"Those Great Stone Architectures in Mountains (Casa Pirihueico)." *LIFE ELEMENT* (Shanghai, China), no. 120: 98–103.

"Across The Board 4. 2010 – ELEMENTAL ARCHITECTURE." *architecturenz* (Kinsland/Auckland, New Zealand), 18.
"Eine Million neue Auftraggeber/betrifft Erdbeben in Chile." *Bauwelt* (Berlin, Germany), no. 15: 6–8.
"The leaders Issue: Alejandro Aravena." *Plan* (Dublin, Ireland), 44–45.
"Un apunt sobrel'urbanisme sostenible." *VISIONS, LO PEQUEÑO ES HERMOSO* (Barcelona, Spain), no. 7: 31–43.
"Mirador Las Cruces, Elemental, Alejandro Aravena." *ARQUINE* (Mexico City, Mexico), no. 53: 54–55.
"Casa Etlin." *GA HOUSES, PROJECT 2010* (Tokyo, Japan: A.D.A. EDITA Tokyo), no. 115: 16–18.
"Cañón Cartesiano, Nva. Residencia y Comedor De La Univ. De St. Edward's." *SUMMA+* (Buenos Aires, Argentina), no. 106: 18–25.

2009
"Alejandro Aravena – Ricardo Torrejón, Residenze Universitarie St'Edward." *Materia* (Milan, Italy), no. 64: 130–141.
"Alejandro Aravena." *MATERIA* (Milan, Italy), no. 64: 49.
"Suelo Urb. Accesible Y Prevenc. De Asentamientos Irreg. La Tierra, El Recurso Escaso." *Construir Ciudades, Mejoramiento de Barrios y Calidad de Vida Urbana* (Washington D.C., USA), 68–69.
"Chile Slum Reconstruction." *The Outlook Magazine* (Hong Kong, China), no. 91: 66–69.
"Cajas Rusticas Con Colores Escondidos, St. Edwards University." *El Clarin, ARQ* (Argentina), 16–21.
"Nào é o Talento Que Faz um Bom Arquitecto." *Revista Unica Expresso* (Portugal), no. 195: 78–81.
"Elemental Iquique, Alejandro Aravena." *Chile Territorio Para La Arquitectura* (Santiago, Chile), 6–9.
"Alejandro Aravena: Soy Ejemplo Que La Meritocracia Funciona." *Vivienda y Decoración* (Santiago, Chile), No. 681: 44–51.
"Viviendas Sociales En Iquique." *Revista Detail* (Spain), 2009-3: 303–304.
"La Casa Que Elemental Diseña Para Brad Pitt." *Qué Pasa* (Santiago, Chile), 4.
Philip Jodidio, "Elemental/Alejandro Aravena." *Architecture Now! Houses* (Taschen), 150–155.

2008
"20 New Heros." *MONOCLE* (UK), no. 19: 30–36.
"Dream Team 2009." *D'LA REPUBBLICA DELLE DONE* (Italy), no. 628: 40.
"Alejandro Aravena, Architecture For The Billions." *ICON MAGAZINE* (Loughton, UK).
"Elemental." *IGLOO* (Rumania), December 2008: 8–60.
"25 Tendencias para los Próximos 10 Años." *SABADO* (Chile), 110.
"Proyecto Elemental Iquique." *ECOLOGIK* (France), 24–26.
"The Chilean Architecture Phenomenon." *INTERNI* (Russia), 7.
"Lider de los Campamentos: El Poder de Cecilia." *REVISTA YA* (Chile), 28–32.
"¿Necesita Santiago un Solo Alcalde?" *Qué Pasa* (Chile).
"Elemental Quinta Monroy." *DETAIL* (Germany), 944–945.
"Acerca de Elemental Chile." *ELEMENTAL, Reflexiones en Torno a la Vivienda Mínima* (Barcelona, Spain: ETSAB), 96–97.
"Alejandro Aravena: El Arquitecto Elemental." *SABADO* (Chile), 18–21.
"Alejandro Aravena (Elemental) La Mia Idea di Social Housing." *Il Magazine dell architettura* (Italy), no. 12: 26–30.
"Conjunto lo Espejo en Revista ARQ." *ARQ* (Chile), 24–27.
"Especial Jóvenes Arquitectos Latinoamericanos." *AU* (Brasil), 48-56.
"Less Money. More Creativity." *MARK MAGAZINE* (the Netherlands), 174–181.
"50 Influyentes del 2008." *Qué Pasa* (Chile), no. 1944: 26–27, 32.
"Elemental Quinta Monroy." *ECOLOGIK* (France), June 2008: 60–63.
"Nuevos Aplausos para Elemental." *VIVIENDA Y DECORACIÓN* (Chile), 54–57.
"Rescatar el Cerro San Cristóbal." *REVISTA CAPITAL* (Chile), 230.
Verb Crisis (Spain: ACTAR), 54–59, 160–167, 278–281.
"Elemental Quinta Monroy." *ARCH* (Slovakia), 50.
"El Gran Parque." *REVISTA PODER* (Chile), 15.
"Iacobelli, Allard y Aravena, Dentro de las 75 Ideas para Mejorar Chile." *Qué Pasa* (Chile), no. 1829: 27.
"The 20 Essential Young Architects." *ICON MAGAZINE* (Loughton, UK), no. 58: 68–73.
"Elemental." *ARQUINE* (Mexico), no. 43: 32–43.
"Ciudades: Minas de Oro o Bombas de Tiempo." *Qué Pasa* (Chile), 18-21.

Credits

Photography credits 写真クレジット

Aravena, Alejandro	7, 8, 19, 27, 44 (middle left and bottom left), 56 (middle left and bottom left), 59 (top right and bottom left), 60 (bottom right)
Baan, Iwan	72 (bottom right), 74, 75–76, 77, 78 (top), 79
Bravo, Martín	43 (middle right and bottom right), 44 (bottom right), 49, 50, 51, 133 (middle right)
Cerda, Juan	137 (bottom and 2nd from bottom left), 139 (bottom left two interior photos), 157 bottom
Combeau, Alberto	47 (bottom left)
Cortese, Tomas	122, 128 (bottom left), 130 (middle), 133 (middle left)
Dusuzean, Ludovic	130 (bottom), 131 (bottom)
Elemental	151, 152, 153, 160, 162
Halbe, Roland	31–32, 34 (top right), 35 (top left and bottom right)
Hsu, Michael	56 (top), 57–58
Jalocha, Tadeuz	22 (except middle left), 23, 34 (bottom), 35 (top right and middle left), 47 (except bottom left), 125 (top), 126 (top), 128 (top and bottom right), 130 (top), 131 (top left)
Maestrello, Sara	131 (middle two photos)
Oddó, Víctor	22 (middle left), 35 (middle right and bottom left), 40 (bottom left), 43 (top), 53 (top), 70 (five brick photos), 81 (middle left), 133 (top and bottom two photos), 134, 135, 137 (except bottom and 2nd from bottom left), 139 (except bottom left two interior photos), 157 (top)
Palma, Cristóbal	40 (except bottom left), 41–42, 43 (bottom left), 44 (top left and top right), 45, 56 (middle right and bottom right), 59 (top left and bottom right), 60 (except bottom right), 61, 123–124, 127, 129, 194
Pérez, Elvira	34 (top left)
Ramirez, Ramiro	141, 142, 143
Stein, Karen	81 (bottom right)
Sacher, Bernardo	9, 80 (Ayoreo Indian photo), 165
Vitra (photo by Nicole Bachmann)	81 (top and bottom left)
Vitra	80 (two Chairless images)

Although we have tried to indicate copyrights as accurately as possible for the photos used in this book, it was not possible to contact all of the copyright holders. Interested parties should contact TOTO Publishing.
本書で使用している写真の著作権者については、できる限り正確な表記をするよう努めましたが、著作権者のうち連絡をとれない方がいます。お気づきの方は、TOTO 出版までご連絡ください。

Japanese Translation 和訳

Doi Jun 土居純

English Proofreading 英文校正

Oshima, Ken Tadashi ケン・タダシ・オオシマ

ALEJANDRO ARAVENA
THE FORCES IN ARCHITECTURE
アレハンドロ・アラヴェナ　フォース・イン・アーキテクチャー

2011年7月28日　初版第1刷発行
2020年3月25日　初版第5刷発行

著者：アレハンドロ・アラヴェナ
コンテンツ作成：ヴィクトール・オッドー
発行者：伊藤剛士
デザイン：榮元正博
印刷・製本：株式会社東京印書館
発行所：TOTO出版（TOTO株式会社）
〒107-0062　東京都港区南青山 1-24-3 TOTO 乃木坂ビル 2F
［営業］TEL: 03-3402-7138　FAX: 03-3402-7187
［編集］TEL: 03-3497-1010
URL: https://jp.toto.com/publishing

落丁本・乱丁本はお取り替えいたします。本書の全部又は一部に対するコピー・スキャン・デジタル化等の無断複製行為は、著作権法上での例外を除き禁じます。本書を代行業者等の第三者に依頼してスキャンやデジタル化することは、たとえ個人や家庭内での利用であっても著作権上認められておりません。定価はカバーに表示してあります。

© 2011 Alejandro Aravena　Printed in Japan　ISBN978-4-88706-320-4